# A LORD WITHOUT LIMITS

## Sermons for the Easter Season Series C

### John Thomas Randolph

A LORD WITHOUT LIMITS (SERIES C)

Copyright © 1979 by
The C.S.S. Publishing Company, Inc.
Lima, Ohio

All rights reserved. No portion of this book may be reproduced or utilized in any form or by any means, electronic or mechanical including photocopying, without permission in writing from the publisher. Inquiries should be addressed to: The C.S.S. Publishing Company, Inc., 628 South Main Street, Lima, Ohio 45804.

ISBN 0-89536-393-3       PRINTED IN U.S.A.

*To my mother,*

*whose boundless love*

*introduced me early in*

*life to*

*A Lord Without Limits.*

# Table of Contents

Acknowledgments ............................. 7
Preface ...................................... 9

Christ is Alive! ............................. 13
*Easter*

"Stop Being Afraid" .......................... 23
*Second Sunday of Easter*

Worthiness and Worship ....................... 33
*Third Sunday of Easter*

On a Dark Day You Can See Forever ............ 43
*Fourth Sunday of Easter*

The City of Hope ............................. 53
*Fifth Sunday of Easter*

The Perfect Church ........................... 63
*Sixth Sunday of Easter*

A Lord Without Limits ........................ 73
*The Ascension*

Come! ........................................ 83
*Seventh Sunday of Easter*

## Acknowledgements

Scripture quotations are reprinted by permission of the following:

*The New English Bible.* © The Delegates of the Oxford University Press and The Syndics of the Cambridge University Press, 1961, 1970.

J. B. Phillips: *The New Testament in Modern English*, Revised Edition (© J. B. Phillips 1958, 1960, 1972)

*The Revised Standard Version of the Bible*, copyrighted 1946, 1952, © 1971, 1973.

## Preface

This is a book of pastoral sermons for the Easter Season, based on the second lessons in the Lectionary.

Easter, you know, is a season. It is not an isolated Sunday, although we have often regarded it as such. Nearly twenty years ago, William F. Dunkle, Jr., wrote in his book, *Values in the Church Year:* "The problem about Easter no longer lies in any failure to observe Easter Sunday itself, but rather in our failure to observe Easter adequately as a season extending long after Easter Sunday and culminating in the glorious commemoration of our Lord's ascension." The sermons in this book aim at overcoming this problem by taking seriously the fact that Easter is indeed a whole season. The themes of the Ascension and "the Second Coming" are dealt with, but they are viewed as aspects of the larger Easter theme that "Christ is Alive!"

It is my prayer that the sermons will be helpful to you and, perhaps, even contribute a bit to a fuller experience of that glorious New Life which is available through Jesus Christ, our Risen Lord. Therefore, I invite you to read the sermons and, then, to share them in appropriate ways with your friends.

I wish to thank my wife, Maubra Jane, for her consistent helpfulness, and Mrs. Joyce Stockslager for typing the manuscript.

John T. Randolph<br>
Advent — 1978

*Easter*

And now, my brothers, I must remind you of the gospel that I preached to you; the gospel which you received, on which you have taken your stand, and which is now bringing you salvation. Do you still hold fast the Gospel as I preached it to you? If not, your conversion was in vain.

First and foremost, I handed on to you the facts which had been imparted to me: that Christ died for our sins, in accordance with the scriptures; that he was buried; that he was raised to life on the third day, according to the scriptures; and that he appeared to Cephas, and afterwards to the Twelve. Then he appeared to over five hundred of our brothers at once, most of whom are still alive, though some have died. Then he appeared to James, and afterwards to all the apostles.

In the end he appeared even to me; though this birth of mine was monstrous, for I had persecuted the church of God and am therefore inferior to all other apostles — indeed not fit to be called an apostle. However, by God's grace I am what I am, nor has his grace been given to me in vain; on the contrary, in my labours I have outdone them all — not I, indeed, but the grace of God working with me. But what matter, I or they? This is what we all proclaim, and this is what you believed.

*1 Corinthians 15:1-11*
*New English Bible (1961)*

# Christ Is Alive

R. W. Dale was a minister who had preached many Easter sermons. Year after year he had stood in his pulpit and recounted the glorious events of the first Easter morning. He had spoken of the Resurrection. But it had never become a personal reality for him. Then one Easter Sunday as he was in his study, making some final preparations on his sermon, the Good News struck him like a flash of lightning: "Christ is alive!" He was so overcome by this fresh realization that all he could do was to walk back and forth across his study, saying over and over again: "Christ is alive! Christ is alive!"

That is our message this morning. As Howard G. Hageman says, "On Easter morning it is the sheer proclamation of the . . . victory of God in the resurrection of Jesus Christ from the dead that is the business of Christian preaching."* We affirm that this morning. We will not argue or debate. We simply rejoice in the good news of Easter: Christ is alive!

We should have known it would happen. Jesus had said it would happen. And in this case, as in others, when people have taken Jesus at his word and have acted on it "they have found it as he told them." Even on the darkness of Good Friday we should have known that the cross would not have the last word, and that New Life would arrive just on the other side of an Easter sunrise.

Evelyn Waugh has written a marvelous story about "The Man Who Liked Dickens."† It's about Mr. Todd who lived by himself in a little clearing in the

---

*Proclamation: Aids for Interpreting the Lessons of the Church Year, "Easter" Series C (Philadelphia: Fortress Press, 1974) p. 6.
†Condensed from "A Handful of Dust," Reader's Digest, June 1978, pp. 197-204.

Amazon jungle. He could not read, but his father, an educated man, had read to him while he was alive. He had read the complete works of Charles Dickens — many times — and Mr. Todd had come to love them. After Mr. Todd's father died, a man named Mr. Washington had continued to read Dickens to him for two hours every afternoon. Then Mr. Washington died and there was no one to read to him — until a man named Mr. Last stumbled, half-dead, into his clearing. As you might guess, the price Mr. Last had to pay for being nursed back to health was to read the books of Dickens to Mr. Todd. But there is an interesting scene that takes place in the story shortly after Mr. Last's arrival. Mr. Todd takes Last to see Mr. Washington's grave and says, "He was very kind to me. Every afternoon until he died, for two hours, he read to me. I think I will put up a cross — to commemorate his death and your arrival — a pretty idea."

And that is what I like — that cross: a symbol of death to be sure; but also a symbol of arrival! Look again at the cross in the sanctuary. It is empty. Jesus was there and death was a reality. But, by the power of God, death was overcome by the arrival of New Life on Easter morning.

You have read the story in the Gospels, but the earliest account of the Resurrection is in verses one through eleven of the fifteenth chapter of 1 Corinthians. We have chosen to read this passage from the *New English Bible* because that particular version expresses the story in three logical paragraphs. They suggest the peg words around which the rest of this sermon will be developed: fact — faithfulness — and fitness.

### 1. Fact

Paul is talking about the Resurrection as a fact. It is

not a dream or a private illusion. He tells the Corinthians and us: "I handed on to you the facts which had been imparted to me: that Christ died for our sins, in accordance with the scriptures; that he was buried; that he was raised to life on the third day, according to the scriptures; and that he appeared to Cephas, and afterwards to the Twelve."

Just the facts, that's all: by the power of God Jesus "was raised to life on the third day."

The Resurrection was a fact. It had the support of consensus. It had been checked out by a whole community and they had affirmed it as a reality. Then that community had passed the news of the Resurrection on to Paul and he passed it on to the Corinthians. Paul didn't invent the Resurrection. He simply received it as a fact and then "handed it on."

Furthermore, the Risen Christ had appeared to Peter and the Twelve. He had appeared to James. Then he had appeared to over five hundred persons at once — some of whom were still alive to verify Paul's account. And, wonder of wonders, the Risen Lord had finally appeared personally to Paul! I don't know how it happened. I don't care how it happened. But it happened. That is a fact.

And, because it is a fact, we are able to sing:

*I serve a risen Savior,*
  *He's in the world today;*
*I know that He is living,*
  *Whatever men may say;*

*You ask me how I know He lives:*
  *He lives within my heart.*
                               Alfred H. Ackley

There are more profound Easter hymns than this one by Ackley, but I like Ackley's hymn because it affirms the Resurrection as a fact of our own personal experience.

## 2. Faithfulness

When we are faithful to this gospel, says Paul — when it becomes personally meaningful to us — then it gives us "a place to stand" and it "brings us our salvation."

As Paul puts it, the gospel with its good news of resurrection gives us a foundation on which we can "take our stand." It gives us stability. As William Barclay writes, in a slippery world it keeps us on our feet. In a world that is filled with temptations it gives us the power to resist. In a world where so many people are hurting, it enables us to endure broken hearts and agonized bodies and not to give in. In a world where there are so many forces that are affirming death, it gives us the power to say yes to Life.

It is the power of the God who raised Jesus from death to new life — and not our own strength — that keeps us stable and keeps us from crumbling under the pressure of life's winds and storms.

In his book *Some Gall — and Other Reflections on Life . . .*, James Buckingham tells about the Eddystone Lighthouse which stands off the shore of Plymouth, England. Actually, there have been two Eddystone Lighthouses. The first was built by an architect named Winstanley. It was a masterpiece of workmanship and Winstanley was so confident of the permanency of his structure that he placed this inscription on the cornerstone: "Blow, O ye winds! Rise, O ocean! Break forth, ye elements, and try my work!" The elements took him at his word and destroyed the lighthouse — and Winstanley — and also carried nine other men to their deaths.

Years later, a new Eddystone Lighthouse was built by John Smeaton. He found a new site for the lighthouse and dug deep to build its foundations upon solid rock. Smeaton was a sincere Christian and had these words from the Scriptures chiseled into his cornerstone: "Except the Lord build a house, they labor in vain that build it." And, says Buckingham, this second lighthouse is still standing. It has stood every test. No storm has been able to shake it because it is founded upon a rock.*

Let us affirm it clearly on this Easter morning: the Resurrection of Jesus Christ is the rock on which we take our stand — the rock which gives us the stability we need. Indeed, the Resurrection means "that the identical divine energy which at the first took Christ out of the grave is available still — available not only at journey's end to save [us] in the hour of death, but available here and now to help [us] to live."†

Paul goes on to say that when we are faithful to this Resurrection gospel of ours it not only gives us a stable place to stand, but it also becomes the source of our salvation. It is clear to us by now, isn't it, that we cannot save ourselves.

I like the cartoon which pictures two gaunt and bearded convicts in a very high and very narrow cell. Far above them, near the ceiling, is a window that is so small that even their thin figures could not pass through it. The convicts are strapped to the wall by their arms, neck, abdomen, and legs, and a ball and chain is thrown in for good measure. In the midst of all this, one of the convicts turns to the other and announces, confidently, "Now, here's my plan!"

This is a picture of how foolish it is to think that our own wit or ingenuity can save us. Only the God who raised Jesus from the dead can make the same divine energy available to us now and lift us up and save us and lead us on to the fullness of perfect health and

---

*Waco, Texas: *World Books*, 1970, pp. 26-27.
†James S. Stewart, *A Faith To Proclaim* (New York: Charles Scribner's Sons, 1953) p. 126.

wholeness.

### 3. *Fitness*

Having affirmed the Good News of Easter — that Jesus Christ is indeed alive — there is only one thing that remains to be done, both today and for the rest of our lives: to go out and share the good news, and the power of new life, with others. The only question we may have about this task is the same question that Paul had — our fitness to undertake it.

In his early days, Paul had "persecuted the church of God" and he thought that he was "not fit to be called an apostle." And, of course, he was right. No one is fit, by the merits of his past record or his present behavior, to be a Christian witness. However, as Paul discovered, it is God's grace that has permitted us to experience the good news of Easter and it is by the grace of God that we are empowered to share it with others.

Recently, a young minister told an older colleague about his growing feelings of inadequacy. The young man was becoming increasingly aware of the heavy demands placed upon him by his ministry, and he was beginning to doubt his ability to meet the demands. The older minister surprised the young man by confessing that he often shared the same feelings of personal inadequacy. But what kept him going, he said, was the deep conviction that God had chosen him and called him to share the Good News. God had taken the initiative and, having called him, had provided whatever adequacy was needed.* The older minister had discovered, with Paul, that his personal adequacy was basically a matter of God's grace working with him and through him.

---

*See, for example, *John* 15:16, *1 Corinthians* 1:27, *1 Corinthians* 9:17-18, *1 Peter* 2:9, and *Revelation* 17:14.

That is the way it works for all of us. It is God alone who gives us our fitness to be a witness. Let us remember this especially at Easter, because Easter simply isn't complete until we share it with others.

My mind keeps coming back to two lines from that story about "The Man Who Liked Dickens." As Mr. Todd recalls a certain chapter from one of Dickens' books, he says, "It was an extremely distressing chapter. But, if I remember rightly, it will all turn out well."

Make no mistake about it: the cross "was an extremely distressing chapter." But, thank God for Easter: it "turned out well." Jesus Christ is alive!

# Second Sunday of Easter

John, to the seven Churches in Asia:

Grace and peace be to you from Him Who is and Who was and Who is coming, from the Seven Spirits before His throne, and from Jesus Christ the faithful Witness, Firstborn of the dead, and Ruler of kings upon earth. To Him Who loves us and has set us free from our sins through His own blood, Who has made us a kingdom of priests to His God and Father, to Him be glory and power for timeless ages, Amen!

See, He is coming in the clouds and every eye shall see Him, even those who pierced Him, and His coming will mean bitter sorrow to every tribe upon the earth. So let it be!

> "I am Alpha and Omega," says the Lord God, "Who is and Who was and Who is coming, the Almighty."

I, John, who am your brother and your companion in the distress, the kingdom and the faithful endurance to which Jesus calls us, was on the island called Patmos because I had spoken God's Message and borne witness to Jesus. On the Lord's Day I knew myself inspired by the Spirit, and I heard from behind me a voice loud as a trumpet call, saying,

> "Write down in a book what you see, and send it to the Seven Churches — to Ephesus, Smyrna, Pergamum, Thyatira, Sardis, Philadelphia and Laodicea!"

I turned to see whose voice it was that was speaking to me, and when I turned I saw seven golden lampstands, and among these lampstands I saw someone like a Son of Man. He was dressed in a long robe with a golden girdle around his breast; His head and His hair were white as snow-white wool, His eyes blazed like fire, and His feet shone as the finest bronze glows in the furnace. His voice had the sound of a great waterfall, and I saw that in His right hand He held seven stars. A sharp two-edged sword came out of His mouth, and His face was ablaze like the sun at its height.

When my eyes took in this sight I fell at His feet like a dead man. And then He placed His right hand upon me and said:

> "Do not be afraid. I am the First and the Last, the Living One. I am He Who was dead, and now you see Me alive for timeless ages! I hold in My hand the keys of Death and the Grave."

*Revelation 1:4-18*
*J. B. Phillips*

# "Stop Being Afraid"

One of the main problems we face is fear. We are afraid of many things. We are afraid of being alone in the universe, both in times of crisis and in the ordinary events of everyday living. We are afraid of that final curtain we call death which signals the end of so much that we have worked and hoped for. And we fear the possibility that there is nothing after death; that life is essentially empty and meaningless, that it has no purpose, that history has no goal.

But thank God that this is the Easter Season and John has a special message for us on this particular Sunday. It is that we do not have to be afraid any longer. The statement has force because John quotes it straight from the lips of the Risen Christ: "Do not be afraid," or, as William Barclay quotes the words, "Stop being afraid."

Jesus had spoken the same words of good news on other occasions. When the disciples had seen him walking toward them on the water, they thought he was a ghost and cried out in fear. But immediately Jesus spoke to them: "It's all right! It's I myself, don't be afraid!" (Matthew 14:27, J. B. Phillips.)

When God spoke to Jesus on the Mount of Transfiguration, the disciples fell on their faces, "overcome with fear." And Jesus touched them and said, "Get up and don't be frightened." (Matthew 17:7, J. B. Phillips)

And when John, overcome by his vision of the Risen Lord, fell down like a dead man, Jesus placed his right hand on him and said, "Stop being afraid."

And now, through John, the Risen Christ is personally telling us that we can stop being afraid.

If Jesus had stopped there and said no more, we

might have dismissed his statement as being superficial and little more than a brave attempt at positive thinking. But Jesus didn't stop there! He goes on and, by way of a kind of self description, gives us sound reasons to stop being afraid.

## REASONS FOR NOT BEING AFRAID

### Christ as Companion

We can stop being afraid because the Risen Christ is our companion. Jesus says, "I am the first and the last." Jesus is saying that he is with us from A to Z, from the beginning to the end. He is there when we are born and he is there when we die. He is with us in the good times and he is with us in the bad times. He is with us at the beginning of the Christian life and he is with us when we complete the course. We are not alone in the world. The Risen Christ is our constant companion.

John certainly wanted the first readers of his letter to get this message loud and clear! Remember the situation. John was writing to Christians who were being persecuted because of their Christian faith and witness. The Roman Emperor had assumed the status of a god and was demanding to be worshiped. Christians who insisted on remaining loyal to Christ, and refused to pledge allegiance to the Emperor, were tortured and murdered. John, himself, was imprisoned on the Island of Patmos because of his unflinching faithfulness to Jesus Christ. Nothing would have destroyed the Christians quicker than to think that God had abandoned them to the enemy and left them alone in the struggle. So John writes to his "brothers in tribulation" and gives them strength to endure by reminding them that they are not alone. The Risen Christ is with them. He was their companion. If that doesn't put courage in your blood and iron in your backbone, then nothing will.

Helmut Thielicke, a German theologian and preacher, who knew what it was to suffer persecution for being a Christian in Hitler's Germany, writes:

> Jesus Christ did not remain at base headquarters in heaven, receiving reports of the world's suffering from below and shouting a few encouraging words to us from a safe distance. No, he left the headquarters and came down to us in the front-line trenches, right down to where we live and worry about what the Bolsheviks may do, where we contend with our anxieties and the feeling of emptiness and futility, where we sin and suffer guilt, and where we must finally die. There is nothing that he did not endure with us. He understands everything.*

We can stop being afraid because Jesus Christ is alive and he is our companion through all of life — even in "the front-line trenches" of life — and his presence completely transforms the situation.

### Christ as Conqueror

We can stop being afraid because the Risen Christ is the conqueror of death. Jesus says, "I am he who was dead, and now you see me alive for timeless ages [for evermore]." Jesus is telling us here that, on Easter, he conquered death and he is alive for evermore to be with his people.

We sometimes give Thomas a hard time because he doubted that the visitor to the Upper Room was really the same Jesus who had been crucified. It was not until Thomas touched the nail-scarred hands and put his hand into the wound in Jesus' side that he accepted

---

*Christ and The Meaning of Life.* Translated by John W. Doberstein (New York: Harper & Brothers, 1962) p. 18.

Jesus as the Risen Christ. (John 20:28) But it was important to Thomas that the Risen Christ really was the same person as the crucified Jesus, because that meant that Christ really had conquered death!

The Reverend Charles L. Koester summarizes the message of Easter this way: "God isn't dead — Death is dead." It may not always seem to us that this is true, just as it may not always have seemed true to those who first listened to John. But faith affirms that it is true.

Someone has said that the message of Revelation for today's reader may be expressed in the words of James Russell Lowell:

*Though the cause of Evil prosper,*
*yet 'tis Truth alone is strong . . .*
*Truth forever on the scaffold,*
*Wrong forever on the throne, —*
*Yet that scaffold sways the future,*
*and, behind the dim unknown,*
*Standeth God within the shadow,*
*keeping watch above his own.*

We can stop being afraid because Jesus Christ is alive and he has conquered our "final enemy," death.

## Christ as Keeper of the Keys

We can stop being afraid because the Risen Christ holds the keys to Eternal Life. "I hold in my hand the keys of death and the grave," said Jesus. As Christians, we believe that Christ not only conquered death for himself, but he also unlocks the door of the grave and ushers us through it into that life which is eternal. Because Christ lives we shall live also (*John 14:19*). As Bishop Arthur James Moore used to say, "A Christian cemetery is the loneliest place in the world because nobody is there!" For those who believe in Jesus Christ and remain faithful to his Lordship even when the going is tough the bitterness of death is forever past.

One of the independent television stations in this area keeps running a commercial by a company called "Unlimited Doors." They sell steel doors, aluminum doors, wooden doors, swinging doors, sliding doors and also other kinds of doors. But the most important door that we will ever face is the door of death. It is fortunate for us that Jesus Christ holds the keys to that door. And he has the authority to let us pass through it into "the shining possibilities of the life that is eternal." (2 *Timothy 1:10,* J. B. Phillips)

This is not to say that we must wait until we die to enter eternal life. Indeed, eternal life is basically a quality of life that is so filled with hope and meaning that nothing can destroy it. It begins when we believe in Jesus Christ and actually commit ourselves to following him as the Lord of Life. But it is so abundant that the small boundaries of this lifetime cannot fully contain it and its fullness necessarily overflows into a deeper relationship with Christ on the other side of the grave.

Do we see what this means? It means that life has a purpose. History has a goal. We are not just going round and round in meaningless circles.

Sometime ago, there was a man named Wahlstrom who loved to tinker with mechanical things. A friend gave him a bombsight and Wahlstrom took it apart to see what made it work. When he put it together again, he decided to incorporate some spare parts that were left over from other projects. He enjoyed this so much that he decided to make it a full-time hobby. When his friends and neighbors heard what he was doing, they also gave him spare parts that were laying around their garages and workshops. Wahlstrom incorporated all of these into his growing machine. Eventually, it had 10,000 parts and was known as "Wahlstrom's Wonder." When he pushed a button, 3000 of the parts would begin to move. Lights would flash, bells would ring, and little gears would drive big gears. And the whole thing revolved on a turntable. Everybody agreed — Wahlstrom was a genius. There was only one problem! The machine didn't do anything. It had no purpose. It was useless.

Thank God we don't have to be like Wahlstrom's Wonder! We have a purpose. We are going somewhere. Our energies are tied up with constructive Christian tasks. In the language of John, there is another age beyond this present age and it will begin when Jesus Christ comes in the fullness of his power. For those who remain faithful in their discipleship, it will be an age that is filled with vindication, peace, prosperity, and righteousness. And new and useful work for us to do.

Perhaps a statement by Victor Hugo will bring this whole matter closer to our own language and experience:

> The nearer I approach the end, the plainer I hear around me the immortal symphonies of the world to come. I will not say when the last moment comes that I have finished my life. For half a century I have been writing my thoughts in prose and verse; but I feel that I have not said one-thousandth part of what is in me. When I have gone down to the grave I shall have ended one day's work; but another day will begin the next morning.

We can stop being afraid because Jesus Christ is alive and he holds the keys to increasingly meaningful life — both on this side of the grave and on the other side of the experience we call death.

If any question remains at this point it is probably this: Is there any way that we can improve our chances of personally meeting this Risen Lord who reveals himself as companion, conqueror, and keeper of the keys? And, based on John's experience, the answer is an emphatic yes.

## Ways of Meeting the Risen Christ

There are many ways of meeting the Risen Christ, but we will look at only two ways that are suggested by John in today's Scripture lesson.

We can meet the Risen Christ through our Sunday worship service.

John had his vision of the Risen Lord "on the Lord's day" when he was "inspired by the Spirit." In all probability, he experienced ecstasy — a kind of religious trance — one Sunday in which he was lifted beyond the world of space and time into the world of eternity.

When I try to translate what happened to John into the terms of my own experience, it comes out like this: the times when I come closest to the Risen Christ — the times when I see him the clearest and know beyond a doubt that he is with me — are the times when I am with others in the worshiping congregation "on the Lord's day." A day like this. With people like you. And we sing the great hymns, and the Word is read, and prayers are offered, and we come together for the sacraments, and we are inspired and we know that the Lord is in our midst.

Sometimes, even a miracle takes place. Albert W. Palmer writes,

> The real miracle of worship is the actual spiritual communion with the divine which may take place, the imparting of transforming peace and power to jangled, beaten, discouraged lives. A worship service into which people have come troubled, defeated, doubtful, and out of which they go with hearts again uplifted and countenance aglow, ready to meet life with new courage and deeper insight — such a worship

service has performed for them the most convincing of all miracles.*

We also meet the Risen Lord in our study of the Scriptures. Please take my word for it: John was thoroughly familiar with the Scriptures of his day. His writing is loaded with the language and images of the Old Testament. We simply have to believe that John's study of the Scriptures provided a channel that Christ could use to make himself known. As William Barclay says, "The best way to prepare oneself for new revelation of truth is to study the revelation which God has already given."†

The marvelous thing about such Bible study is that it not only informs us about Christ, but it also gives him an opportunity to reveal himself anew to us.

Then we know that Christ is indeed alive — for us — and we can stop being afraid.

---

*The Art of Conducting Public Worship* (New York: The MacMillan Company, 1957) p. 2

†*The Daily Study Bible Series*, "The Revelation of John," Revised (Philadelphia: The Westminster Press, 1976), p. 45.

# Third Sunday of Easter

Then in my vision I heard the voices of many angels encircling the Throne, the Living Creatures and the Elders. There were myriads of myriads and thousands of thousands, crying in a great voice,

"Worthy is the Lamb Who was slain, to receive power and riches and wisdom, and strength and honor and glory and blessing!"

Then I heard the voice of everything created in Heaven, upon earth, under the earth and upon the sea, and all that are in them saying,

"Blessing and honor and glory and power be given to Him Who sits upon the throne, and to the Lamb, for timeless ages!"

The four Living Creatures said, "Amen," while the Elders fell down and worshiped.

*Revelation 5:11-14*
J. B. Phillips

# Worthiness And Worship

I have known people who stayed away from the worship services of the church because they felt they were not good enough to attend. I confess that, at times, I have felt the same way myself. There are probably many of us who can identify with the woman who said to her pastor, "I am not good enough to be a Christian, to go to church, and to worship."

It may be helpful to such people to recall that many of the great figures in the Bible shared in this same feeling. When the prophet, Isaiah, entered the temple "in the year that King Uzziah died" and "saw the Lord sitting upon a throne, high and lifted up" and heard the seraphim singing, "Holy, holy, holy is the Lord of hosts; the whole earth is full of his glory," he was overwhelmed. And he cried, "Woe is me! For I am lost; for I am a man of unclean lips, and I dwell in the midst of a people of unclean lips; for my eyes have seen the King, the Lord of hosts!" (*Isaiah 6:1-5*, R.S.V.)

One time when Simon Peter had been fishing all night and had caught nothing, Jesus told Simon to push out into deep water and to let down his nets again. Simon resisted at first but finally did as Jesus directed him and then he caught so many fish that his boat nearly sank beneath their weight. When Simon saw this, he fell down at the knees of Jesus and said, "Depart from me, for I am a sinful man, O Lord." (*Luke 5:8*, R.S.V.)

You remember Jesus' story of the Pharisee and the tax collector. Both men prayed. But the Pharisee used his prayer as an opportunity to tell God how good he was. The tax collector, on the other hand, would not even lift his eyes to heaven, but beat his breast, saying, "God be merciful to me a sinner!" (*Luke 18:13*, R.S.V.)

And Jesus said that it was the tax collector, rather than the Pharisee, who went home justified in God's sight.

So, if we do not feel worthy to worship, at least we are in good company. Nevertheless, our feeling that we cannot worship God because we are not worthy represents a complete misunderstanding of Christian worship. To be sure, there is a relationship between worthiness and worship. "Worship" literally means "worth-ship." *But the reference here is not to our worthiness to worship; the reference is to the worthiness of Jesus Christ to be worshiped.* In fact, it is precisely because we are not worthy that we come to the house of the Lord to worship Jesus Christ as the Risen Lord and the Savior of our lives.

There are many reasons why Christ is worthy of our worship, but we will focus on only three of the reasons that are mentioned in today's Scripture lesson.

### The Worthiness of Christ

1. Jesus Christ is worthy of our worship because he gave his life for us. "Worthy is the Lamb who was slain," writes John.

We need not dwell upon John's imagery of blood and sacrifice in order to get his point. The Risen Christ who now guides his Church through difficult times through the power of his Spirit, is the same Jesus who loved us so much that he gave himself for our salvation. Paul had written, "But God shows his love for us in that while we were yet sinners Christ died for us." (*Romans 5:8*, R.S.V.) And on one occasion Jesus had said, "Greater love has no man than this, that a man lay down his life for his friends." (*John 15:13*, R.S.V.)

C. FitzSimons Allison tells of an automobile accident that occurred in a rural county and the family was taken to a small hospital. Fortunately, the only one who was hurt was the little girl. She had lost a lot of blood and the small hospital did not have the type of blood that was needed for a transfusion. Her small brother was the only immediate source of the kind of blood she needed. The doctor suggested that the father approach the boy and tell him that his sister was quite ill and ask him if he would give her a transfusion. The little boy was not sure of what was involved but he did not hesitate for a moment. He hurried into the hospital where he was placed on a table next to his sister. Since he was young and might wiggle around with the needle in his arm, the doctor decided to put him to sleep while the transfusion was in process. As his blood flowed into his sister, her color returned and she began to recover. Later, as he was waking up, his father entered the room and said, "Son, I just want to thank you for giving some of your blood to your sister." Looking up from his pillow, the boy replied, "My blood? I thought I was gonna give my life."

"Worthy is the Lamb that was slain," said John. Jesus Christ loved us so much that he gave his life to save us — to forgive us our sins and lead us back to fellowship with God. His worthiness is the only worthiness that counts. It inspires our worship. It gives us whatever worthiness we may have.

2. Jesus Christ is worthy to be worshiped because he possesses the answers to our needs. The seven things of which the angels sing in our Scripture lesson have been called the "possessions" of the Risen Lord. They are power, riches, wisdom, strength, honor, glory, and blessing. From his well stocked storehouse of possessions, the Risen Christ is able to minister to all our needs with an extravagance and effectiveness that transcends our wildest dreams.

When we are weak and feel worn-out, then we call upon Christ and he gives us the *power* we need to cope with life.

When our spirits are discouraged and nearly

bankrupt, then he renews us and makes us more than millionaires with what Paul calls "the unsearchable *riches* of Christ." (*Ephesians* 3:8)

When we have enough knowledge to comprehend the problems of life, but not enough understanding to solve them, then we call on Christ and he shares his *wisdom* with us. It is "the wisdom of God" and helps us to solve not only the problems we have but also (as Paul Scherer said) the problems we are.

When we are nearly ready to crumble and to give in to the devilish temptation to compromise our Christian principles — or to make a full scale surrender to the enemy — then the Risen Lord gives us more than enough *strength* for victory, if we only ask him for it.

When we are drifting about in life with a lot to live *on* and not much to live *for,* he gives us a Lordship and a teaching and a life-style that inspires our *honor* and commitment.

When we forget who we are — and whose we are — then Christ shares his *glory* with us and it is the glory of God. And we know that our lives are tied up with a special divinity that we cannot escape even when we try.

And the *blessing* — the blessing is that Jesus Christ does not selfishly clutch his possessions to himself, but freely shares them with us. And, thereby, he enables our lives to become a blessing to others.

I'll tell you this: the Christ who ministers so generously to us and our needs, and thus enables us to minister to others, is worthy of our worship!

3. Jesus Christ is also worthy of our worship because he has unique authority. John says that the Lamb who was slain is now Risen and "sits upon the throne" for evermore. He shares the authority of God "and he shall be King for timeless ages." (*Rev. 11:15,* J.B.P.)

Sometimes I think that we are like the boy who stood looking at the royal hothouse gardens in Sweden.

His mother was sick and he wanted to take her some grapes he saw hanging on the vines. He finally gathered enough courage to ask the gardener if he could buy a bunch, but was sternly refused. A young man who had been standing nearby and heard the request cut off two fine bunches of grapes and handed them to the boy. When the boy offered to pay for the grapes the young man, who was really the prince, refused to accept the money, saying, "My father is not a merchant who sells; he is a king who gives."

Our Lord is like that, says John. When he offers his possessions to us — when he gives his life for us — his gifts are meaningful and effective because he has the authority to give them.

And that is the only way we can receive them: as gifts. They cannot be bought or earned. Only the Risen Christ who "sits upon the throne" can give them to those who are receptive. And he is generous.

Truly, Jesus Christ is worthy of our worship.

But what is the nature of our worshipful response?

### The Worship of Christ

1. The dominant note of our worship is praise. John does not use the word praise, but it undergirds everything that he says. You can feel it in your bones. It sings out from between the lines. And that is no surprise. When you consider the worthiness of Christ to be worshiped, then there is little choice but to respond with praise.

Raymond Abba says that praise is the "characteristic note" of worship. Indeed it is "the very essence of all true worship."* When God reveals himself to us through Jesus Christ, it is such a marvelous experience

---

*Principles of Christian Worship* (New York: Oxford University Press, 1960) p. 132.

that we have to sing.

Like many other ministers, I always join with our senior choir for a prayer before we enter the worship service on Sunday morning. When I lead in the prayer, I often include a phrase that goes like this: "We thank you, God, for giving us a faith that is so vital and alive that it needs to be sung."

When Carl F. Burke invited some kids from city streets to translate parts of the Bible into their own language, here is the way they paraphrased Psalm 117:

*Everybody give the Lord a cheer*
*Everywhere in the world.*
*Tell the good things about Him*
*(They ain't no bad things anyway.)*
*His love is just great!*
*And is strong and for sure*
*And it lasts longer than red bricks.*
*Give a cheer to the Lord.*\*

"Everybody give the Lord a cheer": that is a good expression of praise as the dominant note of our worship.

2. Our worship is characterized by humility. John says the elders "fell down and worshiped." While our worship is not dependent upon any particular physical posture, many of us feel that kneeling is still an appropriate part of worship because it expresses a humble and receptive spirit.

Personally, I cannot comprehend a worship service that omits the Prayer of Confession. Where I came from, everybody on the block had "sinned and fallen short of the glory of God." And it's a good thing just to recognize that fact and get it out in the open where the cool breeze of God's forgiving love can make us clean again.

---

\*From: *Treat Me Cool, Lord,* Copyright © 1968 by National Board of YMCA. Used by permission of Follett Publishing Company.

This doesn't mean that we wallow in a morbid sense of guilt and unworthiness. God forbid! But it does mean that, as Theodore Parker Ferris put it, there is "a healthy sense of unworthiness." When we see ourselves against the backdrop of God's perfection, as Isaiah did in the temple and as Peter did in the boat, then we know how far short we have fallen from God's intention for our lives.

It is this acknowledgment of our dependence and this "healthy sense of unworthiness" that drives us to the humility of spirit which provides an opening for God to enter our lives.

3. Our worship is also inclusive. "Everything created" worshiped the Lamb on the throne, says John. Those on earth worshiped. Those in Heaven worshiped. Those who had died worshiped. Even the animals and creatures of the sea worshiped. Talk about "the ecumenical spirit"! The John of Revelation makes John R. Mott and St. Francis of Assisi look provincial.

How great is our Lord and how vast the whole company of those who worship him!

I like the story that Raymond Abba tells about the cynical English Colonel who was billeted in a French village during the First World War. The Colonel took great delight in teasing the old village priest. One Sunday morning he passed the church as a handful of faithful people were leaving Mass. "Good morning, Father," he called to the priest at the door. "Not very many at Mass this morning, Father — not very many!" "No, my son, you're wrong," replied the priest. "There were thousands and thousands and tens of thousands!"*

The priest was right, of course. We are "surrounded by so great a cloud of witnesses" (*Hebrews 12:1*) and when we worship we are joined by "the angels and the

---
*Abba, p. 12.

archangels and all the company of heaven." That is what we mean when we say that our worship is inclusive.

4. Finally, our worship leads to obedient action. "Amen" cried the creatures in John's revelation. "Let it be so." Our verbal consent to the risen Christ implies that our words will be confirmed by our deeds. The worthiness of the Lamb to be worshiped must be affirmed with our lives as well as our lips.

The Christians who first heard John had to live out their "Amens" in the midst of a hostile environment. When they said, "Worthy is the Lamb who was slain and is risen," they very well may have been signing their own death warrants. But, if they suffered with Christ and for Christ, then that suffering would be one more cause for rejoicing. The worthiness of the one they worshiped would give them all the worthiness they wanted or cared about.

We do not take our own worship lightly. When the minister says the "Amen" at the conclusion of the Benediction, he is giving us our marching orders. The service is just beginning!

# Fourth Sunday of Easter

After this I looked, and behold, a great multitude which no man could number, from every nation, from all tribes and peoples and tongues, standing before the throne and before the Lamb, clothed in white robes, with palm branches in their hands, and crying out with a loud voice, "Salvation belongs to our God who sits upon the throne, and to the Lamb!" And all the angels stood around the throne and round the elders and the four living creatures, and they fell on their faces before the throne and worshiped God, saying, "Amen! Blessing and glory and wisdom and thanksgiving and honor and power and might be to our God for ever and ever! Amen."

Then one of the elders addressed me saying, "Who are these, clothed in white robes, and whence have they come?" I said to him, "Sir, you know." And he said to me, "These are they who have come out of the great tribulation; they have washed their robes and made them white in the blood of the Lamb.

Therefore are they before the throne of God, and serve him day and night within his temple; and he who sits upon the throne will shelter them with his presence.

They shall hunger no more, neither thirst any more; the sun shall not strike them, nor any scorching heat.

For the Lamb in the midst of the throne will be their shepherd, and he will guide them to springs of living water; and God will wipe away every tear from their eyes."

*Revelation 7:9-17*
*R.S.V.*

# On A Dark Day You Can See Forever

"On A Clear Day You Can See Forever." That was the title of a play that was popular a few years ago. I must confess to you that I never saw the play, but I have always been fascinated by the title. It came to mind again as I was preparing this sermon, because it suddenly dawned on me that if you change one word in that title you have a good description of John's vision as it is recorded in today's Scripture lesson: On A *Dark* Day You Can See Forever!

"On A Clear Day You Can See Forever" has a nice sound to it, but there is no virtue in it. On clear days — those days when it is sunny and there are no clouds in the skies and everything is going well — then anyone can see forever. The clearness itself inclines us to a spirit of optimism. It is easy for us to think that because things are going well for us now they will continue to go well forever.

In his book, *Six Men*, Alistair Cooke writes of Edward VIII: "The most damning epitaph you can compose about Edward — as a Prince, as a King, as a man — is one that all comfortable people should cower from deserving: he was at his best only when the going was good." Of course, it is easy for us to be at our best on the "clear days" when the "going is good." But what about the dark days when the going is tough? Those are the days that test our faith and create character.

And this brings us back to John. He was writing in dark days — in days when the clouds of persecution and oppression were dark and the sun hid its face from him and others who were members of the Christian Church. The Roman Emperor demanded that he be worshiped instead of Christ, and when Christians refused to conform to his demands they were persecuted and killed. It is not surprising, therefore, that John spoke so harshly of Rome, referring to her as "Babylon . . . mother of harlots and . . . drunk with the blood of the saints and the blood of the martyrs of Jesus." (Revelation 17:5, 6, R.S.V.)

The darkness of the days did not defeat John, however, and beyond the darkness he could see forever. He could see that all the cruelties and injustices suffered by the faithful on earth would ultimately be straightened out. John had sneaked a peek at the end of his history book and now he knew that God was going to win in the end. Therefore, it was important for the church to remain patient and faithful and to wait for God's final victory, which had already been foreshadowed in the Resurrection victory of Jesus Christ.

On a dark day John saw forever because he saw the eternal glory of the Risen Christ.

We should remember this and take heart on our own dark days — on those days when the odds seem stacked against justice and truth, and our own efforts at Christian witnessing seem to be bouncing ineffectively off the walls of an unreceptive and, at times, hostile environment. We may not experience the intense persecution that many of our Christian brothers and sisters still face in many parts of the world, but our lives are tied up with theirs and we suffer with them. And we know the personal pain of our own frustration and discouragements.

John is telling us and the whole Church to take heart and remain faithful because he had looked out on a dark day and he had seen forever. He looked down the road and he saw what was in store for the faithful and it was victory and satisfaction and comfort — forever.

## Victory

Those who are faithful to Christ in the diffcult times will experience ultimate and eternal victory.

There is nothing that keeps us going on, even in the face of great pain, like the hope of victory. We want to be winners. We don't want to be losers. Some time ago, a magazine showed the photographs of several faces. They were twisted beyond recognition by what appeared to be excruciating pain. The reader of the magazine was supposed to guess what caused such severe facial distortions. Had they been run over by a bus? Were they boxers whose faces had just been hit by gloves that were loaded with lead? No. They were runners who were pushing themselves almost beyond human limits in order to cross the finish line before the other competitors. They were running that hard because they wanted to be victorious in the race, and, I feel sure, the winner would say that the victory was worth all the pain.

John is telling us that though the Christian Church may face some vicious "competition" in this present age, in the end she is going to win the victory. As someone has said, John has given us "a marvelous picture of the church militant which has become the church triumphant."

The oppression had been terrible, but those who had remained faithful to the Risen Lord had "come out" of it. They had survived! I like the way the *New English Bible* expresses this point. It says, "These are the men who have *passed through* the great ordeal." Doesn't that remind you of the twenty-third Psalm where it says, "Even though I *walk through* the valley of the shadow of death, I fear no evil; for thou art with me . . ." God doesn't take away all of our difficulties, but he never permits them to be dead ends! He helps us to *pass through* them and to come out victorious on the other side.

For the faithful, according to John's vision, are more than mere survivors. They have been "saved." When they "came out" they "came out" shouting: "Salvation belongs to our God who sits upon the throne, and to the Lamb!" God had not only kept them from falling apart, he had actually made them whole. God had not only taken away their pain, he had actually restored them to perfect health. And God had done it through his Son Jesus Christ.

We need not get bogged down in John's imagery of how the faithful would be saved through "the blood of the Lamb." The point he is making is that through the life and death of Jesus Christ the Christian experiences a purity and victory that he could never achieve for himself. The evidence of the Christian's victory is the fact that he is dressed in white robes, which are Christian symbols of victory.

Dr. Carl Michalson was a brilliant Christian teacher and preacher. I have heard that he once told a class in Systematic Theology that his favorite television program was "Gunsmoke." He said that he liked that program because it was easy to tell the good guys from the bad guys. The good guys always wore white and the bad guys always wore black. And, although the good guys and the bad guys were always engaged in a battle, you knew that in the end the good guys — the fellows in white — were going to win.

John believed that too. The Church was involved in a battle with the powers of darkness and evil, but in the end the Christians who are "dressed in white robes" — those who remain faithful in their discipleship to the Risen Christ — are going to win.

You may have heard of the man who said that he believed that the world was engaged in a great spiritual warfare between the powers of light and the powers of darkness — between Christ and Satan — and he went to church to let people know whose side he was on.

Those who stand on the side of Christ now can be assured that they are standing on the winning side, because John looked out one dark day and beyond the darkness he saw victory stretching out forever.

*Satisfaction*

Those who are faithful to Christ on the dark days will also come to experience the unending satisfaction of their deepest needs and their highest desires. John writes, "They shall hunger no more, neither thirst anymore." The words remind us of what Jesus had said in the Beatitudes: "Blessed are those who hunger and thirst for righteousness, for they shall be satisfied." (Matthew 5:6, R.S.V.) Or, as the *Good News Bible* translates this verse: "Happy are those whose greatest desire is to do what God requires; God will satisfy them fully!"

We live in a world that promises us satisfaction. Sears, Roebuck and Company, one of the world's largest stores, popularized the slogan: "Satisfaction Guaranteed or Your Money Back." I doubt that any store that provides a product or service would even stand a chance of succeeding unless it offered a similar guarantee. Recently, a political candidate in this area told the voters that he was the only one who could satisfy the community's needs. Such guarantees are great when it comes to exchanging a defective toaster or getting a pot-hole filled in front of your house. But at the deepest levels of our human needs, the world cannot deliver on its promise to satisfy us.

The religion of Hinduism takes an interesting view of this whole matter. It says, for example, that there is nothing inherently evil or wrong in seeking pleasure and worldly success, with its components of fame, wealth, and power. All of these things may be sought and enjoyed within responsible limits. Nevertheless, Hinduism still hopes that a person will mature to the point where he realizes that the problem with pleasure and worldly success is that they are too limited to satisfy his deepest needs. Certainly our Christian faith would agree on the inability of pleasure to completely satisfy us. As Kierkegaard, the Danish philosopher and theologian, expressed it, "In the bottomless ocean of pleasure, I have sounded in vain for a spot to cast anchor." Or, if Kierkegaard is too fine for our taste, then we can get the same message from the country-western singer who had "done it all" and still concluded, "I can't get no satisfaction."

Augustine was right, you know, when he said that God has made us for himself, and our hearts are restless until they find their rest in him. So hold on, Church — and hold on, Christian — fight the good fight and run the race with patience and faithfulness, and Christ will give you the prize of complete and unending satisfaction. He is the only one who can guarantee that and actually deliver it: "I am the bread of life; he who comes to me shall not hunger, and he who believes in me shall never thirst." (*John 6:35*, R.S.V.)

On a clear day, we may not be able to see that because we are probably sailing along on the pleasant delusion of self-sufficiency. But on a dark day we can see forever, and we know that the Risen Lord is the only One who can fully satisfy our deepest needs and our highest desires.

### Comfort

Finally, those Christians who remain faithful in their witness to the lordship of Jesus Christ will be comforted by God himself. John says that the Risen Christ "will be their shepherd, and he will guide them to springs of living water; and God will wipe away every tear from their eyes."

Oh what a joy that will be! We will know that the struggle was worth it, the sacrifices were worth it, the suffering was worth it. We will know the joy of comfort that never ends.

You may be interested to know that this particular Sunday, which used to be called the Third Sunday After Easter, is traditionally referred to as *Jubilate*. The theme is joy and a special kind of joy. It is "the exuberance of sorrow which has been turned into joy."*

And what will turn our sorrow to joy? The eternal comfort of God.

Like the Good Shepherd that he is, Jesus Christ will lead the weary "to springs of living water." He will lead those who were wounded in the battle "beside still waters" where he will "restore their souls." (*Psalm 23:2*, R.S.V.) He will nourish their bodies by providing for all of their physical and spiritual needs.

And their hearts — our hearts — will be comforted for "God will wipe away every tear from their eyes." He will personally usher us into (what Lynn Harold Hough called) "The Land Where Tears are Only a Memory."

If you have ever known the pain of sorrow as a little child, and then experienced the joy of a loving mother holding you on her lap and gently wiping away your tears, then you will have a tiny inkling of that comfort that comes from God — and will come forever to those who remain faithful to his Son.

In October of 1978, a major event took place in the Church of England. After seventy-four years, Liverpool's Anglican Cathedral — England's "last great cathedral" — was finished and finally dedicated by Queen

---
*Reginald H. Fuller, *Preaching the New Lectionary* (Collegeville, Minnesota: The Liturgical Press, 1974) p. 28.

Elizabeth II. Her great-grandfather, King Edward VII, laid the foundation stone on July 19, 1904. The building of the cathedral has survived two world wars and the German's bombs. It has continued through bankruptcy, labor strife and rising costs. The work was once stopped for two years by a strike. Thieves broke in and stole the bronze bars for the last big stained glass window, so that it was not installed until just a few days before the dedication.

During the darkest and most difficult years of the war, King George VI visited the cathedral builders and told them, "Keep on with the work, if only in a small way. Refuse to be beaten."

King George was only talking about a church building. But the words could be John's as he speaks to the people of the church militant on their way to becoming the church triumphant: "Keep on with the work, if only in a small way. Refuse to be beaten." "And," he would add, "if you do that you will come to know the joy of eternal victory, unending satisfaction, and everlasting comfort."

If you keep your eyes on the Risen Christ, then, like John, even on a dark day you can see forever!

# Fifth Sunday of Easter

Then I saw a new heaven and a new earth; for the first heaven and the first earth had passed away, and the sea was no more. And I saw the holy city, new Jerusalem, coming down out of heaven from God, prepared as a bride adorned for her husband; and I heard a great voice from the throne saying, "Behold, the dwelling of God is with men. He will dwell with them, and they shall be his people, and God himself will be with them; he will wipe away every tear from their eyes, and death shall be no more, neither shall there be mourning nor crying nor pain any more, for the former things have passed away."

And he who sat upon the throne said, "Behold, I make all things new." Also he said, "Write this for these words are trustworthy and true."

*Revelation 21:1-5*
R.S.V.

# The City Of Hope

Robert A. Mann tells of passing through the Idaho towns of Hope and East Hope. A few minutes later he noticed a sign in the midst of a small cluster of buildings. It read: "Beyond Hope."

Today's cities are increasingly characterized as being places that are "beyond hope." That seems to be the judgment of Lewis Mumford, an expert on metropolitan areas, who decries the tendency in cities to regard what is pathological as normal. It is also the judgment of the "average citizen" who has to contend on a daily basis with rising costs, rising taxes, rising rates of crime and violence, and rising pollution. The list could go on and on; everything seems to be rising except hope.

Of course, there are many fine values in our cities and we are thankful for them, but these do not solve the problems that are there. Neither does money. In a recent "Mr. Tweedy" cartoon, two well dressed businessmen have just passed a poor man who is dressed in rags and is "down and out" on the sidewalk. One of the businessmen says to his friend, "I gave him a nickel even though I don't think we can solve problems by throwing money at them." We know too many people who are "up and out" to sincerely believe that increased amounts of money are going to solve all the problems and make the situation more hopeful.

John, on the other hand, has caught a vision of another city — "the holy city, new Jerusalem, coming down out of heaven from God" — and it is a city of hope. It hasn't been completed yet, but it has been established in principle through the resurrection of Jesus Christ, and it is anticipated in the life of the church. This new city will be the place of ultimate happiness for all those who have been faithful to Christ in those cities where they now live.

Now, we may live in cities that are characterized by sin and weakness and failure, but it is the essence of the Christian hope that the lives of individuals may be so transformed and that, indeed, the whole creation may be so radically transformed that it will ultimately become the completed community of perfect love.

This city of hope, that John talks about in today's Scripture lesson, is characterized by two things: the nearness of God and the newness of men. These two things are very important to us in the here and now because to the degree that we experience them in our own lives we are already participating in the city of hope.

### The Nearness of God

John reports, "Behold the dwelling of God is with men. He will dwell with them, and they shall be his people, and God himself will be with them." Note the repetition in this brief report. John wants to be sure we get the message. He says the same thing three times: God himself is with us! The city of hope, therefore, is the city to which God has drawn near in order to establish his personal residence with his people. God is not just "The Man Who Came to Dinner"; he is near to us on a permanent basis.

There is no question about the reality of God's presence with us, but we are not always able to perceive his presence. In fact, we will never be permanently and continuously aware of his presence until the city of hope is fully experienced in heaven. Nevertheless, here in this world, we do catch occasional glimpses of God's presence.

I read of such a glimpse in a recent newspaper.

"Run!" was the last sound to reach Maria Brown before the lightning bolt struck her. The jolt knocked her to the ground, stopped her breathing and her heartbeat, and sent her into a coma. Ms. Brown's neck was badly burned where the lightning struck her necklace and fried her skin. Her skull was scorched and there were long jagged burns where the electricity traveled down her stomach and leg and out between the toes of her right foot. There were other injuries, but she survived! Dr. Brooks Gilmore, a heart specialist, said, "She's doing amazingly well for the amount of injury she had. It's a miracle she survived." And Dr. Richard Bloomfield, the physician who treated her in the emergency room of the hospital, said, "Basically, she survived (because) God was with her."*

We are thankful that the presence of God is usually experienced in less dramatic ways. We catch glimpses of him in our worship — through the Word and Sacrament. We know he is near when we are with people who truly "love one another even as Christ loved them." We catch other glimpses of God's presence when his Spirit communes with our spirits and when his Spirit really comes alive in the church and in the family. Surely, "the dwelling place of God is with men and God himself will be with them."

Such nearness — such fellowship — should not come as a surprise to us. It is the fulfillment of scriptural promises. Following the Exodus, God had promised Moses, "And I will make my abode among you . . . and I will walk among you, and will be your God, and you shall be my people." (*Leviticus 26:11, 12*, R.S.V.) Both Jeremiah (*31:33*) and Ezekiel (*37:27*) had echoed the same promise. Now, in his vision of the city of hope, John is saying that this promise has been fulfilled. And

---

*Reported in *The Wilmington Morning News*, Wilmington, Delaware, November 3, 1978, p. 41.

even now we can begin to experience a deep and meaningful fellowship with God.

The nearness of God, of course, is a central theme of our Christian faith. We are still in the Easter Season, but it is difficult to keep our minds from racing back to Christmas. Then we affirmed that, the word of God "became a human being and lived among us." (*John 1:14*, J. B. Phillips) Then we knew that Jesus was Immanuel which means "God with us." And we know it still. Our God is no dim and distant deity; he has drawn near to us through Jesus the Christ, and he is present with us even now through the power of his Spirit.

He is with us in our suffering, weakness and failure. Certainly the cross tells us that.

He is with us in our joy and the victory of new life. Indeed, he is our joy and victory. Certainly the Resurrection tells us that.

And he walks beside us as the Unseen Companion in every experience of every day. Certainly the story of the Emmaus Road tells us that. (*Luke 24:13-35*)

The God revealed in Jesus Christ our Lord is with us always and in all ways. (*Matthew 28:20*)

Our fellowship with him is the basis of the Christian community and the essence of our worship. "For where two or three are gathered in my name," said Jesus, "There am I in the midst of them." (*Matthew 18:20*, R.S.V.)

God's nearness to us, and our fellowship with him through the Risen Christ, is also a moral and spiritual challenge to each one of us to translate God's presence into thoughts, words, and actions that are pure and loving and just.

Let us make no mistake about it. Our perception of the truth may grow dim at times, but the truth remains: "the dwelling of God is with men . . . and God himself will be with them."

But, in spite of all that we have said so far, the best thing still remains to be said.

## The Newness of Men

When God draws near to men, and they are open to receive his presence and to welcome him, he always makes them new!

John reports God's thrilling intention for us: "Behold, I make all things new." The report is even more impressive when we realize that it is God himself who makes it. This is the first time that John announced a direct statement from God, and it is a promise to make us into new persons!

One of the finest sermons I have ever heard was preached by D. Reginald Thomas, when he was the minister of the First Presbyterian Church in Germantown, Philadelphia. He told of his school days and of how he was far from being the favorite of his mathematics teacher. He had the dubious distinction of arriving at more incorrect answers than any boy in class. And, on the infrequent occasions when his answers were right, it was usually discovered that he had used the wrong methods. The smudges in his exercise book that were caused by erasing so many incorrect answers became his badges of disgust. Time after time, the teacher said to him, "Turn over a new leaf, boy, and start again."

Thomas was reminded of that experience years later when he was serving a church in Wales, and for the first time in his ministry he was faced with a life in ruins. Through sheer lack of experience, Thomas tried to counsel the troubled man by telling him that his prospects for the future were going to be brighter. Finally, after many talks, one day the man shouted at Thomas angrily, "It's no use. If only you knew everything that I've been." Then it dawned on Thomas that "this man was crying not for a new leaf but for a brand-new beginning."

That is what we want too, isn't it? At least, when we are deeply troubled and our lives are in ruins we know that "turning over a new leaf" is not enough; we need a whole new book and a whole new start. And, by the grace of God, that is exactly what we may have: "Behold, I make all things new."

You may have heard of the workman who was criticized by his workmates because he lived a life of strict sobriety, never gambled, and always spoke of the Bible with reverence. They teased him by saying, "If you believe in the Bible, you must believe that water was turned into wine?" "I believe more than that," he said. Then, as his mind wandered back over his early evil days before he met Christ, he added, "I have seen beer turned into furniture. Betting slips into food. I have seen a woman, miserable because she was married to a gambling addict, made radiantly and permanently happy because her man was changed before her eyes. Of course, I believe in miracles."

The story of that workman, incidentally, is included in a sermon by W. E. Sangster, a great English preacher. And you will not be surprised to learn that his sermon was also based on Revelation 21:5: "Behold," said God, "I make all things new."*

The God who is near to us is also the God who makes us new! The God who draws near to us in the Risen Christ "will wipe away the tears from [our] eyes, and death shall be no more, neither shall there be mourning nor crying nor pain anymore, for the former things have passed away."

Last summer, my wife and I took our young son to an outdoor program in Dover, Delaware. One of the

---

*Sangster's *Special Day Sermons* (Nashville: Abingdon Press, 1960) p. 42.

entertainers was a clown by the name of Professor Auguste. He "blew" his big red nose which was really a horn, stumbled over imaginary obstacles, and did all kinds of other things that made the "children of all ages" laugh. But the most interesting thing to my own curious eyes was a button with the initials "P-B-P-W-M-G-H-F-W-W-M-Y" that was pinned to Professor Auguste's lapel. Just before the program was over, he told us what the initials meant: "Please Be Patient With Me — God Hasn't Finished Working With Me Yet."

We have not yet reached the perfection of the city of hope — "the holy city . . . coming down out of heaven from God." But we have seen the sign, the resurrection of Jesus Christ our Lord, and we are on the way.

Therefore, as we continue to live in faithfulness to our Lord in the midst of our present cities, let us be patient and hopeful. For the God who draws near and makes all things new "hasn't finished working with us yet."

# Sixth Sunday of Easter

And in the Spirit he carried me away to a great, high mountain, and showed me the holy city Jerusalem coming down out of heaven from God, having the glory of God, its radiance like a most rare jewel, like a jasper, clear as crystal. It had a great, high wall, with twelve gates, and at the gates twelve angels, and on the gates the names of the twelve tribes of the sons of Israel were inscribed; on the east three gates, on the north three gates, on the south three gates, and on the west three gates. And the wall of the city had twelve foundations, and on them the twelve names of the twelve apostles of the Lamb.

\*\*\*

And I saw no temple in the city, for its temple is the Lord God the Almighty and the Lamb. And the city has no need of sun or moon to shine upon it, for the glory of God is its light, and its lamp is the Lamb.

*Revelation 21:10-14, 22-23*
R.S.V.

# The Perfect Church

A few years ago, there was a church in a southern city that had nearly fallen to the ground. The roof of the building had collapsed. The paint had peeled off the shingles and several windows had been broken. The yard was full of weeds and the bulletin board, which had once proudly announced the services of the church, had rotted. Still posted on the board, however, was the title of the last sermon that had been preached there: The Perfect Church.

The scene is symbolic. The distance between the truly perfect church that God intends for us and the church as we know it in our own experience is great. In fact, the contrast nearly overwhelms us at times.

Perhaps the only perfect church may be called "the once and future church." It existed *once* in the mind of John the Seer and he shares his vision of it with us through today's Scripture lesson. And, if we take John's vision seriously — as surely we must — then it will exist again, in fact, at some time in the *future*. It is significant that John uses the number "twelve" so often in his description of the once and future church because that number is a biblical symbol of perfection. But, in the meantime, we know that the church is not so perfect.

One sign of our imperfection, as Bishop Lance Webb points out, is the lack of vitality in our worship. He tells the story of the little boy who asked his pastor to explain the names on the bronze plaque in the narthex of his church. The pastor replied, "Those are the names of the men who died in the service." And the boy asked, innocently, "Which service, the nine or the eleven o'clock?" Webb goes on to say that there are hopeful signs of new life in the church today; however, we are not being unfair to recognize the fact that the church is still a long way from perfection.

This fact does not need to overwhelm us. It may even motivate us to become a better church. For, as D. Elton Trueblood says, "it is the unsatisfactory character of the Church as we know it that spurs us to the work of completion."

So, we look more closely at John's vision of the perfect church in the hope that it will spur us on to a closer approximation of that church in our own time and place.

Thus we notice that the perfect church:

*Comes From God and is Christ-Centered.*

John writes that he saw "the holy city Jerusalem coming down out of heaven from God." To be sure, John is writing about a city, but it is a "holy city" that is so filled with the presence of God that it has become identical with the Christian Church. And if the imagery of this church "descending from God out of heaven" means anything, it surely means that the church originates from God.

Human beings did not invent the Christian church. They did not create the church. The church is not the product of any human architect. The church is essentially a gift that is given to us by God, through his Son Jesus Christ.

In the United Methodist Church, *The Order For Confirmation and Reception Into The Church* begins with these words:

"Dearly beloved, the Church is of God, and will be preserved to the end of time, for the conduct of worship and the due administration of his Word and Sacraments, the maintenance of Christian fellowship and discipline, the edification of believers, and the conversion of the world. All, of every age and station, stand in need of the means of grace which it alone supplies."

That whole statement is worth pondering, but we are especially interested in the part that affirms "the Church is of God." Certainly our participation is desired, but only as we remember that the Church is God's creation and not our own.

I may refer to this particular congregation as "my church," but that is not an accurate statement. This particular congregation is actually one local expression of God's church, and it happens to be the one with which I choose to identify myself.

Not only does the church come from God, but it is also Christ-centered. Referring to the perfect church, John tells us that "its temple is the Lord God the Almighty and the Lamb." It is obvious, isn't it, that it is the presence of *Christ* which defines the *Christian* Church?

We have not yet obtained perfection and we need buildings in which the worshiping congregation can gather, but buildings do not make the church. We need liturgy, but liturgy does not make the church. We need an organization to implement our ministry, but organizations do not make the church. As William Barclay expresses it: "The one thing which makes a Church is the presence of Jesus Christ. Without that there can be no such thing as a Church; with that any gathering of people is a real Church."

As we try to approximate the perfect church in terms of our own experience, therefore, we will not forget that it comes from God and is Christ-centered.

The perfect church is also:

*Catholic.*

We are using the term here in its original sense, meaning worldwide or universal. If you read John's verses (21:15-21) which are sandwiched in between the beginning and the end of our Scripture lesson, you are impressed by the tremendous size of the city-church. It has enough room for everybody! It is big enough to include everybody in the whole world! Furthermore, the perfect church has "twelve doors" which stand as a generous invitation for all to enter. And the doors are "never shut"; they "shall stand open day after day" (Rev. 21:25, J. B. Phillips).

Thank God, we have come a long way in the last few years. But it is not easy to forget that not so long ago persons were barred from worshiping in so-called Christian churches because of their race. Discrimination has also raised its ugly face in other more subtle ways and slammed all "twelve doors" in the faces of those who only wanted to worship the Christ who also died and rose again from the dead for them.

In T. S. Eliot's play, *Murder in the Cathedral*, the priests bar the door against those who want to assassinate Thomas the Archbishop. Even though Thomas knows they have done it to protect him, he will not permit it. And he commands,

"Unbar the doors! throw open the doors!
I will not have the house of prayer, the
Church of Christ,
The sanctuary, turned into a fortress . . .
The Church shall be open, even to our enemies.
Open the door!*

When will we learn that Jesus Christ regards no person as an emeny? He defeated his "enemies" on the cross and rose victorious over them on Easter morning. Now his church is open to all. John reminds us that there are some who "deal in filthiness and lies" (Rev. 21:27, J. B. Phillips) who will not choose to enter.

---

* T.S. Eliot, *Murder in the Cathedral*, (New York: Harcourt, Brace and Company, 1935) p. 73.

But the door is open to all those who are faithful to the Risen Christ as the Lord and Savior of Life.

As we strive to embody the perfect church here on earth, we will not forget that it is truly catholic and is big enough to include everybody.

We will also remember that the perfect church is a:

*Community of Witnesses.*

John writes that the walls of the church are built on twelve foundations and the names of the twelve apostles are inscribed upon them. In other words, the church is literally founded upon the disciples' witness to the Lordship of the Risen Christ. Sometimes we sing "The Church's one foundation is Jesus Christ her Lord." And that is true. But how are others to know that unless someone tells them? Our responsibility as witnesses, therefore, is basic and necessary.

It is not happenstance that John says that "the glory of God is its light, and its lamp is the Lamb." Light shines for a purpose. In this instance, the light shines in order to help "the nations walk" in the path of faithfulness to Jesus Christ.

God himself is the light. Christ is the lamp from which the light shines. And we are the bearers of the lamp to all the peoples of the world.

Robert Louis Stevenson records the delightful memory of a summer that he spent in Northern Scotland, as a boy of twelve. Toward the end of September, when school time was drawing near and the nights were already black, Stevenson and his friends would equip themselves with tin bullseye lanterns. They would buckle the lanterns to their waists and button their top coats over them. The lanterns smelled of blistered tin, never burned right, and would always burn their fingers, but the boys didn't mind.

When they met in the darkness of the night, there

would be an anxious, "Have you got your lantern?" and a gratified "Yes!" Then the boy would open his coat, pull down the slide on his lantern, and let his light shine! Stevenson entitled this story about his boyhood experience, "The Lantern Bearers."

Well, that is what we are. That is what the Christian Church is. We are a community of Lantern-Bearers. We bear witness, in all we say and do, to the glory of God and to his Son Jesus Christ. They are the source of the light by which the nations walk. But what a privilege is our's to bear witness to the light.

We are not perfect and our lanterns grow dim at times. People who are experiencing "the dark night of the soul" cry out for light, and our response is not always as bright or gratifying as it ought to be. We are too much like the painting in a New York City exhibition. The critic who evaluated the painting said that it was excellent in many ways, but it was too dark. He said that when you looked at the painting you wanted to cry out, "Light! Light! Give me more light!" That is also the cry of a world that is walking in darkness: they want more light! Thank God that, as a community of witnesses to the glory of God and his Son, Jesus Christ, we are in a position to respond affirmatively!

Some of us remember the words of an old song: "This little light of mine, I'm gonna let it shine . . . Gonna shine it around the neighborhood . . . I'm gonna let it shine everywhere I go." When we let the light of Christ shine through us, it is our prayer that others will see the good things we do and give praise to our Father in heaven. (See John 5:16).

When we consider the perfect church, we will remember that it is basically a community of witnesses.

Finally, the perfect church is:

## Conducted by the Spirit

John does not say that the Holy Spirit is a characteristic of the perfect church, but it is clear from the Scripture lesson that his vision of the church and his participation in it were made possible only through the power of Christ's Spirit. If John had not been "in the Spirit," as he puts it, then he would never have had his vision of the perfect church and we would not have the book of Revelation which grew out of that experience.

Surely, the perfect church will never come upon the face of the earth unless it comes as a gift from God by the power of his Spirit. And his Spirit is the Spirit of Jesus Christ, working in and through people like you and me. As the Korean Creed puts it: "We believe in the Holy Spirit, God present with us for guidance, for comfort, and for strength."

It is clear, isn't it, that we cannot save ourselves? When we try to save ourselves, we are as pathetic as that proverbial fellow who tried to lift himself from the ground by pulling on his own bootstraps! Or we are like the small boy who got up into his high chair and then tried to pull himself up to the table by reaching around and tugging on the back of his chair. He grunted and groaned and made the most sincere effort, but of course he did not move. Finally, his father had to lift the chair, with him in it, and place it nearer to the table.

Even our sincerest efforts will not save us. They will not even move us one inch closer to the final goal of wholeness or perfection. If we are going to move in that direction — as individuals or as a church — then the Heavenly Father will have to move us. The power of his Spirit will have to lift us, as it lifted John, and move us along the road toward perfection.

The fact is that, by nature, we are not programmed for perfection. There was an interesting illustration of this at the 1976 Olympic games in Montreal, Canada.

When Nadia Comaneci, the amazing little fourteen year old gymnast, scored a perfect ten (10), the computers nearly blew a fuse and finally registered the score as ten one hundreds (.10). Quite a difference! This happened because the people who programmed the computers had been told that a perfect score of ten was an impossibility on the opening night of gymnastics. The computers simply were not programmed for perfection.

Neither are we!

The only way we are ever going to get anywhere near to perfection is to open ourselves to the Spirit of the Risen Christ who transforms our lives and guides us in the paths of obedient and faithful discipleship.

When ministerial candidates are admitted into the membership of a United Methodist Annual Conference, the Bishop asks the candidates a series of questions related to their character and commitment. A few minutes later he asks them another question: "Are you going on to perfection?" Usually, the candidates will squirm a bit uneasily as they consider the loftiness of the goal in the light of their human weaknesses. Occasionally, the Bishop will prompt them to a response by asking, "If you are not going on to perfection, then where are you going?"

John says that we should at least be aiming for the perfect church. Certainly we will come closer to it if we aim for it than we will come if we do not aim for it.

And, if we are not "going on to perfection," then where are we going?

# The Ascension

I thank God continually for you and I never give up praying for you; and this is my prayer. That God, the God of our Lord Jesus Christ and the all-glorious Father, will give you spiritual wisdom and the insight to know more of Him: that you may receive that inner illumination of the spirit which will make you realize how great is the hope to which He is calling you — the magnificence and splendor of the inheritance promised to Christians — and how tremendous is the power available to us who believe in God. That power is the same divine energy which was demonstrated in Christ when He raised Him from the dead and gave Him the place of supreme honor in heaven — a place that is infinitely superior to any conceivable command, authority, power of control, and which carries with it a Name far beyond any name that could ever be used in this world or the world to come.

God has placed everything under the power of Christ and has set Him up as Head of everything for the Church. For the Church is His body, and in that Body lives fully the One Who fills the whole wide universe.

*Ephesians 1:16-23*
J. B. Phillips

# A Lord Without Limits

If you were asked to name the four major festivals of the Christian year, what would you say? From the earliest times the Christian church has affirmed that these festivals were Christmas, Easter, Pentecost, and Ascension. I wonder how many of you knew all four of them. Most of you probably named Christmas and Easter immediately. Some of you probably even named Pentecost. But, unless I miss my guess, only a few, if any, remembered the Ascension.

One writer points out that Ascension Day was once an English holiday. It was the day on which the House of Commons adjourned. But, as time went on, the members of the House decided to work on Ascension Day and granted themselves a holiday, instead, on Derby Day. We have heard it said that "things were going to the dogs." But here was a case where a major Christian festival came in second place to the horses! This is only one of the signs of our increasing neglect of the Ascension.

Such neglect is surprising when we consider the prominent place the Ascension occupies in The Apostles' Creed. That creed devotes only one comma to the entire public ministry of Jesus Christ! There is nothing in that creed between the virgin birth of Jesus and his suffering under Pontius Pilate except a comma. And yet two whole lines are devoted to the Ascension: "he ascended into heaven, and sitteth at the right hand of God the Father Almighty; from thence he shall come to judge the quick and the dead."

If you want the biblical evidence for the Ascension, you will begin in *Luke 24:44-53* and *Acts 1:1-11*. Both of these accounts were written by Luke. According to the Gospel account, Jesus appeared to his disciples shortly after the resurrection and led them out as far as Bethany and "while he blessed them, he parted from them." According to the account in Acts, Jesus appeared to the disciples forty days after the resurrection and told them they would receive power when the Holy Spirit came upon them. "And when he said this, as they were looking on, he was lifted up, and a cloud took him out of their sight." It is further explained that Jesus "was taken up . . . into heaven."

And, of course, we must not overlook today's lesson in Ephesians which affirms that God "raised [Christ] from the dead and gave him the place of supreme honor in Heaven." Or, as the *Revised Standard Version* expresses it, God raised Christ from the dead "and made him sit at his right hand in the heavenly places."

But what does the Ascension of Christ mean for our lives? Perhaps you are willing to affirm a creed and to let the matter rest there. Millions have done that, but some of us feel a need to go on and try to translate the biblical material about the Ascension into a statement that will be of practical help to us in our daily living.

So, today we are suggesting this translation: The Ascension means that, as Christians, we worship a Lord without limits. The "same divine energy which was demonstrated in Christ when [God] raised him from the dead" also enables Christ to transcend the limitations of space and time and power.

### Not Limited by Space

It is certainly clear that we are limited by space. We can go very far very fast, but the fact remains that we can only be in one place at one time. An automobile manufacturer recently boasted that his company has produced a car that will travel 240 miles per hour. Thirteen years ago, R. L. Stevens set a new speed record for a landplane by traveling 2,070.1 miles per hour.

And the rockets that carried our astronauts to the moon would make Stevens look like he was standing still! In spite of the incredible speed with which we can travel from one place to another, we can still occupy only one space at any given time.

Such spacial limitation may be very frustrating to us at times. We may receive a telephone call informing us that a loved one has become seriously ill in a distant state. We would like to be *there* immediately. But we are *here*, and travel arrangements must be made.

Sometimes we think that we would like to have lived when Jesus of Nazareth was actually performing his ministry "in the flesh." We would like to see his face, hear his voice, and feel the touch of his hand. But we may not stop to think that in those days Jesus, also, was limited by space. If he had been preaching or teaching or healing in Galilee while we were shopping in Jerusalem, we would have missed him! You remember how Mary and Martha got so upset when their brother, Lazarus, had died before Jesus was able to get to him.

But, thank God, the Ascension has changed all that! For the Lord we worship *now* is no longer limited by spacial considerations. He has ascended to the Father who "made him sit at his right hand in the heavenly places."

If we have thought that "heaven" referred to the remoteness of God, then we have made a great mistake. For, indeed, heaven refers precisely to the nearness of God. Gerhard Ebeling, a German theologian, has written some words about the Lord's Prayer that are helpful at this point. He writes:

> To proclaim God as the God who is near, as Jesus did, is to put an end to the idea of heaven as God's dwelling place and to reverse the relation of God and heaven. It is not that where heaven is, there is God, but rather where God is,

there is heaven . . . For "Our Father, who art in heaven" means precisely, "Our Father, who art present here on earth." For the fact that God is near is not to be measured in terms of space. God is so near to us that he is nearer to us than we are to ourselves.*

When we say, with the writer of Ephesians, that the Risen Lord is "in heaven" we mean that he is with God. And, because God is near to us in all places, we know that Christ is with us also. He is no longer limited by space. He is present everywhere at once through the power of his Spirit. His words, "lo, I am with you always," (Matthew 28:20) take on a new meaning.

Now, we know that if a loved one becomes ill in another state or country, Christ our Lord is equally present with both of us. We will still have to make travel arrangements, but he will not! There is a human need here and he is here. There is a human need there and he is there. Our risen and ascended Lord is as near as a receptive heart; he is as near as a prayer.

I cannot imagine a more helpful or comforting thought: our ascended Lord is not limited by space.

### Not Limited by Time

Just as we are limited by space, we are also limited by time. This is true for all of us irrespective of our age or sex or income or anything else. Each one of us has sixty seconds in every minute, sixty minutes in every hour, twenty-four hours in every day, and seven days in every week. This much and no more. In this sense, we are prisoners of the clock and the calendar. We have so much time to work and play and then we must rest. We may not like it very much, but the fact remains that we

---

*On Prayer. Translated by James W. Leitch with an Introduction by David James Randolph. (Philadelphia: Fortress Press, 1966) p. 50.

are limited by the amount of time we have.

We live in a culture that values youth and the cosmetics industry has concocted all kinds of marvelous creams and lotions to help us deny the reality of growing older. But in our heart of hearts we know we are fighting a losing battle and that, as Tennessee Williams has said, youth is like a "sweet bird" that flies away. We may even share the feelings of a young lifeguard in one of John Updike's short stories:

> Each of our bodies is a clock that loses time. Young as I am, I can hear the protein acids ticking; I wake at odd hours and in the shuttering darkness and silence feel my death rushing toward me like an express train. The older we get, the fewer mornings left to us, the more deeply dawn stabs us awake.*

There is nothing like the consciousness of our own mortality to remind us that our time on earth is indeed limited.

But we thank God that our risen and ascended Lord does not share our limitations of time. For, as the writer of Ephesians reminds us, the ascended Christ now has a name "far beyond any name that could ever be used in this world or the world to come." Our Lord is the Lord of the past. He is the Lord of the present. And he is the Lord of all our tomorrows. And because of this we are able to sing the words of John Greenleaf Whittier with confidence:

> *I know not what the future hath*
>     *Of marvel or surprise,*
> *Assured alone that life and death*
>     *His mercy underlies.*

Jesus Christ has opened the door of death and, through our devotion to God and obedient service to his

---

*Pigeon Feathers and Other Stories* (Greenwich, Conn.: A Crest Book by Fawcett Publications, 1963) p. 148.

Son, we are enabled to walk through it. Jesus Christ is not running on a schedule that is ticked out by a Timex; he is running on God's time and it is only one more sign of his grace that he is willing to share it with us.

Our time on earth is still limited, of course, but now we are able to view it from a new perspective. Now we know, as Dr. Claude H. Thompson put it, that every day has "a delicate significance." The hours are filled with holy potential. Every second is sacred. We will not waste time or "kill it." We will count each day as a precious opportunity to love and serve others in the name of Christ.

When Dr. William E. Sangster was dying of a terminal illness and his time on this earth was growing increasingly limited, his belief in the Ascension of Christ gave him great comfort and hope because it reminded him that "on the other side of death is a known and dear Friend."

That is what the Ascension means: our time is limited but the love of Christ is not.

### Not Limited in Power

In addition to our limitations of time and space, we are limited in our power. Such super-heroes as Wonder Woman and the Incredible Hulk are enjoying great popularity on television, probably because they possess the kind of power that we would like to have for ourselves. But, alas, it is not so. While I was working on this sermon, I had to move a large object from the church to the parsonage and succeeded in this task only because a friend was kind enough to help me.

On a deeper level, we are limited in our power to cure illness. We are grateful for the contributions of doctors and nurses, but they have not yet found a cure for the common cold or for cancer. I was reminded of that again recently as I called on members of our congregation who are in the hospital.

And we are limited in our power to create a human community that transcends itself through its outgoing love and service to God and neighbor. For awhile, many people thought that Jim Jones had created such a community in Guyana, South America. This agricultural community appeared to be exemplary in its religious devotion and in its generosity to people in need. It received the congratulations of mayors, governors, a Vice-President, a U. S. Cabinet officer, and a President's wife, among others. But then the lid blew off and over 900 members of the Peoples' Temple followed their leader in the largest mass suicide-murder in modern history.

Such a tragedy defies easy explanations, but one suspected that at least part of the problem was due to Jones' sick and inflated notions of himself. A former associate of Jones said, "Jim stopped calling himself the reincarnation of Jesus and started calling himself God. He said he was the actual God who made the heavens and earth."*

We are limited in our power, even in the power to accomplish the best of human intentions. And we are certainly limited in our power to play God. Nothing but tragedy can result from such preposterous attempts.

But God, the True God, the God revealed in Jesus Christ, is not limited in power. This is what the Ascension means. The power of God which "raised Christ from the dead and made him sit at his right hand in the heavenly places" knows no bounds. This God is infinitely superior to any power on earth or beyond it. And this God "has placed everything under the power of Christ."

Our Lord is a Sovereign Lord. How badly we Christians need to trumpet-forth this theme again! This

---

*Time Magazine, 12/4/78, p. 27.

world is not a car that is careening wildly out of control. Our Lord's hand is on the steering wheel and he is in charge. He is the source of our strength. He is the source of our healing. And he is the only One who has the power to bring unity to our disorder, by reconciling us to God and to the human community.

We have not yet witnessed the fullness of such strength and healing and unity, but they are "God's plan" for us and, as the writer of Ephesians says, "when the time is right," God will complete his plan "to bring all creation together, everything in heaven and on earth, with Christ as head." (See *Ephesians 1:10, Good News Bible*.)

The best definition of power that I have ever heard is "the ability to accomplish purpose." It is God's purpose that Jesus Christ shall reign as Sovereign Lord over the whole creation, and he has the ability to accomplish that purpose. His power is not limited.

But, finally, we must ask ourselves what responsibility the Ascension places upon us as members of the Christian Church. It seems clear that our responsibility is great, because the writer of Ephesians says that the Church is the body of Christ. Therefore, we are to be the "instruments" through which the ascended Lord reveals himself to the world. We are to function, with our varied gifts, as the hands and feet and voice of Jesus Christ. A great deal depends upon our faithful discipleship.

As we move out into the world in ever-widening circles of witness and service, then we are actually assisting Christ to "fill the whole wide universe."

And, through our faithfulness, we are affirming to the whole world that the risen and ascended Lord we worship is not limited by space or by time or in power!

*Seventh*

*Sunday*

*of*

*Easter*

"Behold, I am coming soon, bringing my recompense, to repay every one for what he has done. I am the Alpha and the Omega, the first and the last, the beginning and the end."

Blessed are those who wash their robes, that they may have the right to the tree of life and that they may enter the city by the gates. Outside are the dogs and sorcerers and fornicators and murderers and idolaters, and every one who loves and practices falsehood.

"I Jesus have sent my angel to you with this testimony for the churches. I am the root and the offspring of David, the bright morning star."

The Spirit and the Bride say, "Come." And let him who hears say, "Come." And let him who is thirsty come, let him who desires take the water of life without price.

*** 

He who testifies to these things says, "Surely I am coming soon." Amen. Come, Lord Jesus!

*Revelation* 22:12-17, 20
R.S.V.

# Come!

The word that stands out above all the other words in today's Scripture lesson is the word "come." John uses "come," or "coming," six times in only seven verses. It announces his theme and it concludes his theme.

In light of John's emphasis on this word, I decided to look it up in *Webster's New Collegiate Dictionary* and here are some of the definitions that are listed for "come":

1. To move hitherward; approach; as, he is coming . . .
2. To appear or arrive, as on a scene of action . . .
3. To arrive at or reach the point of being . . .
4. To take place or have its place in a series . . .

If I wanted to bore you, we could go on for at least another four definitions. But there is no real purpose for extending the list. It seems clear that John's fascination with the word "come" goes beyond dictionary definitions and springs to life only as he relates the word to his Christian faith.

In that context, the word begins to bristle with excitement as John relates it to a prayer, a promise and a program.

### A Prayer

When John says "come," he is expressing a prayer: "Come, Lord Jesus!" It is a personal prayer. It is also a prayer that is offered on behalf of the whole church. The simple inclusion of the exclamation point suggests the excitement and urgency of John's voice when he first uttered the prayer.

You will remember that John was living and writing

in a time when the Christian church was experiencing a great deal of persecution. "Martyrdom" is a seldom used word in our vocabulary, but it was a brutal reality in John's day. Christians were murdered because they dared to give public expression to their faith. Acts 7:55-60 reports the martyrdom of Stephen, who was stoned to death for preaching a fiery sermon. Multiply that situation several times and you will have a picture of the situation that John was facing.

In the midst of such crushing persecution, the one thing that John wanted most was the speedy return of Jesus Christ.

Jesus had lived, ministered and died. God had raised Jesus from the dead and exalted him by enthroning him at his own right hand in heaven. Now, John wanted the Christ to return to earth in power and glory and victory. In other words, John knew all about the Crucifixion and the Resurrection and the Ascension. Now, he longed for the Parousia, or the Second Coming of Christ into the world. John firmly believed that when Christ returned he would set things right again. Therefore, John eagerly prayed, "Come, Lord Jesus!"

It is the prayer of a faithful, confident Christian. It is the prayer of someone who is sure of the ground on which he stands.

I fear, sometimes, that we may be a bit too glib when we say that we want Jesus Christ to return to earth. I heard a song on the car radio the other day that was really a prayer that Christ would come into the world again, and the song made it sound as though such an event would be all sunshine and roses. But the truth, which John recognized and affirmed, is this: while the return of Christ would be great joy for some, it would be severe judgment for others.

A college student scratched these words on a lounge wall: "Jesus is coming. Be good!" I will not say that the author of that brief "sermon" is a great theologian, but he had put his finger on a great truth. The coming of Jesus Christ has moral and ethical implications for our lives.

Those who have "washed their robes," says John — those who have appropriated Christ's saving power and have faithfully followed Christ as Lord — will experience Christ's coming as joy and gladness. But those who have lived lives of immorality, persecuted or slaughtered others, worshiped false gods, or loved and lived falsehood, will be "shut out" from the joy of Christ's returning.

Blessed are they who know all of this, but can still join with John when he prays, "Come Lord Jesus!" (Those who are not yet able to affirm John's prayer will want to consider "getting their robes cleaned"!)

### A Promise

We should not overlook the fact that John's prayer has added weight because it is based on a promise. Indeed, John's prayer was simply a faithful response to our Lord's promise: "Surely I am coming soon."

One of the first "preachers' stories" I heard was based on this promise. It told of how a young minister had been graduated from seminary and had been assigned to serve his first congregation. He was quite excited as the day approached for him to preach his first sermon. He wanted to do a good job so he wrote out his sermon in full and committed it to memory. When Sunday morning came, he left his manuscript at home and went to the church and greeted the members of his little rural congregation. Everything went well until he stood up to preach. Then he panicked. His mind went blank and he could not recall a single word of his sermon. Then he had an idea: if he repeated the words of his text perhaps that would help to recall the sermon. So, he quoted the text as it was recorded in the King

James Version of the Bible: "Behold, I come quickly." But nothing happened. Then he grabbed hold of the shakey lectern that served as a pulpit and repeated the text more forcefully: "Behold, I come quickly!" But nothing happened. His mind was still a blank. Finally, in desperation, he grabbed the pulpit again and leaned forward with all his strength as he shouted, "Behold, I come quickly!"

The pulpit broke loose, and the young preacher was humiliated as he fell into the lap of a sweet, little, old lady who was seated in the front pew. He apologized as quickly as he could, but she replied gently, "That's all right young man; I should have moved; you warned me three times that you were coming!"

Along with many other people of his day, John believed that Jesus was going to "come quickly." In fact, John believed the promise that Jesus Christ would visibly return to the earth from heaven. And he believed that it was going to happen soon.

We tend to interpret that promise in spiritual terms. That is, we tend to interpret the "Second Coming" to mean that Christ will reveal himself to us again through our worship or through our faith or through our human relationships. And all of that is true, I am sure. But that does not exhaust what John believed. It seems quite clear that John also believed in a speedy, physical, visible return of Jesus Christ to earth.

It was the promise of just such a return that kept John and others going in the face of tremendous persecution. It gave them hope. It gave them courage. It added fuel to their Christian faithfulness. For when Christ returned, he was going to defeat "the enemy" — all those persons and powers who had been hostile or indifferent to him — and he was going to vindicate and fulfill all those who had remained faithful to him through long and difficult days. For this latter group, the return of the Lord would be a time of victory and glory and power.

There are many people today who believe, as John did, in the speedy, physical, visible return to earth of Jesus Christ. Such a point of view is often characterized by some slogans that were written by a class of church school students:

"Be prepared because time is running out!"
"The End is near — Sinners repent!"
"Be prepared to meet your DOOM!"
"The World is coming to an End!"
"Be forgiven before time runs out!"
"Time is running out — Prepare to abandon ship!"

The difficulty with the theology of such slogans, at least for me, is that it is so negative and fear-oriented and manipulative. It also tempts us to start setting specific dates on which, it is believed, Christ will return. You may have read the recent news report of the midwestern farmer who left his farm and started "preaching" that the world would end and Christ would return to earth on this past Labor Day. According to the last report I read, on the day after Labor Day the fellow gave up "preaching" and went back to the farm.

As I recall, Jesus himself said that nobody knew the specific time for his return to earth except his heavenly Father — and the Father wasn't about to share the schedule, not even with his Son!

I say it reverently and humbly, but it seems clear that John was wrong about one thing: Jesus Christ did not return to earth in the speedy, physical and visible way that John had expected.

But — and hear this well for this is the really important matter — John was not mistaken about the promise! His timing of the promise may have been off, but the promise itself is still operative and valid.

As Christians, we believe in the Parousia or the "Second Coming" of Christ. As a great theologian, Emil Brunner, expressed it: "Whatever the form of this event, the whole point lies in the fact that it will happen . . . Faith in Jesus Christ without the expectation of his Parousia is a voucher that is never redeemed, a promise that is not seriously meant." A Christian faith without the expectation that Christ will come again in glory as Lord, says Brunner, "is like a ladder which leads nowhere but ends in the void.*

My friends, we are not without hope because we are not without a future. God has a future and he is inviting us to share it with him through our continuing faithfulness to his son, our Lord, Jesus Christ.

But what are we to do in the meantime?

That is the question that brings us to John's final use of the word "come."

### A Program

For, on the lips of John, the word "come" is also a program: "And let him who hears, say, 'Come.' And let him who is thirsty come, let him who desires take the water of life without price."

Every Christian is a missionary. Every Christian is an evangelist. It is our high privilege, and responsibility, to go out into the world and invite all the people to come to Jesus Christ, who is already moving to meet them.

Christ is the One who satisfies the thirsty spirits of the people. He is the One who feeds the deepest hungers of the human heart. He is the One that many are seeking, even though they may not know his name. His "kitchen" is full and the only "ticket" that is needed is the desire to enter. And, believe it or not, the food and the water there — which are the only food and water that give eternal satisfaction to the soul — are "without price."

---

*See *Eternal Hope* (Philadelphia: The Westminster Press, 1954) pp. 138-139.

When I was very young, my older brother, David, took me to hear Dr. William Sangster preach in Philadelphia. I was so thrilled by Sangster that I still remember his outline. It was simple: Come; Tarry; Go! First, we respond to the invitation to come to Christ. Then, as we tarry with him, our own needs are fulfilled and our commitment to him grows. And, then, we go and issue the great invitation to others. And the cycle goes on, until the whole world has heard the invitation and had a chance to respond to it.

Come! It's a great word to have in our hearts and on our lips as we face the future. It creates an excitement that can't be captured in dictionaries. But it really springs to life only when our Christian faith translates it into a prayer, a promise, and a program!

To Blanche and Mainey

Cliff Lake – Sky Lakes Wilderness (Ch. 56) (USFS Photo)

# 76 Day-Hikes
## Within 100 Miles of the Rogue Valley

**by Art Bernstein**

New Leaf Books • 1450 N.E. 'A' St. • Grants Pass, OR 97526

1st Printing - May 1987
2nd Printing - July 1987

Copyright © 1987 Art Bernstein

All rights reserved. No part of this publication may be reproduced or transmitted in any form or by any means, electronic or mechanical, including photocopy, recording, or any information storage and retrieval system, without permission in writing from the publisher.

Library of Congress Cataloging-in-Publication Data

Bernstein, Art.
  76 Day-Hikes Within 100 Miles of the Rogue Valley

  1. Hiking--Oregon--Rogue River Valley Region--Guide-books.
  2. Rogue River Valley Region (Or.)--Description and travel
Guide-books    I. Title.
GV199.42.072R643    1987       917.95'21       87-20240
ISBN: 0-9617525-1-3

Cover: Mt. McLoughlin (Ch. 59)
Watercolor by Yvonne Gentry

Printed in the United States of America
Springs Printery, Rogue River, OR

# Contents

**Part One: Introduction**

|  |  |  |
|---|---|---|
| I. | Why day hikes? | 1 |
| II. | Why 76 hikes? | 2 |
| III. | How to use this book | 3 |
| IV. | Hiking rules | 5 |
| V. | The land | 6 |
| IV. | Thank yous | 7 |

**Part Two: Trails**

|  |  |  |
|---|---|---|
| 1. | Humbug Mountain (Humbug Mtn. State Park) | 9 |
| 2. | Indian Sands (Boardman State Park) | 10 |
| 3. | Vulcan Lake (Kalmiopsis WA) | 12 |
| 4. | Mislatnah Peak (Kalmiopsis WA) | 13 |
| 5. | Windy Valley | 15 |
| 6. | Game Lake Loop (Kalmiopsis WA) | 17 |
| 7. | Azalea Lake/Coquille Falls | 18 |
| 8. | Johnson Creek | 20 |
| 9. | Mt. Bolivar (Wild Rogue WA) | 21 |
| 10. | Illinois River/Pine Flat (Kalmiopsis WA) | 23 |
| 11. | Illinois River/Buzzards Roost | 24 |
| 12. | York Butte (Kalmiopsis WA) | 26 |
| 13. | Silver Falls | 28 |
| 14. | Silver Creek | 29 |
| 15. | Rogue River Trail/Whiskey Creek | 30 |
| 16. | Rogue River Trail/Blossom Bar (Wild Rogue WA) | 31 |
| 17. | Pearsoll Peak (Kalmiopsis WA) | 34 |
| 18. | Eagle Mountain | 35 |
| 19. | Babyfoot Lake (Kalmiopsis WA) | 36 |
| 20. | Umpqua Joe Trail (Indian Mary Park) | 38 |
| 21. | Shan Creek | 39 |
| 22. | Mungers Butte | 40 |
| 23. | Rabbit Lake | 41 |
| 24. | Kerby Peak | 43 |
| 25. | Big Tree Loop (Oregon Caves NM) | 44 |
| 26. | Bigelow Lake/Mt. Elijah | 46 |
| 27. | Tannen Lake (Red Buttes WA) | 48 |
| 28. | Tannen Mountain (Red Buttes WA) | 49 |
| 29. | Black Butte (Siskiyou WA) | 50 |
| 30. | Raspberry Lake (Siskiyou WA) | 52 |
| 31. | Devils Punchbowl (Siskiyou WA) | 54 |
| 32. | Grayback Mountain | 55 |
| 33. | Miller Lake | 57 |
| 34. | Collings Mountain | 58 |
|  | **Locator Map** | 60 |
| 35. | Stein Butte | 62 |

| 36. | Azalea Lake (Red Buttes WA) | 64 |
|---|---|---|
| 37. | Middle Fork Applegate | 66 |
| 38. | Frog Pond Loop (Red Buttes WA) | 67 |
| 39. | Red Buttes (Red Buttes WA) | 68 |
| 40. | Tunnel Ridge | 70 |
| 41. | Wagner Butte | 72 |
| 42. | Lower Table Rock | 74 |
| 43. | Upper Table Rock | 76 |
| 44. | Boundary Springs (Crater Lake NP) | 78 |
| 45. | Upper Rogue Trail/Winding River | 79 |
| 46. | Upper Rogue Trail/Natural Bridge | 81 |
| 47. | Upper Rogue Trail/Takelma Gorge | 82 |
| 48. | Toad Lake (Rogue-Umpqua Divide WA) | 83 |
| 49. | Cliff Lake (Rogue-Umpqua Divide WA) | 85 |
| 50. | Fish Creek Valley (Rogue-Umpqua Divide WA) | 86 |
| 51. | Mt. Thielsen (Mt. Thielsen WA) | 88 |
| 52. | Mt. Bailey | 90 |
| 53. | Mt. Scott (Crater Lake NP) | 91 |
| 54. | Garfield Peak (Crater Lake NP) | 93 |
| 55. | Red Blanket Trail (Sky Lakes WA) | 94 |
| 56. | Seven Lakes Basin (Sky Lakes WA) | 95 |
| 57. | Blue Canyon Basin (Sky Lakes WA) | 97 |
| 58. | Cold Springs Trail (Sky Lakes WA) | 99 |
| 59. | Mt. McLoughlin (Sky Lakes WA) | 100 |
| 60. | Varney Creek Trail (Mountain Lakes WA) | 102 |
| 61. | Pilot Rock | 104 |
| 62. | Whitney Falls (Mt. Shasta WA) | 105 |
| 63. | Black Butte | 107 |
| 64. | Mt. Shasta (Mt. Shasta WA) | 108 |
| 65. | Marble Valley (Marble Mountain WA) | 110 |
| 66. | Paradise Lake (Marble Mountain WA) | 112 |
| 67. | Wright Lakes/Shackleford Creek (Marble Mountain WA) | 114 |
| 68. | Paynes Lake (Russian WA) | 115 |
| 69. | Duck/Eaton Lakes (Russian WA) | 116 |
| 70. | Trail Gulch/Long Gulch Lakes (Trinity Alps WA) | 118 |
| 71. | Hidden Lake (Trinity Alps WA) | 119 |
| 72. | South Fork Lakes (Trinity Alps WA) | 120 |
| 73. | Caldwell Lakes | 121 |
| 74. | Deadfall Lakes/Mt. Eddy | 122 |
| 75. | Toad Lake | 125 |
| 76. | Upper Sacramento Lakes | 126 |

# 76 Day-Hikes
## Within 100 Miles of the Rogue Valley
### by Art Bernstein

## Part One: Introduction.

### I. Why day-hikes?

Before going further, I should explain the hyphen between "day" and "hike" in the book's title. When I first came up with the name "76 Day Hikes," everyone admonished me to make it clear that the subject was not hikes which are 76 days longs, as in "76-Day Hikes." Hence, the clarifying hyphen.

Writing this book was not easy. Apart from problems with hyphen juggling, all nature writers face one inescapable truth: John Muir, the famous naturalist, exhausted every possible superlative to describe nature as long ago as 1895. Thus, conveying a mountain sunset or the morning mist off a lake with originality, can be a challenge.

I hasten to point out that Muir's complex sentences, full of words like "wondrous" and "glorious," helped inspire my interest in the outdoors. His book, *The Mountains of California*, was the first natural history book I ever read. Without it, I might still be back in Detroit, Michigan.

I'm obviously not interested in competing with Muir. In fact, I like to think of myself as fleshing out the details of areas he missed. The only place in this book Muir wrote about was Mt. Shasta, which he considered "glorious." I'm sure he'd have found the rest of our region, if not glorious, then at least wondrous.

This book "fleshes out the details" of 76 day-hikes within 100 miles of Oregon's Rogue Valley. A day-hike is defined as one to five miles one way or a two to 10 mile loop.

Why day hikes? I've been addicted to southern Oregon and northern California's back country since moving here in 1970. My compulsion to take to the trails has never abated, even though I'm presently bounding wildly into middle age. I've concluded in my bounding, however, that long routes such as the Rogue River Trail or Pacific Crest Trail are best accomplished on vacation. One doesn't jump into the car on Saturday morning, drive to the Mexico border, and expect to hike to Canada by 3:00 PM Sunday.

Every trail in this book may be done spur of the moment, except possibly the Mt. Shasta climb. Some require that you rise fairly early and camping out may be advisable to avoid arriving home at midnight.

One small gift advancing age has given me is a slight back problem. Day-hiking doesn't bother it but sleeping on boulders, dirt or waterbeds

**2    Introduction**

can be painful. I haven't camped out in eight years as I write this but have logged, nevertheless, countless trail miles.

Day-hiking is among the least environmentally damaging back country uses. The horrible overuse problem in some areas of the Sky Lakes, for example, is largely the result of competition for campsites and horse pasture. Not enough people realize that it's possible to comfortably hike to the heart of the Sky Lakes, have a great time, and be home in time for dinner.

## II. Why 76 hikes?

While reasonably thorough, this book is by no means comprehensive. Instead, it offers a potpourri of pedal pathways. The selection criteria were largely subjective, based on my particular (or peculiar) taste. But I can convey a sense of my standards:

First, all trails are nature oriented. While several pass near old mines, homesteads and bigfoot traps, that is not their focus. Drop by the local Chamber of Commerce or Historical Society for information on places like the Gin Ling Trail which tours an old Chinese gold mine, or walking tours of Jacksonville's historic buildings.

Second, it makes no sense to me to hike to a place to which one can drive, or to walk a trail paralleling a road. A trail should reveal wonders unattainable by other means.

Finally, I prefer trails which are scenic, varied and lead to well defined objectives. I like what landscape architects call "edge," where different types of visual images meet. A flat expanse of forest soon grows tiresome to me. But stick in a meadow, lake, cliff or waterfall and you have a wonderland.

I realize people have differing motivations, likes and dislikes. Being compulsive and results oriented, I'm most comfortable on trails which climb mountains or lead to lakes. I've attempted to balance this, however, with trails following rivers or creeks, one which follows a mining ditch and one which leads to the ocean. Avoided are trails which simply lead off through the woods like the Dutchy Creek Trail. Strolling through woods can be rejuvenating, educational and even spiritual. But for this book, I've stuck to paths emphasizing our region's many highlights.

Many routes in this book follow either combinations of trails or segments of longer trails. Hiking only the best chunks of our more notable long trails should enhance the experience for many. The Pacific Crest Trail, for instance, sometimes goes 20 miles between highlights. The hikes herein include portions of the Rogue River Trail, the Illinois River Trail, the Upper Rogue Trail, the Siskiyou Boundary Trail, the Sky Lakes Trail, the Clear Creek Trail, the Panther Ridge Trail, the Sisson-Callahan Trail and the Rogue-Umpqua Divide Trail. Only three segments of the Pacific Crest Trail are included but the trail is crossed numerous times.

**Introduction** 3

## III.  How to use this book.

The goal of this book is to provide not only a factual reference but interesting reading with which to curl up on a winter's eve. To enhance your "winter's eve" reading, paragraphs containing only detailed road directions are printed in slightly smaller type. You may skip such paragraphs, if you like, until ready to jump in the car and take off for the trailhead.

Several other items should be noted about the information in each chapter:

**A.  Maps.** The reader should be able to reach most objectives using the maps and descriptions in this book. Maps include only the trail itself and the last connecting road. All maps are oriented with north up and the scale varies with the trail length.

You may wish to obtain supplementary material. National Forest maps, for example, cost a dollar and are strongly recommended since road and trail signs on the ground can be confusing or absent.

The Forest Service also puts out Recreational Opportunity Guides for selected trails. While helpful, they vary in quality and availability and can be confusing. The nine mile loop trail in Chapter 49, for instance, included information from seven Recreational Opportunity Guides. Only four of the seven National Forests crossed by this book's trails put out such guides.

**B. Trail Length.** Each trail heading gives length either as distance from the trailhead to the farthest objective or as a "loop" distance. The latter means the trail returns by a different route than it went out on. Loops may or may not end at the same trailhead where they began.

Most distances were obtained from the agency in charge and not all are reliable. In several instances, they were estimated. In attempting to present information in its most useful form, it has never mattered to me if a trail was 3.2 or 3.3 miles.

**C. Access.** Since life doesn't begin when you step out of the car, I've treated the drive to the trailhead as part of the experience. In a couple instances, reconnaisance by car beforehand is crucial to understanding the trail.

The "ease of access" rating is the least subjective and most easily defined herein. "One" means the road is paved to the trailhead. A wide, well graded gravel road for the last mile might also rate a "one." "Three's" are recommended for four-wheel drive. Although a two-wheel drive vehicle may survive, look for steep grades, blind curves, no shoulders, single lanes, ruts, mud and jostling. "Two," of course, is everything in-between.

In most cases, only a rough mileage estimate is given, or no mileage at all, unless an exact figure is crucial to locating the trailhead.

**4    Introduction**

**D. Difficulty.** This "one to three" rating is fairly subjective since one person's mountain is another's molehill. "Ones" are easily defined. If the trail is level or mostly level throughout, it's a "one." River routes fall into this category.

"Three's" are harder to pin down. I rated a trail "three" if I felt people in poor physical condition or with medical problems should stay off it. In most instances, somebody from the agency in charge agreed.

The majority of trails are rated "two," which covers a lot of ground, so to speak. "Two's" may vary from almost easy to rather difficult.

**E. Scenic quality.** I attempted to apply a three point rating to scenic quality but were I the reader, I'd ignore it. "One's" aren't unscenic and "three's" may require too much exertion to appreciate. Also, I prefer high drama over gentle communing with nature but who's to say that a 1000 foot cliff is more scenic than a moss covered rock.

On a scale of one to ten, nothing herein would rate less than a six. Other than that, "three's" are more scenic than "two's" and "two's" are more scenic than "one's."

**F. Water.** If a trail is less than two miles, it's less than 65 degrees out, or the trail's difficulty rating is "one," I wouldn't worry about carrying water on the trail, although you might consider leaving some in the car. As for drinking from creeks, my personal rule is never to drink if there's habitation between me and the stream source. Also, if I can't get across a creek in a step or two or the water is stagnant, I won't drink from it.

Don't quote the above. Any water can make you sick and the means through which bacteria spread are numerous. So my "official" advice is never to drink unpurified water.

**G. Season.** Weather varies so greatly that the seasons indicated are based strictly on formula. Trails below 3500 feet elevation are considered accessible pretty much year round, although if it snowed in Medford the day before, you may wish to make local inquiry before setting out. Look for mud and high water in the wet season. For trails between 3500 and 4500 feet, the seasons are given as May through November. Those above 4500 feet are shown as June through October.

However, the numerous last minute trail excursions in preparing this book were accompanied by marvelous weather. I hiked into the Sky Lakes (6000 feet), in mid-November; visited Game Lake (4200 feet), two days after Christmas; and checked out the Rogue-Umpqua Divide Wilderness in January.

**H. Elevation.** Elevations are given in feet and most are rounded off to the nearest 100 feet. Where two numbers are indicated, they represent the trail's lowest and highest points. A single number means the elevation change is insignificant.

**Introduction    5**

**I. Use.** While this book is hiker oriented, other permitted uses are noted. Unfortunately, my experience with such uses is limited. I've been cross-country skiing twice and have never been on a pack trip or ridden a trail bike. All require too much planning for my temperament. Most of my trail ventures are conceived either the night before or the same day.

If cross-country ski is indicated under "use," it means the trail is usually snowed over in winter, isn't too steep and the access road is either plowed or often driveable to within a mile of the trailhead. Motorized vehicles are prohibited in Wilderness Areas. Permitted uses may not always be feasible uses.

In addition to use designations, the text generally indicates if there's room at the trailhead to park and turn around a trailer.


**IV. Hiking rules.**

No hiking book is complete without a rules list. Dozens come to mind: Never hike alone. Always bring matches. Let someone know your destination. Always bring a map. Never drink unpurified water. Get a Doctor's OK before undertaking strenuous exercise. Always wear Vibram soled shoes. Always carry toilet paper.

Unfortunately, I've rarely observed the above. I've gotten sick, lost, injured and stuck on my excursions but somehow always made it home. I usually go alone, rarely remember to tell anybody and half the time I forget map, camera, canteen, lunch and gas money. Perhaps the element of risk is part of the adventure to me.

I once got lost on Mt. McLoughlin and spent the night at 8000 feet with no matches, food, flashlight, or water. After that, I vowed never to leave home without a basic survival kit. Once in a while, I actually remember my vow. I haven't forgotten my lunch in years.

The once popular, heavy hiking boot with non-skid, Vibram soles, is out of vogue. They're considered environmentally damaging and should be worn only if rock climbing, in snow, or if you intend to hike off-trail in wet weather. Otherwise, a soft soled sneaker is more comfortable and easier on the trail surface.

Speaking of environmental damage, the Forest Service has some rules which are far more important than mine. As part of "no trace" camping, they ask the following:

1. Pack out all litter.

2. For human waste, select a spot at least 200 feet from open water and dig a hole six to eight inches deep. Cover it with dirt when done.

3. If a fire is absolutely necessary, build it in a safe spot where fires have been built before. Wood collection can be environmentally damaging and portable stoves are recommended. I suggest cold meals on day-hikes.

4. Pitch tents so no drainage ditch is required and replace rocks and other material removed from sleeping areas. Camp sites should be at least 100 feet from open water and animals should be pastured at least 200 feet from open water.

**6    Introduction**

## V. The land.

Understanding where you are and what you're walking on increases one's appreciation of the outdoors. Our region, unfortunately, is far too complex to go into great detail here. Still, a little background is better than no background.

**A. Geology.** Two mountain building processes are important in southern Oregon and northern California. Most obvious is the recent volcanic activity of the Cascades. Outpourings of lava and ash created most of its high peaks.

Less obvious are the vast areas of rock which solidified underground, then became exposed through erosion, faulting and folding. These intrusive granites usually intermingle with ancient lavas and sedimentary rock to form the complex and very rugged peaks and canyons of the Siskiyou and Marble Mountains. Some of the older lavas and sedimentary deposits have metamorphized, or altered, into metavolcanics, schists, and marble.

Two geological terms which arise frequently in the trail descriptions are "serpentine" and "glacial cirque."

Serpentine is a type of granitic rock lacking calcium and rich in heavy metals. Our region contains more serpentine than any other in the country. The substance is lousy for tree growing but contains significant concentrations of nickel and chrome.

Douglas-fir, ponderosa pine, madrone and other common species won't grow on serpentine. Some species will, however, including several found nowhere else. Jeffrey, knobcone and western white pine; and Port Orford and incense cedar, seem to love serpentine. So do many shrubs and some exceedingly rare flowers such as kalmiopsis and Waldo gentian. Nitrogen poor bogs populated by insect eating plants are common.

To spot serpentine, look for scraggly, open forests with lots of manzanita. The rock itself is black but weathers to a rough tan.

While the word "serpentine" is used whenever the above plant associations are encountered, both the mineral makeup of the rock and the specific plant associations vary considerably. Serpentine-type ecosystems may be found not only on serpentine but on related rock types called "periditite" and "gabbro."

All mountains in southern Oregon and northern California have experienced galciation. Glaciers are formed when annual snowfall exceeds melt and ice starts oozing down the mountain. The only glaciers these days are the ones on Shasta and a few tiny ones in the Trinity Alps. Remnants of former glaciers scar many higher peaks, however.

On mountain slopes, glaciers carve out round-bottomed valleys as they move downward. But they also gouge sharply backward into the peak. The result is "cirque basins" with steep, amphitheater headwalls rising above a bowl. Our region's hundreds of small, alpine lakes are found almost entirely within glacial cirques.

**Introduction** 7

**B. Geography.** Now that you know how the land formations got there, here is a brief overview of how people have categorized and named them.

Most significant are the Cascade Mountains, a string of fairly young volcanic peaks extending from Calfornia's Mt. Lassen to Canada. They include Mts. Shasta, McLoughlin and Thielsen, as well as Crater Lake. Look for cinder cones, lava flows, pumice and tuff and rock with bubbles in it. Except for isolated high peaks, this range is rather gentle with broad basins and vast panoramas. Shasta, at 14,161 feet, towers over all other Cascade peaks in our area. McLoughlin is second at 9500 feet.

The Rogue-Umpqua Divide area, north of the upper Rogue River and west of Diamond Lake, though part of the Cascades, contains many elements similar to the Siskiyous and Marbles. Complex and rugged, it is composed mostly of volcanic rock but is a remnant of an older system called the Western Cascades.

The Siskiyous, Marble Mountains, Trinity Alps, Salmon-Scott Mountains and Trinity Divide are all segments of a complex granitic uplift called the Klamath Mountain system. The peaks north and west of the Klamath River, east of the Cascades and south of about Bandon, are considered the Siskiyous. Mt. Ashland, at 7400 feet, is the Siskiyous' highest summit.

The Marble Mountains, south of the Klamath and north of California's Salmon River, are similar to the Siskiyous but higher — up to 8200 feet. The Trinity Alps, between the Salmon and Trinity Rivers, reach 9000 feet and contain some of America's most impressive scenery. Mt. Eddy, in the Trinity Divide between the Sacramento and Trinity Rivers, is the Klamath system's highest peak at 9025 feet.

**C. Botany.** The trail descriptions try to point out important plant associations and unusual species. Descriptions are avoided, however, as they would take up too much room.

Different species which grow together in similar kinds of places are called "associations." Look for riverbank associations, upland associations, bog associations, fire associations, north slope associations (shady), south slope associations (sunny), elevational associations, serpentine associations, geographic associations, etc. Geographic associations in our area include elements of the Sierra Nevada forest region, the Pacific coast forest region and the Pacific Northwest forest region. Our mountains also boast several unique species such as Brewer spruce and Baker cypress. The area is even more complex ecologically than it is geologically.

**VI. Thank yous.**

In preparing this book, I learned quicky that hiking a trail doesn't necessarily provide everything needed to write about it. I often required information on an area's natural history, descriptions of side trails or alternate routes, information on recent or pending changes, a memory refresher if I hadn't been on a trail in several years and suggestions on what to include.

**8    Introduction**

Those who helped out are myriad. Above all, there's my wife, Patricia. If she didn't agree that my writing should be a priority, I'd be an emotional mess. Second, there's Bonnie Clark, receptionist at Siskiyou National Forest, whom I bothered several times a week for months with requests for such oddball items as aerial photos of Humbug Mountain. She uncomplainingly attempted to provide whatever I needed and usually succeeded.

Kurt Berger, Joan Peterson-Bratt and Randy Wainscott were especially helpful and encouraging. So were several bookstore owners.

Finally, there are the agencies, all of whom offered carte blanche to whatever resources they had. I've named a few particularly helpful agency people in the text but their actual number runs into the dozens. In writing this, I interviewed people at the BLM, the Oregon State Parks, the Josephine County Parks, seven National Forests, 15 Ranger Districts and the National Park Service. Virtually all greeted me with patience and encouragement.

# Part II: Trails

## 1. Humbug Mountain
### (Humbug Mountain State Park)

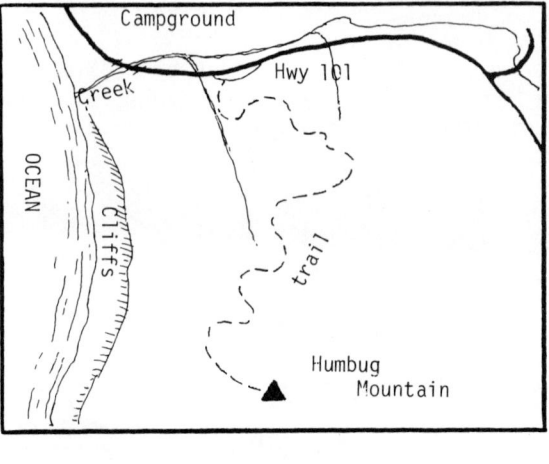

**Length:** 3 miles
**Water:** Lots
**Access:** 1
**Season:** All
**Difficulty:** 1
**Elevation:** 0 to 1756 ft.
**Scenic Qual.:** 2
**Use:** Hikers only

This book's first trail description should have a strong lead paragraph, with adventure, witty quips and philosophical insights. Unfortunately, nothing out of the ordinary occurred the day I hiked up Humbug and no brilliant philosophical insights came to mind.

However, Humbug Mountain itself is pretty out of the ordinary. As the highest point rising directly from the Oregon Coast, its west flank crashes some 1700 feet into the surf just south of Port Orford.

Much of the surrounding area is also out of the ordinary. Driving north on Highway 101 from Gold Beach, Humbug's black, forested dome soon appears in the distance, 20 miles away. Past the emerald tidal flat at Ophir, the highway cuts behind the mountain, follows a little creek past park and waterfall, then re-emerges at the ocean.

Port Orford, just north, is a pretty fishing village with many historic buildings and a small harbor tucked inside a rocky peninsula. Port Orford Headlands State Park can be explored by car or on foot. It offers vistas of the coast and of several lakes nestled amid the dunes. Beyond Port Orford, another state park merits a look. The desolate, grassy expanses at Cape Blanco, Oregon's westernmost finger, are lovely and mysterious, although the actual point is closed to the public.

Back at Humbug Mountain, also a state park, the trailhead parking lot is situated off Highway 101, immediately before the road meets the coast on the north side.

**10    Indian Sands**

Despite its considerable rise, the trail is virtually level except near the beginning, due to many switchbacks. The wide path offers an intimate look at a coastal rain forest. It begins in a moss draped maple and myrtlewood grove and winds past waterfalls and fern covered rock faces. The dominant tree species is Douglas-fir, mixed with grand fir, western hemlock and, of course, Port Orford cedar. Look for red alder near the creeks and lots of rhododendron.

Towards the summit, the forest grows a little drier but this is still a very wet place. It is also an unstable place with blown over trees every few yards. It's no place to linger during high winds and heavy rain.

The views aren't as good as one might expect. Nevertheless, you will catch glimpses to the north from time to time, first of the highway and nearby hills, then of the Port Orford headlands. The grassy opening at the summit offers a view predominantly southward towards Gold Beach. Vistas in other directions are blocked by trees.

# 2. Indian Sands
## (Boardman State Park)

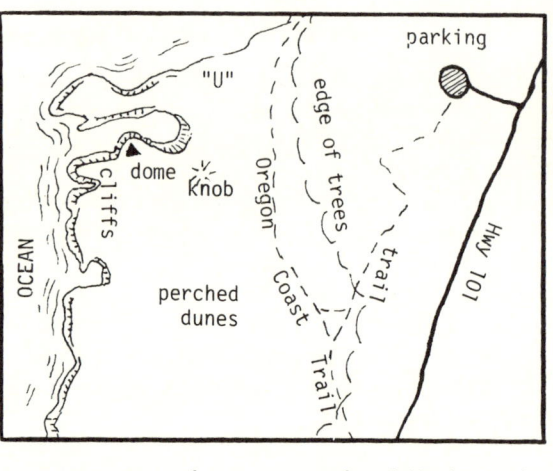

**Length:** 1 mile
**Water:** No
**Access:** 1
**Season:** All
**Difficulty:** 2
**Elevation:** 50 to 300 ft.
**Scenic Qual.:** 3
**Use:** Hikers only

Numerous trails criss-cross the cliffs above the southern Oregon coast. Although some are well marked, others, like the trail to the right at Natural Bridge, just pop up. Most of the "pop up" variety are extremely steep and brushy and some are dangerous. The Oregon Parks and Recreation Division is attempting to consolidate these trails into a single route called the Oregon Coast Trail. While much progress has been made, many links are yet to be completed.

The Indian Sands Trail is a quarter-mile access link to a two mile segment of the Coast Trail. It leads to what is, in my opinion, the most

Indian Sands    11

**Indian Sands - Oregon Coast Trail (Ch. 2)**                    (Bernstein Photo)

beautiful — and weird — spot on the Oregon coast. The trailhead, located a few miles north of Brookings off Highway 101, is well marked from the road. A short turnout leads to a parking area and viewpoint. The trail takes off through the woods to the south.

The access trail is actually more tunnel than trail, cut through an almost impenetrable mat of shore pine and Sitka spruce. The often muddy and slippery path winds steeply downhill through a sheltered jungle before emerging into daylight.

Where it emerges requires explanation. Most coastal sand dunes are formed from beach sand washed in from the ocean. The dunes at Indian Sands, however, are perched on a small plateau atop sheer cliffs. The formation appears to be a layer of soft sandstone above much harder rock. Wind has eroded the sandstone into a small amphitheater while whipping much of it back into sand. The area is not visible from the highway, except for an instant if you have a very sharp eye.

The trail opens into a tiny alcove of loose sand where the Coast Trail can be seen leading off in both directions. While there's much to be explored, including natural arches and archaeological sites, I suggest following the path to the right, towards the large "U" which looks out to the north. At the "U," you'll find a secluded perch above the beaches with a view of the Thomas Creek Bridge, supposedly Oregon's highest.

Just before the trail enters the large bowl in front of the "U," a dune crest trends off to the left. It ends at a little rocky knob which drops straight down into a small but spectacular inlet with sheer cliffs, crashing

**12    Vulcan Lake**

surf and sea caves. To the right of the knob, loose sand spills over the cliff. To the left, the huge dune face drops down to a little grassy flat and is great fun to play on.

Nearby stands a large rock dome with an enticing patch of green on top. The rock is attached to the mainland and makes a challenging objective. Climb down the sand, or the rocks beside it, to a low spot where you can walk across.

The low spot sits at the head of a large notch with waves spouting up it. A smaller notch nearby offers a window through a 50 foot, perpendicular black cliff which drops straight into the churning foam. Don't fall.

For a longer, alternative route, pick up the Coast Trail at the Thomas Creek Bridge and follow it through the aforementioned "U" into the Indian Sands. South of the access trail, the Coast Trail winds through a stand of mature shore pine, disappears into the woods and continues south to Whalehead Beach.

# 3. Vulcan Lake
## (Kalmiopsis Wilderness Area)

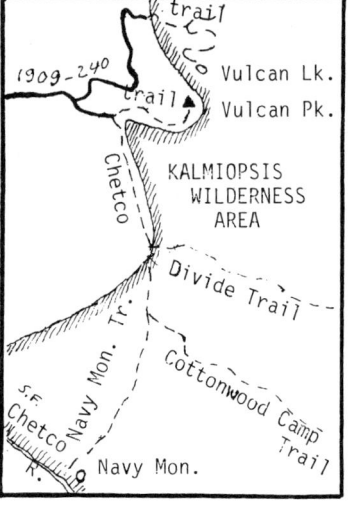

**Length:** 1½ mi.
**Water:** Yes
**Access:** 3
**Season:** May to Nov.
**Difficulty:** 2
**Elevation:** 3600 to 4200 ft.
**Scenic Qual.:** 3
**Use:** Non-motorized only

My wife found Vulcan Lake spooky and didn't like it at all. I found it fascinating; a lovely blue-green lake set on a rocky terrace overlooking the upper Chetco basin.

The tan, weathered bedrock in which the lake is nestled, and Vulcan peak overhead, contain such a high percentage of serpentine that the

area is a virtual desert. The few trees and shrubs are stunted and bizarre. Yet from the ridge above the lake, one can see the Pacific Ocean and the lush vegetation of the coastal mountains.

Of the many mountain glacial lakes in southern Oregon and northern California, this is the only one reached from the coast. To get there, drive up the Chetco River out of Brookings (Roads 784 and 1736). Turn right on Road 1909, which takes off up the mountain past Polliwog Butte and Red Mountain Prairie. Along the way, one sees vast Douglas-fir forests broken by occasional grassy openings. The openings afford views of the ocean, the Chetco Valley and surrounding peaks such as the Big Craggies. Even if you skip the trail, it's a beautiful drive. The last mile, on spur 260, used to be rather hair-raising but I'm told it's been improved.

The trail is only about 1½ miles long. It climbs up and over a rocky ridge from which one can see across the Kalmiopsis Wilderness to Pearsoll Peak. There are steep spots but the walk isn't difficult. The trail then descends sharply to the lake. Look for serpentine adapted plants such as Sadler oak, manzanita, Jeffrey pine, western white pine and azalea. This is a great place for botanizing, with many rare shrubs and flowers, so bring a good plant guide. Fishing in Vulcan Lake, I'm told, can be frustrating, although it's home to a few trout.

Two other trails may be of interest. Both require backtracking to the beginning of spur 260 where the Vulcan Peak Trail is clearly marked. The Vulcan Peak Trail is a steep, mile hike over brush and rock to an old lookout site offering a panorama of the Kalmiopsis and the coast.

The Chetco Divide Trail takes off from the same trailhead. About 1½ miles down, a side trail leads to the Navy Monument and Cottonwood Camp. This route, actually an old cat track, drops from 3000 feet elevation to 800 feet in 2½ miles. It ends near the South Fork of the Chetco at the wreckage of a World War Two Navy transport plane which crashed in 1944. The Monument stands nearby.

Much longer trails in the Vulcan Lake area lead to Chetco Peak to the south, and Valen Lake and the upper Chetco River to the north.

## 4. Mislatnah Peak
### (Kalmiopsis Wilderness Area)

Some places do not lend themselves to trails. The Empire State Building, for example, is best admired from the bottom. A trail up its side would be impractical. The same is true of the 3000-acre Big Craggies Botanical Area on the northwest edge of the Kalmiopsis Wilderness. These formidable outcroppings, like a series of stoneware platters stacked on end, comprise the visual focal point of the entire region. Big Craggie, 4600 feet high, soars 4000 feet above the Chetco River.

**14    Mislatnah Peak**

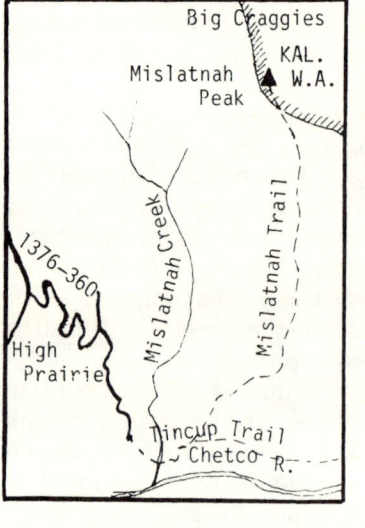

**Length:** 4½ mi.
**Water:** No
**Access:** 2
**Season:** All
**Difficulty:** 2
**Elevation:** 600 to 3124 ft.
**Scenic Qual.:** 2
**Use:** Non-motorized only

Not only that, in the scattered patches of thin soil between the cliffs, lurk several extremely rare plants. The periditite rock is similar to serpentine and supports similar flora. The Botanical Area was created to protect these plants and the lack of trails had the same objective. The most sensitive plants include Brewer spruce (discussed in other chapters), kalmiopsis (see the Illinois River/Pine Flat chapter), Cascade sedge, Siskiyou fritillaria, Howell's manzanita and other species.

The Mislatnah (pronounced "mis-lay-tna") Trail offers the closest views of the Big Craggies and is the only route to penetrate even a corner of the Botanical Area.

To reach the trailhead, drive up the north bank of the Chetco, from Brookings, almost as far as the road will take you. One can also reach the trailhead from Hunters Creek out of Gold Beach or via Bear Camp Road from Grants Pass.

I'd recommend the Brookings route. Pick up Road 784, the North Bank Road, just north of the Brookings bridge. Road 784 soon becomes Road 1736. Follow it past the turnoff to Vulcan Peak to a side road just beyond High Prairie.

From High Prairie, spur 360 drops through Douglas-fir forest to the trailhead. The landing at High Prairie affords a good view of Mislatnah Peak while the Big Craggies pop into view briefly at the first curve on spur 360. Except for the last mile, spur 360 is better than the main road, if a little more curvy. The last mile is somewhat bumpy. Bear right at a sign directing cars to the Tincup Trail.

Beyond the roomy trailhead, the trail winds down to Mislatnah Creek, crosses a newly built log bridge, then begins its long, steady climb. Though considered a steep trail, the last mile is the worst. The remainder is steep only in spots, although it ascends 2500 feet.

A mile down the trail, the Tincup Trail peels off to the right. It eventually joins the Upper Chetco Trail, an extremely long, rugged pathway emerging at several points on the Cave Junction side of the Wilderness.

Beyond the Tincup junction, the Mislatnah Trail passes Mislatnah Prairie, then reenters the woods. This is a transitional area between the periditite ecosystem and the coastal Douglas-fir forest so look for a fairly open canopy to start to develop, with a high percentage of pines. Shortly before the summit, the route breaks into the open.

The trail ends at an old lookout site. While the views are supurb and this is as close as its possible to get to the Big Craggies, the actual view of the Craggies is blocked by some of the near peaks. On returning to your car, continue up the road towards Snow Camp for a better look.

Atop Mislatnah, look for a faint, quarter-mile trail leading into the Botanical Area. This is an interesting little hike, although it doesn't pass any kalmiopsis or Brewer spruce. It is, however, a good jumpoff point for some off-trail scrambling up the peaks of the Big Craggies.

## 5. Windy Valley

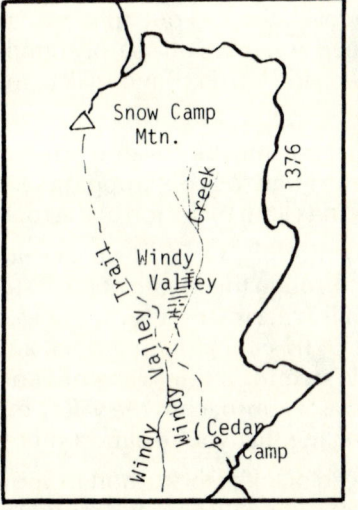

**Length:** 2 mi.
**Water:** Gallons
**Access:** 2
**Season:** All
**Difficulty:** 1
**Elevation:** 3100 to 2800 ft.
**Scenic Qual.:** 2
**Use:** Non-motorized only

Before I describe this secluded, easy trail located amid some of the most bizarre country anywhere, you must promise to first check out some things by car.

Windy Valley can be reached via Brookings or Bear Camp. Bear Camp is shorter from Grants Pass but driving time may be longer. Best is to take Highway 199 south to Highway 101 north, from Grants Pass to Brookings. At Brookings, follow Road 784 and 1376 up to the north bank of the Chetco River. Turn left towards High Prairie at the appropriate junction.

The road between High Prairie and Snow Camp Mountain is a must. Just past High Prairie, the dense, almost rain forest of Douglas-fir sud-

## 16   Windy Valley

denly opens into a vast expanse of orange peridite and serpentine rock, sparsely covered with manzanita and stunted Jeffrey and western white pines.

Just beyond High Prairie, the Big Craggies appear on the right. See the Mislatnah Peak chapter for more on the Big Craggies. Suffice to say, the Craggies are so steep and the rocks so mineral poor, that the area contains few trees except in the draws. Several rare plants grow in the Big Craggies, including the kalmiopsis flower.

Views are spectacular along Road 1376. Past High Prairie, it winds around Mineral Hill. Immediately beyond, at a small saddle, spur 220 comes in on the left. Just beyond the junction, up the bank on the left, a sign marks the trails to High Prairie and Windy Valley. The actual Windy Valley trailhead is shortly beyond, at a metal gate in a little hollow near a culvert. Parking is best a couple hundred yards back, at the junction.

Before setting out on foot, I suggest driving the rest of the way up to Snow Camp Lookout, the terminus of the Windy Valley Trail. The two mile walk from Windy Valley to the lookout is grueling and not recommended. The 4200 foot lookout offers views of the Windy Valley, every peak within 100 miles, and the ocean. To reach the lookout, follow Road 1376 to where it becomes narrow and steep and takes off sharply uphill. Look for a gated road a mile or so beyond on the left. Park and walk to the lookout.

The Windy Valley Trail is charming. After passing the collapsed shelter at Cedar Camp, the route passes behind the huge rock outcropping seen from the trailhead. It's an easy and rewarding climb to the top of the rock.

Just past the rock, a vista unfolds to the left. On a clear day, it's supposed to be possible to see the ocean through the mouth of the Pistol River. The trail contours around a steep hillside, crosses several creeks, a myrtlewood grove or two, two patches of fly eating darlingtonia, and countless azaleas and rhododendrons. Watch for a brief view of Snow Camp Lookout. The way steepens a little as it approaches the valley but Windy Creek soon comes into view, signaling that you're almost there.

To reach Windy Valley, go straight instead of left at the turnoff to Snow Camp. Beyond the turnoff, the trail grows rather indistinct and muddy in spots. But the woods and grassy meadows are enchanting and it's difficult to become lost. Finally, the large prairie comprising Windy Valley proper unfolds in front of you. It's necessary to cross the creek which, in winter, can be calf deep.

I visited on a sunny December 28th. Being soaked to the knees from two creek crossings and several marshy areas, I didn't spend much time exploring. But I'm told the ruins of an old homestead grace the north end of the prairie and there are supposed to be good swimming holes and fair fishing in Windy Creek. The spot is popular in summer.

Game Lake Loop    17

# 6. Game Lake Loop
## (Kalmiopsis Wilderness Area)

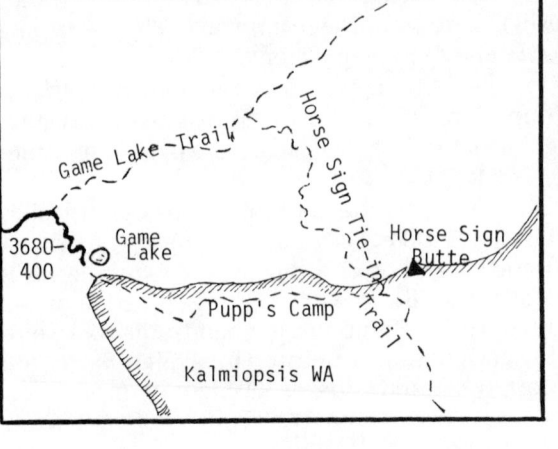

**Length:** 6½ mi. loop
**Water:** OK
**Access:** 2
**Season:** May to Nov.
**Difficulty:** 2
**Elevation:** 3900 to 2800 ft.
**Scenic Qual.:** 3
**Use:** Non-motorized only

High in the coastal mountains, on the ridges between the Rogue and Illinois Rivers, lies some of southern Oregon's most unusual country. Two important trails originate there, which careen down to the Illinois River in some of the steepest descents in this book. Both trails involve either fording the Illinois or attempting an impossible hike back up.

Fortunately, the Forest Service has recently constructed a connecting tie between these trails so there is now an easy loop through the rocky crests of the Game Lake country.

From the Illinois looking up, all one sees are looming slopes textured by dense, old growth Douglas-fir. It's very formidable. Unseen above these slopes are rocky summits, sheer cliffs, grassy prairies and sparsely forested serpentine ridges. From the top looking down, the views are fantastic.

Getting up to the peaks tends to be a long, slow project, although the gravel roads are decent. The best route from Grants Pass is over Bear Camp to Agness (see the Illinois River/Buzzards Roost chapter for a description of Bear Camp). Take I-5 north one exit to Merlin and follow Merlin-Galice Road to Galice Creek Road. Look for a sign pointing left to Agness and Gold Beach. You'll come out on Road 33 opposite Agness. Follow the pavement left, to either Road 3318 or 3313 (both gravel routes), uphill to the left. 3318 winds through Wildhorse Prairie while 3313 climbs Quosatana Butte.

From Gold Beach, go up Hunters Creek, just south of town. The road soon meets Road 3680. This is a very long, unpaved route which doesn't become scenic for 20 miles. However you get there, Road 3680 is your objective.

Beyond the junction with 3318, 3680 evolves into one of the more interesting auto excursions. Bear right at all ambiguous looking junctions as Game Lake is approached. Aside from much logging activity, this road offers closeup views of Collier Butte and the Big Craggies, not to mention

virtually every peak within 100 miles. The barren and impenetrable Big Craggies are especially interesting (see the Mislatnah Peak chapter).

Game Lake is a pleasant little pool in a wooded flat. It's quite popular so expect lots of summer traffic. The last half-mile of the road is rather rough and the lake shore is brushy. There are campgrounds at the lake, Fairview Meadow, Wildhorse Prairie and Quosatana Creek.

Bill Sherearth, of the Gold Beach Ranger District, recommends picking up the loop trail at the Pupps Camp end, following it around to the Game Lake Trail and returning. The latter hits the Game Lake road ¾ of a mile before the lake, at a well marked trailhead.

The equally well marked, roomy trailhead of the Pupps Camp Trail is located on the east end of Game Lake, across a grassy field. It follows a fairly level ridge, with some steep ups and downs, for two miles as it makes its way towards Horse Sign Butte while skirting the edge of the Kalmiopsis Wilderness Area. Horse Sign Butte is a handsome rock spire resembling an inverted sugar cone. Just before Horse Sign Butte, the Pupps Camp Trail drops off into infinity, losing 3000 feet in three miles.

Fortunately, the reasonably level Tie-in Trail cuts left immediately prior. It joins the Game Lake Trail after 1½ miles. Turn left on the Game Lake Trail and follow it 2½ miles back to the road. A right turn onto the Game Lake Trail will land you at Oak Flat, 12 miles down the Illinois from where the Pupps Camp Trail meets the river.

The entire loop is fairly uniform in that it mostly dips up and down through rock outcroppings, brush and grass openings, and scattered forest. Panoramas are frequent. The Tie-in Trail crosses creeks surrounded by Douglas-fir pockets. Game Lake also sits in a pocket of Douglas-fir. The rest of the route traverses two parallel ridges composed mainly of serpentine-type rock. Look for thin soil, manzanita, Jeffrey pine and western white pine. In occasional marshy areas or along streams, you'll see darlingtonia or flycatcher plants and other rare bog flowers, along with azalea and rhododendron.

# 7. Azalea Lake/Coquille Falls

These are actually two trails about two miles apart. The Coquille Falls Trail, while spectacular, is too short to include by itself. The Azalea Lake Trail is more intimate than grandly scenic but botanically interesting. Both trails are located in an area deserving more attention than it receives.

There are many ways to reach the trailheads, located on the South Fork of the Coquille River, south of Powers, Oregon. You can travel to Galice from Grants Pass and Merlin and take the road uphill left at the Grave Creek Bridge. From there, simply follow the signs to Powers and Agness. Or you can go over Bear Camp from Galice to Agness and continue on to Powers. For an all weather route, take I-5 north to Winston and follow the signs to Coquille. Turn off at the road to Powers.

**Azalea Lake/Coquille Falls    19**

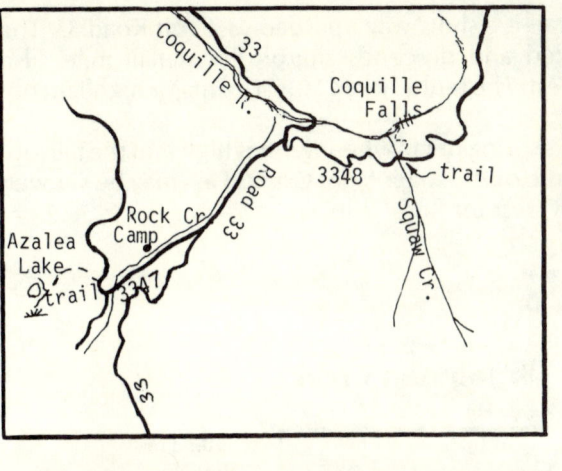

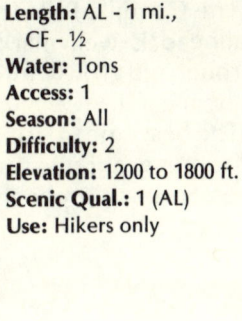

**Length:** AL - 1 mi.,
   CF - ½
**Water:** Tons
**Access:** 1
**Season:** All
**Difficulty:** 2
**Elevation:** 1200 to 1800 ft.
**Scenic Qual.:** 1 (AL)
**Use:** Hikers only

By whatever route, your goal is the spot where Road 33, south from Powers, meets Road 3348, the road to Glendale and Galice. Road 33 is especially scenic in the wet season. Its last few miles, along the Coquille River, are lined with high bluffs and countless seasonal waterfalls, not to mention some year-round waterfalls. None compare to Coquille Falls, however. Road 33 continues on to Agness.

To reach Azalea Lake, follow Road 33 a mile or so beyond the 33-3348 junction and turn right on Road 3347. Follow 3347 past Rock Creek Campground. There's a "T" intersection just beyond the campground near a bridge across Rock Creek. The trailhead can be seen just to the right, over the bridge. The Forest Service map shows it to the left.

It's a little over a mile to Azalea Lake, up a closed logging road. The trek is rather steep, although the Forest Service plans to reroute it, adding switchbacks to make it a little longer but lessening the gradient. After a mile, the trail crosses a little creek, then forks. Both forks lead to the lake but the right fork is more direct and less muddy.

The ridges and canyons around Azalea Lake are dramatic and heavily forested but there are no good observation points from the trail. It's a pleasant walk, however, through typical lush coastal forest. Look for salal covering the ground and lots of rhododendron. The main trees are Douglas-fir, of course, plus western hemlock and tanoak. There is also much of the uniquely Oregonian Port Orford cedar, with its fernlike foliage.

Azalea Lake doesn't compare to the dazzling cirque lakes of the Marble Mountains. It's more of a brushy lily pond in an upland swamp. A nice little marsh sits immediately adjacent. The lake is lined with azalea, rhododendron and coffeeberry and is splendid when all are in bloom. While natural, the lake's summer water level is maintained artificially by a system of pipes from nearby creeks. The Forest Service hopes to establish a fish population.

**20    Johnson Creek**

The Coquille Falls Trail is a short way up Road 3348, off Road 33. The trailhead is well marked and descends sharply for a half-mile, also through old growth forest. The multi-tiered falls are a major highlight not to be missed.

The best time to visit is spring or fall when water is high and the falls are all running, altough some of the roads from Grants Pass may be snowed over. Spring is probably best for floral displays.

# 8. Johnson Creek

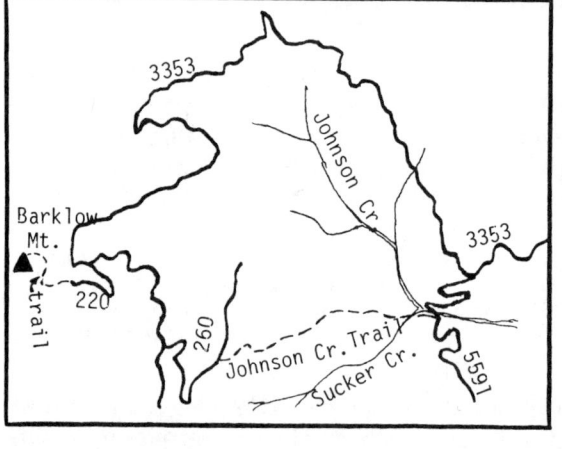

**Length:** 3 mi.
**Water:** No
**Access:** 2
**Season:** May to Nov.
**Difficulty:** 2
**Elevation:** 1200 to 1760 ft.
 (Barklow - 3579 ft.)
**Scenic Qual.:** 2
**Use:** Hikers only

Bernstein's Book of Naturalist Cliches contains two inviolate rules. The first is that the word "panorama" must always be preceded by "spectacular" (or by "vast"). The second is that "coastal forests" must always be described as "lush."

Both are the case on this trail above the Coquille River near Powers. It begins on the rocky summit of a mountain with a spectacular panorama, winds through lush coastal forest, and ends in a steep walled, moss lined canyon. If you play your cards right, the whole trip is downhill.

To reach Johnson Creek, one must first find Road 33, south of the town of Powers on the South Fork of the Coquille River. From Grants Pass, you can get there via Galice, Glendale or Winston. See the Chapter on Azalea Lake/Coquille Falls for more detail. Or invest in a state map.

You should also have a current Siskiyou National Forest map before fooling around on the back roads of the Powers Ranger District. To find the Johnson Creek trailhead, cross the Coquille River at China Flat and turn onto Road 3353. It's well marked. After four miles, you will pass Road 5591, which leads down a very steep, two-mile dirt road into a hole with Johnson Creek at the bottom. Your vehicle should have no problems but the road is so narrow and curvy, it's impossible to see oncoming cars. The trail is just over the bridge to the right.

Mt. Bolivar    21

I recommend leaving a vehicle at the bottom and driving a second rig to the upper trailhead. That way, you won't have to hike back up. I also recommend having a look at Johnson Creek if you're planning a one-way hike down. When water is low, crossing it poses no problem and can usually be done without getting your shoes wet. The first time I visited, in November, the water was hip deep and very uninviting. It's only a couple hundred feet from the lower trailhead to the creek crossing.

From Johnson Creek, return to 3353 and continue on for about 10 miles to a small saddle between the Coquille and Sixes Rivers. Look for a short spur on the right, called 220, which leads to the Barklow Mountain trailhead. The "spectacular panorama" referred to earlier is the top of Barklow. The upper Johnson Creek trailhead is a couple miles down the road. The Barklow Mountain Trail is only a half-mile long but should not be missed.

Beyond Barklow, 3353 winds along the ridgetop amid much logging. The surrounding slopes are densely forested and very steep. Some three miles past Barklow Mountain, you'll arrive at a logging spur to the left called 260. This road drops sharply into the Sucker Creek drainage and you'll find the trailhead about 1½ miles down on the left.

All but the last quarter-mile of the Johnson Creek Trail follows Sucker Creek, not Johnson Creek. But if they want to call it the Johnson Creek Trail, who am I to argue?

The first half-mile of the trail is quite brushy. It passes an unstable area with much raveling and gravel slides across the trail. According to Rob Batten at the Powers Ranger District, this segment is maintained regularly, although it may look a little precarious. Shortly, you will find yourself in an old growth forest of Douglas-fir and western hemlock. There are few panoramic views on the trail as this lush coastal ecosystem continues for almost two miles. If you were walking uphill, the grade would be considered moderate to steep.

Finally, the trail reaches bottom and ends in a lovely canyon where two creeks coverege. Mossy cliffs soar overhead everywhere.

Except for Barklow Mountain, this excursion is more of a quiet hike in the intimacy of nature than high drama. But beauty and variety are certainly to be found in abundance.

## 9. Mt. Bolivar
### (Wild Rogue Wilderness Area)

The hike to the top of this highest point on the north rim of the Rogue River canyon isn't particularly long but driving to the trailhead takes forever. The trail offers perhaps the best single view of the canyon. Throw in nearby Hanging Rock and you have a pretty full day.

**22    Mt. Bolivar**

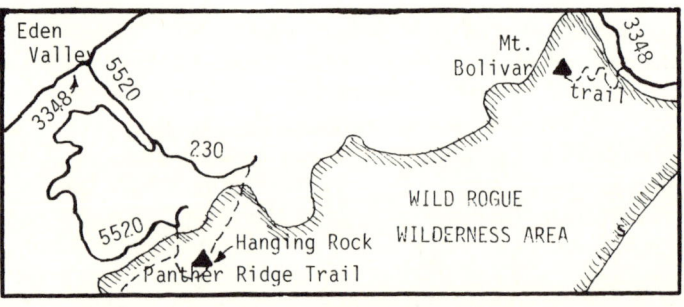

| | |
|---|---|
| **Length:** 1½ mi. | **Water:** No |
| **Access:** 2 | **Season:** May to Nov. |
| **Difficulty:** 2 | **Elevation:** 3000 to 4319 ft. |
| **Scenic Qual.:** 2 | **Use:** Hikers only |

Reaching the trailhead isn't difficult but the road is long, slow and keeps running into major intersections with signs pointing every which way. Without a map, you're never quite sure you're one the right course. Much of the route is paved or oil topped.

> To get there from Grants Pass, take the road to Powers and Agness from either Galice or Glendale. Glendale is 25 miles north of Grants Pass off I-5. Galice is reached via the Merlin exit on I-5, one exit north of Grants Pass. Follow Merlin-Galice Road to the Grave Creek Bridge and turn left up the hill. The first two miles of this road offers excellent views of the Rogue.
>
> The unpaved road levels off beyond the Mt. Reuben junction (stay left), then picks up the road from Glendale a few miles beyond. Most confusing is Anaktuvik Saddle, named for a pass in Alaska's Brooks Range. Just keep straight, following the signs to Powers (Road 3348). You'll run into a few miles of unpaved road but the blacktop soon picks up again. The Mt. Bolivar trailhead is about four miles beyond the aforementioned saddle.

Beyond Bolivar, the road descends into the Coquille River drainage and the forests become lush and coastal. The road is paved from Eden Valley to Coquille Falls, with some notable gaps. For an outstanding side trip, hang a left at Buck Creek Road (5520), to Hanging Rock and the Panther Ridge Trail. The latter is an 11-mile route, most of whose highlights are accessible by road. The signs on 5520 will try to lead you to the Buck Point trailhead but I recommend continuing on to spur 140 where the trailhead for the half-mile Hanging Rock Trail is located. Hanging Rock is a spectacular formation on Panther Ridge.

Back at Mt. Bolivar, the trail is quite steep with lots of switchbacks. But it's short so just take your time. It begins in a forest of Douglas-fir and white fir, with lots of rhododendron decorating the understory. The open, rocky areas are overgrown mostly with manzanita and scrub chinkapin.

The summit looks down Mule Creek to Marial and the Rogue River. Directly opposite, Bobs Garden Mountain can be seen with far more clarity than it can from Bear Camp Road. Look also for the rugged Saddle Peaks radiating southwest of Boilvar.

The foundation of an old fire lookout adorns the Bolivar summit. There is also a small monument with a bronze plaque. The plaque was presented to the people of Oregon from the people of Venezuela in 1984 in recognition of the fact that Mt. Bolivar was named for that country's greatest hero. Simon Bolivar, of course, was the legendary South American general responsible for the independence of many countries, including Venezuela. It's an interesting tribute to democracy in the middle of a vast and beautiful wilderness.

## 10. Illinois River/Pine Flat
### (Kalmiopsis Wilderness Area)

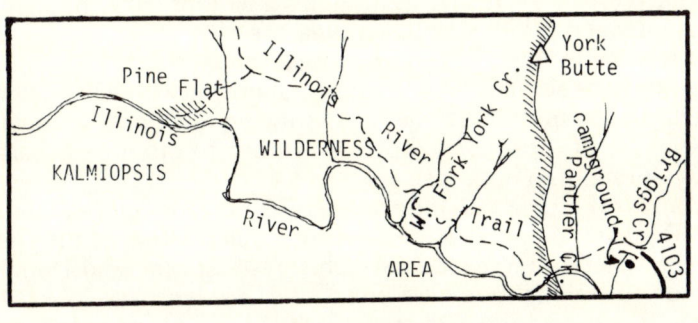

**Length:** 6 miles      **Water:** Yes
**Access:** 2           **Season:** All
**Difficulty:** 1        **Elevation:** 900 ft.
**Scenic Qual.:** 3      **Use:** Non-motorized only

This is my favorite winter hike. In fact, I once camped out at Pine Flat in February. In summer, it is the shortest trail from which to view the rare kalmiopsis plant, after which the Wilderness Area was named. The purple, azalea-like flowers bloom from May through August.

To reach the trailhead, turn right at Selma from Highway 199 out of Grants Pass and drive the Illinois River Road to its end at Briggs Creek. The road is winding, unpaved, and bumpy but affords outstanding views of the river.

The first turnoff to the left (011) is particularly interesting. It leads to no trails but to a huge bog of fly eating darlingtonia plants, lilies, and lady slipper orchids. At the end of this side road, where Deer Creek joins the Illinois, the most beautiful azalea-lined swimming hole I know of may be found. This is a four-wheel drive road.

## 24　Illinois River/Buzzards Roost

Back on the Illinois River Road, the last mile can be very muddy in winter and the last eighth-mile has some steep spots. But you'll make it. The road ends in a tiny campground with an impressive foot bridge spanning Briggs Creek.

The first-half mile of the trail crosses an old ranch with an abandoned orchard. It then emerges high above the river and for 1½ miles, passes sheer cliffs and rockfalls. Far below are the rapids of the Illinois, one of the country's great whitewater rivers. On the other side rise the rocky slopes of Nome Peak and Granite Butte. Canyons and waterfalls crash from their flanks into the river. The trail skirts the base of the York Butte, whose summit is itself an interesting day-hike.

After two miles, the trail crosses the steep, rocky East Fork of York Creek. A quarter-mile beyond, the West Fork is similar looking but has completely different vegetation. Instead of willow and alder, the West Fork is lined with azalea and darlingtonia.

Be absolutely sure to pause where you come around the bend and first view the West Fork. At that spot begins a 60 foot circle of kalmiopsis plants. A dwarf rhododendron or azalea, the plants form a prostrate mat only a few inches high with purple, bell shaped flowers. In the entire world, there are perhaps 15 such clumps, almost all within the Kalmiopsis Wilderness. The spot where you stand is also within the Wilderness. York Creek is one of those special places I return to often and share with friends visiting from back East.

Beyond York Creek the slope to the river becomes more gradual and the trail moves inland. For the next four miles, views of the river are infrequent as the trail winds through forests of pine and Douglas-fir, interspersed with oak and madrone.

Finally, the route forks at the top of a little hill. To the right lies the trail to Bald Mountain and Agness. To the left is the steep, half-mile descent to Pine Flat. Pine Flat is perfectly named. It is quiet and out of the way, with good water, excellent camp sites and an outstanding view of the river.

## 11. Illinois River/Buzzards Roost

Both ends of the Illinois River Trail start at places called Oak Flat. The Oak Flat at the Agness end is flatter, larger and oakier than the one at the Illinois Valley end.

This chapter follows the Illinois River Trail from the confluence with the Rogue river upstream to Buzzards Roost and Indigo Creek. Beyond, the trail climbs several thousand feet to the top of Bald Mountain before emerging at the other Oak Flat.

The downstream Oak Flat trailhead may be reached in two ways. If you happen to be in Gold Beach, it's a beautiful 25 mile drive up the South Bank Road to Cougar Lane, Agness and the Illinois River Bridge.

**Illinois River/Buzzards Roost** 25

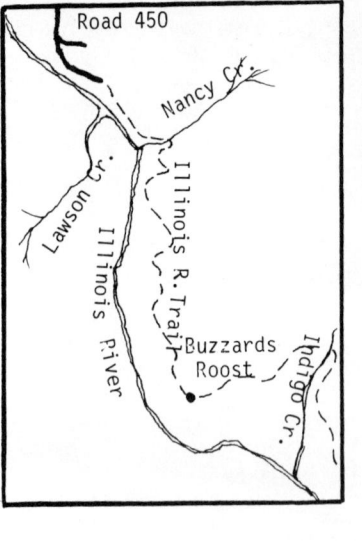

**Length:** 2 miles
**Water:** Gobs
**Access:** 1
**Season:** All
**Difficulty:** 1
**Elevation:** 600 ft.
**Scenic Qual.:** 2
**Use:** Summer — any;
    winter — hikers only

From Grants Pass, take the drive over Bear Camp. This is one of the region's great scenic routes, although closed in winter. Get off I-5 north at Merlin, just past Grants Pass. Take the Merlin-Galice Road to Galice Creek Road and follow the signs to Gold Beach. At the summit, 5400 foot Brandy Peak rises to the south, with its high meadows and craggy outcroppings. One of only three or four clusters of Alaska cedar in the entire Siskiyou Mountains decorates the glacial cirque on the north side of Brandy Peak. The species is fairly common in the upper elevation Cascades from Diamond Lake north.

Just beyond the summit are excellent views of Mt. Bolivar and the Rogue canyon, altough the river itself can't be seen.

Where Bear Camp Road meets the highway near Agness, turn left and proceed a mile or two past Cougar Lane, to the road up the Illinois. It's three miles to the well marked, roomy trailhead, which was recently moved.

The trail is mostly level and wooded with muddy spots in wet weather. There is much horse traffic and trail bikes are permitted in summer to the Wilderness boundary just before Silver Creek. The first quarter-mile of the trail offers views of the river and Lawson Creek. For the next two miles, the trail moves inland, crossing several side creeks, one with a charming myrtlewood grove. The last half-mile to Buzzards Roost is mostly uphill but not terribly steep. Should you continue on to Indigo Creek, the return to Buzzards Roost is steep.

Buzzards Roost, where the trail starts back down, offers a panorama of the river from a high vantage point. The spot was well known to Indians and is now an archaeological preserve. For more information, inquire at the Forest Service.

**26    York Butte**

It's two miles from the trailhead to Buzzards Roost, three to the bridge at Indigo Creek and the side trail to the top of Silver Peak, and two days to the other Oak Flat.

## 12. York Butte
### (Kalmiopsis Wilderness Area)

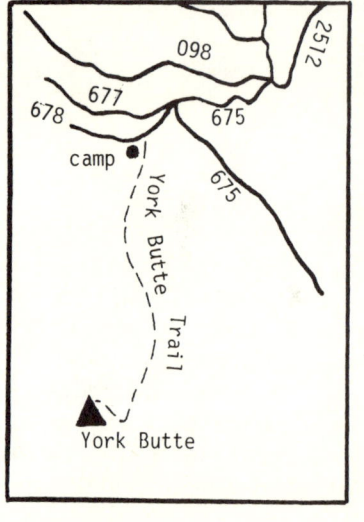

**Length:** 1½ miles
**Water:** No
**Access:** 2
**Season:** May to Nov.
**Difficulty:** 1
**Elevation:** 4100 to 4234 ft.
**Scenic Qual.:** 2
**Use:** Non-motorized only

This is a perfect "bring the kids" day-hike, even if access is a bit long and complicated. The goal is the summit of York Butte. Unfortunately, the best view of York Butte is not from the trail but from the lower Illinois River Road. From that road, the mountain can be seen plopped in the middle of the canyon like a giant horse's hoof. The diverted river forms a mighty whitewater gorge around it and the beginning of the Illinois River Trail skirts its flanks. Elsewhere in the region, York Butte is virtually invisible.

To reach the trailhead, take the Taylor Creek/Big Pine Road off Merlin-Galice Road just north of Grants Pass. Past Big Pine Campground, continue on Road 2512. This makes a fine Sunday drive with panoramas of Briggs Valley and the surrounding peaks.

Much of the area, especially near Chrome Ridge, is serpentine rock, recognized by its rough, weathered, tan surface. Look for odd, dwarfed vegetation and a conspicuous absence of Douglas-fir and madrone.

The road breaks up at Flat Top into a maze of logging roads. Road 2512 curves sharply right and drops into Silver Creek. Another road leads through Mud Springs while still another traverses the front of the hillside

**York Butte**    **27**

**Illinois River from top of York Butte (Ch. 12)**    (Bernstein Photo)

to the left. The latter is the beginning of the controversial Bald Mountain Road.

The object of your quest is the road on the far left which disappears behind the hill. From there, an old jeep road drops into Briggs Creek. Stay off it, whatever you do. Look instead for a primitive but driveable, double-rutted road through the grass into the woods. It ends at a little camp site where the trail begins.

The trail itself winds through the woods, past a little spring, across a saddle and finally up a steep gabbro rock face. The top is level and roomy but rocky, and graced with the elegant and rare Brewer spruce, with its dangling, whiplike branchlets.

The view of the Illinois Canyon is supurb. Look for Pearsoll Peak, Kerby Peak, Pine Flat, Granite Butte and, to the north, the eerie forests of Bald Ridge and South Bend Mountain. It's a great spot to eat lunch, let the kids run loose, and admire the wilds of southern Oregon.

**28    Silver Falls**

# 13. Silver Falls

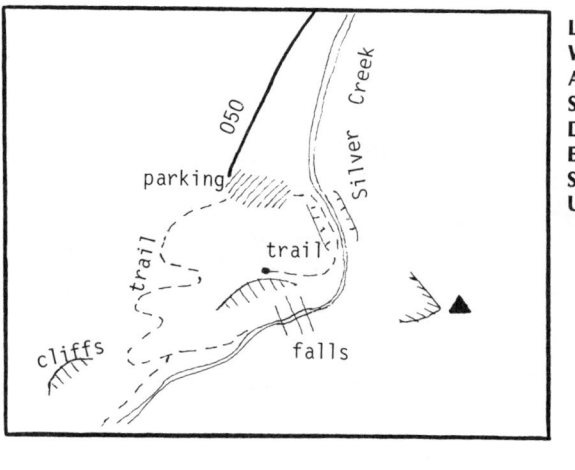

**Length:** 1½ miles
**Water:** Thunderous
**Access:** 3
**Season:** May to Nov.
**Difficulty:** 2
**Elevation:** 1800 ft.
**Scenic Qual.:** 3
**Use:** Non-motorized only

A couple of my half-dozen visits to Silver Falls have ended in unantici-
pated adventure, including pulling stuck motorists out of the mud.
Therefore, I rated the access road a "three" as a warning to stay off in the
wet season.

Even if you get stuck, you won't regret Silver Falls, a thundering,
60-foot plunge set amid towering, steep sided, densely forested peaks
with cliffs and landslides everywhere you look.

To get there, take I-5 north from Grants Pass and get off at Merlin. Proceed up
Merlin-Galice Road to Bear Camp Road, also called Galice Creek Road. Follow Bear
Camp Road about eight miles to the second Chrome Ridge turnoff. Two roads take
off left at that point. Chrome Ridge Road goes uphill and Silver Creek Road goes
downhill. Where Silver Creek Road forks a short way down, take the lower fork along
the creek. Follow the main road to spur 050. Although there are signs to the falls, it's
best to bring a map.

Note the almost pure stand of western hemlock lining the upper creek.
The species isn't that common in the Siskiyous. After passing much
logging activity, you will soon find yourself in a dark, wooded canyon
with Silver Creek flowing gently alongside. Park where the road ends.

The main trail takes off to the right over a little hill. Before starting up,
however, walk from the road end down to the creek on the left, to where
it enters a narrow, rocky — and manmade — gorge. A faint trail passes
through the gorge and comes out directly above the falls. This trail is
unstable and probably dangerous, crossing a couple of gravel falls which
end up at the bottom of the canyon. I didn't follow it all the way.

The main trail rises slightly, then begins a series of switchbacks down to
the creek below the falls. It's a long way down and the view of the falls is
never as good as the view from the other trail. I should add that some
maps do not show either trail and this one is also considered dangerous.
Once at the creek, make your way to the base of the falls, if you can. Then
begin the long, steep climb back up.

# 14. Silver Creek

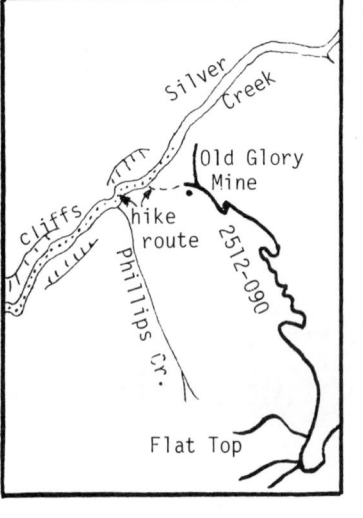

**Length:** 2
**Water:** Lots
**Difficulty:** 2
**Season:** Dry weather only
**Access:** 3
**Elevation:** 1300 ft.
**Scenic Qual.:** 3
**Use:** Hikers only

A different sort of hike, this "trail" follows the most unusual and beautiful of southern Oregon's wilderness streams. Silver Creek is a special place. Even at its headwaters off Bear Camp Road it is different, being lined for three miles with the largest stand of western hemlock in the Siskiyous.

Several miles downstream, from Silver Creek Falls to the confluence with the Illinois River, lower Silver Creek is vastly different from neighboring waterways. For one thing, it is clearer. You can stand in a neck deep pool and look at your toes and the water doesn't even look blue, it's that clear.

In addition, sheer, overhanging walls rise up on either side along most of the lower stream, forming imposing rock faces, eerie passageways, fern grottos and waterfalls. It is possible, wearing an old pair of sneakers for traction, to walk up the creek bed to view these wonders. At least it is in July and August when the water is rarely more than knee deep.

Upstream from Old Glory Mine, where the road ends, the gorge widens a little. Silver Creek Falls is about three miles upstream. Downstream, at least for the first few miles, the canyon is spectacular. Beyond that, the way gets pretty rugged, although the 20 miles or so to the Illinois makes a formidable adventure.

Reaching Old Glory Mine by car may also be a formidable adventure, requiring four-wheel drive and some nerve. Take Taylor Creek Road off Merlin-Galice Road, one freeway exit north of Grants Pass. Follow Taylor Creek past Big Pine and continue on Road 2512 where it swings right at Flat Top Mountain. Eventually, the road narrows and drops sharply downhill and across a creek. From the creek to the mine, the road is not only steep but outsloped, which means your car will be tilted sideways.

**30    Rogue River Trail/Whiskey Creek**

Old Glory Mine is itself interesting. Park at the abandoned gold mine and look around for the road to the creek. Do not attempt to drive to the water in anything other than a bulldozer, however. It is the ony spot where you don't have to climb down a cliff to reach the creek.

Below Old Glory Mine, there's a lovely sand bar with a huge fern grotto above, opposite the creek access. The bar is suitable for fishing, camping and swimming. The best swimming hole is 100 feet upstream. The best scenery is downstream.

## 15. Rogue River Trail/Whiskey Creek

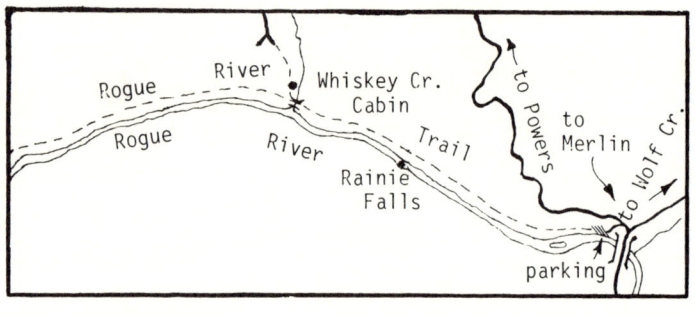

**Length:** 3 miles          **Water:** OK
**Access:** 1              **Season:** All
**Difficulty:** 1           **Elevation:** 650 ft.
**Scenic Qual.:** 2         **Use:** Hikers only

One of the country's most famous river gorges may be seen from this trail. The path's destination, Rainie Falls, is one of the river's scenic highlights and the only spot on the "Wild and Scenic" section of the lower Rogue which forces most boaters out of the water.

Access to the trailhead is paved all the way. Take the Merlin exit off I-5, just north of Grants Pass, and continue out Merlin-Galice Road, past Hellgate Canyon, to the Grave Creek Bridge. Be sure to stop at the Hellgate overlook.

The boat ramp at the foot of the Grave Creek Bridge is the river's most used. It is cramped for space and the short road down is steep. In summer, it's also usually mobbed, necessitating parking on the road and walking down. Another trailhead, on the other side of the bridge, also follows the Rogue for a couple miles.

The main trail begins at the boat launch area. It is well marked, mostly level, and usually cool and shaded. Kids love it. It's two miles to Rainie Falls and three to Whiskey Creek.

**Rogue River Trail/Blossom Bar** 31

The falls are more like rapids but impressive, nevertheless. There's a developed campground there, with pit toilets. To view the falls, hike down through the campground and climb out on the rocks. Boaters can be seen feeding their crafts with ropes through the side channel which bypasses the rapids.

A mile beyond Rainie Falls is the Whiskey Creek Cabin. Occupied from 1880 to 1977, it's now a registered National Landmark and well maintained by the Bureau of Land Management. A sign just past the fancy log bridge spanning Whiskey Creek points to the the cabin, only a few hundred feet from the Rogue Trail. They say fishing in Whiskey Creek is excellent.

It's possible to drive to within ¾'s of a mile of the cabin but I wouldn't recommend it. At Grave Creek, take the road to the left, uphill, and follow the oiltop surface into the Whiskey Creek drainage. The unmarked turnoff to the cabin is a mile past the second bridge along Whiskey Creek. This last road is steep, rutted and muddy in winter. The roads ends at a gate and the walk down follows a steep (though driveable if they'd let you) road. The hike isn't the least bit scenic and it's easier just to walk in from Grave Creek — and much prettier.

It isn't necessary to end your hike at Rainie Falls or Whiskey Creek. Foster Bar, at Agness, is 38 miles away and Marial is only 20. But Marial is another chapter.

There's a chance you'll come away smitten by the whitewater bug. Should that occur, check at the Rand Recreation Site to find out about permit requirements and when and where it's OK to go on the river. Or stop by any of the numerous boat and raft rental and car shuttle services in Merlin or Galice.

## 16. Rogue River Trail/Blossom Bar
### (Wild Rogue Wilderness Area)

Along with the climb up Mt. Shasta and the hike into the Marble Valley, this short, level stretch along the Rogue River is one of this book's three "ultimate hikes." The Marial-Blossom Bar area, halfway between Grave Creek and Agness, offers the ultimate among trails along southern Oregon and northern California's many wild and scenic rivers.

Picking up the trail 23 miles below the Grave Creek trailhead requires adventurous driving. One must drive to the top of the mountain, then make their way to the bottom of one of the deepest and most rugged canyons in the country.

People come from all over the world to run the lower Rogue and it tends to be the domain of boat and raft people. Many also hike in from Grave Creek. Few arrive at Marial by car but I wouldn't worry about that. Enjoy the scenery and cheer the rafters on as they attempt to run some of the Rogue's most difficult rapids.

## Rogue River Trail/Blossom Bar

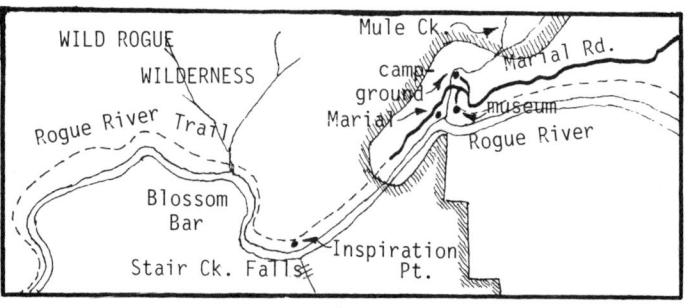

**Length:** 2 miles     **Water:** Lots
**Access:** 3     **Season:** All
**Difficulty:** 1     **Elevation:** 400 ft.
**Scenic Qual.:** 3     **Use:** Hikers only

The trailhead at Marial may be reached via several routes. Easiest from Grants Pass is to get off I-5 at Merlin and proceed past Galice to the Grave Creek Bridge. Turn left just over the bridge and head up the mountain. The road forks a few miles up, with the main fork winding into Whiskey Creek. Both forks emerge on a paved road from Glendale. Turn left onto it, towards Powers. The turnoff to Marial is clearly marked a few miles beyond.

The single lane dirt road into Marial is steep, very winding, and seemingly endless. But the far wall of Mule Creek Canyon will finally appear, followed by the Mule Creek Campground turnoff and the turnoff to the little Ranch and museum, with its neatly tended grounds.

The cramped campground is situated in an area containing much more vertical than horizontal. It's pretty, though, with Mule Creek running through it and much canyon live oak. The museum sits on the canyon's only level spot. Do visit it as the area boasts much history; between pioneers, gold miners and Indians. A nearby archaeological dig has recently uncovered the oldest remains of human habitation in Oregon.

Marial itself is just beyond the museum and over a little bridge. The road bears right, passes a couple buildings, then trails off into the woods for a mile, over some quite bad spots, before ending at the trailhead parking area. Immediately beyond lies the boundary of the Wild Rogue Wilderness Area.

After a short walk through the woods, the trail comes out on a ledge above the river. For the next two miles, the trail is gouged into sheer rock up the side of the gray-green canyon.

Soon after meeting the river, Mule Creek canyon is entered. Look for two monolithic boulders called "The Jaws." The canyon beyond, dubbed "The Narrows," empties into a formation known to river runners as "The Coffee Pot." Look for boats careening from one wall of the canyon to the other or spinning helplessly in the middle. The Coffee Pot is fun in a raft but the tendency to crash into the wall is hard on rigid boats.

Beyond the Coffee Pot, the river calms as it passes Stair Creek Falls and Inspiration Point. The aptly named falls cascade down the narrow gorge

Rogue River Trail/Blossom Bar    33

**Lower Rogue Canyon (Ch. 16)**                          (USFS Photo)

of Stair Creek. Stop at Inspiration Point for views of the falls, canyon and surrounding peaks.

The canyon widens slightly at Blossom Bar. There's not much of a gravel bar at Blossom Bar but there are lots of azalea blossoms in spring and early summer. A small camping site graces the mouth of Blossom Bar Creek.

Blossom Bar is an area of immense boulders, both on the bank and in the water. Blossom Bar Rapids is the most difficult run on the river. In fact, it was impossible until Glen Wooldridge blasted a channel through in the 1920's. Wooldridge is credited with being the first person to run the lower Rogue.

The trail at Blossom Bar is a favorite spectator spot so find a good perch above the rapids and enjoy the show. Every rock, chute, and formation has a name and bystanders will be happy to explain the best routes and the technical prowess necessary to avoid a dunking.

From Blossom Bar, it's another 15 miles to the end of the trail near Agness. Just remember what I said in the last chapter: Prolonged exposures to the wild section of the Rogue could result in an obsession with river running. But I wouldn't worry. There are worse fates.

34    Pearsoll Peak

# 17. Pearsoll Peak
## (Kalmiopsis Wilderness Area)

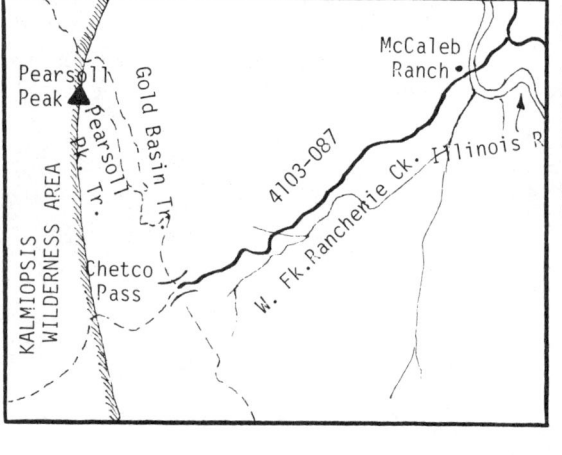

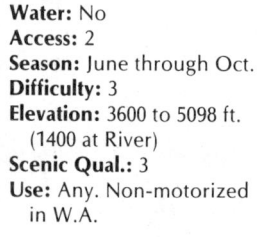

**Length:** 2 miles
**Water:** No
**Access:** 2
**Season:** June through Oct.
**Difficulty:** 3
**Elevation:** 3600 to 5098 ft.
　(1400 at River)
**Scenic Qual.:** 3
**Use:** Any. Non-motorized
　in W.A.

The orange cone comprising the highest point in the Kalmiopsis Wilderness Area is visible from many points in Josephine County. One of the better is from the little bridge over Deer Creek just beyond Selma on Highway 199.

While not Josephine County's highest peak, Pearsoll is among its most prominent at 5098 feet. Comprised mostly of weathered serpentine rock, the lack of vegetation at the summit is due more to poor soil than high elevation. Serpentine is black but weathers to a buff orange. The peak is especially beautiful when its flanks are highlighted by a light mantle of snow.

The road down the Illinois canyon to the trailhead begins in the town of Selma, 20 miles south of Grants Pass on Highway 199. Turn left on Road 4103. A few miles down, 4105 takes off uphill and looks like the main road but isn't. From there to Store Gulch, the road is narrow, rocky, and may remind your stomach of a roller coaster. It's quite scenic, however.

A couple miles beyond Store Gulch, a short, steep dirt road descends to the left, towards the river. The sign directs motorists to Illinois River Falls and the McCaleb Ranch Boy Scout Camp. The low water bridge across the river here can be scary and may be submerged. Once across, McCaleb Ranch lies to the right, through the field. The road to Chetco Pass is straight ahead, up the hill.

The Chetco Pass Road was originally a jeep road. The 1976 Forest Service map showed it as a trail while the latest map shows it as a road again. The four-mile route requires four-wheel drive and some driving skill. It's very steep and deeply rutted, with spots of loose rock. As a hike, it's hot, dusty and tiring.

The two mile Pearsoll Peak Trail takes off to the right from Chetco Pass. It's easy to follow but worse, if possible, than the Chetco Pass Road. There

Eagle Mountain    35

are ruts, steep spots with loose gravel, and the entire route is dusty and out in the open.

One can drive much of the way from the pass to the peak but walking is recommended. One can also hike down to the Chetco River from the Pass, or south along the crest to Whetstone Butte and Onion Camp. The Pearsoll summit is inside the Wilderness Area but the trail isn't.

An old lookout caps the summit, at which to rest, regroup and admire the view. You can't quite see down to the Illinois but almost all the southwest Oregon wilderness, including the entire Chetco basin, is laid out at your feet. Look for York Butte, Vulcan Peak and the Big Craggies.

The trail continues north from Pearsoll over Gold Basin Butte. It then forks and you can either hike down Gold Basin or continue along the craggy ridges. Both trails are long and difficult.

## 18. Eagle Mountain

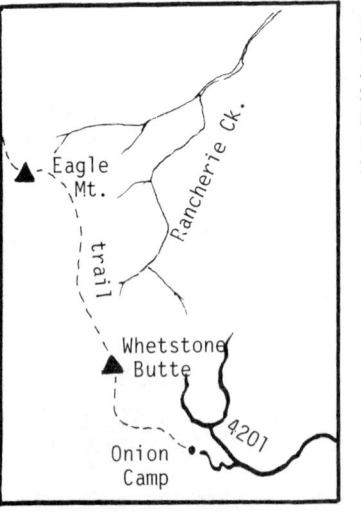

**Length:** 4 miles
**Water:** No
**Access:** 2
**Season:** May through Nov.
**Difficulty:** 3
**Elevation:** 4000 to 4464 ft.
**Scenic Qual.:** 2
**Use:** Any

For those desiring to experience the Pearsoll Peak area without having to drive or hike the Chetco Pass Road, consider the route from Onion Camp to Eagle Mountain. The hike takes in a chunk of the Chetco Rim Trail along the crest of the Chetco-Illinois Divide. The Babyfoot Lake trail begins a quarter-mile south while Chetco Pass lies six or seven miles north. Like the Pearsoll Peak Trail, the Eagle Mountain trek is dry, rugged and offers excellent vantage points.

To reach the trailhead, take Highway 199 south from Grants Pass. A couple miles past Selma, a side road to the right says, "Eight Dollar Road-Kalmiopsis Wilderness Area." Take it over the bridge and up the hill almost to the end, then pull in at Onion Camp.

36    **Babyfoot Lake**

Back near the beginning of the road, where it first heads uphill, a turnoff left leads to a rare hanging bog, formed on a continually oozing hillside instead of a low spot. Look for insect eating plants, such as darlingtonia and the rosette shaped butterwort. In August, look for the extremely rare and beautiful Waldo gentian.

From Onion Camp, I'll turn the story over to my friend Randy Wainscott, who once hiked the trail by accident, carrying a fishing rod while searching in vain for Babyfoot Lake.

At Onion Camp, he says, "a small, wooden arrow, stating simply, 'Trail,' directs you past the rest rooms. Crossing a small bridge, the trail starts in a heavily forested area. It emerges a half-mile later and begins the ascent of Whetstone Butte."

The trail here becomes very steep and indistinct, with much raveling, dust and loose rock. The area is mostly serpentine-type soil and vegetation is sparse. Water is non-existent.

Randy continues, "At the top of Whetstone Butte, the diligent hiker is more than compensated by the spectacular mountain scenery. The trail beyond is once again well maintained. Bending sharply left, it follows the side of Eagle Mountain down through Eagle Pass.

"You can, if you wish, continue on through Chetco Pass to the top of Pearsoll Peak. For us, we were satisfied, after about five miles, that we weren't going to find Babyfoot Lake. We never did catch any fish that day."

# 19. Babyfoot Lake
## (Kalmiopsis Wilderness Area)

If you have a secret yen to just stick a toe inside a national Wilderness Area without working up a sweat, this is the trail for you. The only highway sign pointing to the Kalmiopsis Wilderness, in fact, directs visitors to Babyfoot Lake.

To reach the trailhead, take Highway 199 south from Grants Pass. Just beyond Selma, a sign pointing left reads, "Kalmiopsis Wilderness-17 miles." This road has some interesting highlights described in the previous chapter. Not mentioned in that chapter is a large serpentine-type bog on the right, just before the "Entering Siskiyou National Forest" sign. Look for two jeep roads taking off to the right. Follow the lower road on foot a couple hundred feet, then drop down to the right. You will find darlingtonia plants, lilies, azaleas, coffeeberry, myrtlewood, Port Orford cedar and Jeffrey pine. Be exceedingly careful in this fragile environment.

Back on Eight Dollar Road, as the route to Babyfoot Lake is called, cross the Illinois River bridge and proceed uphill. It's steep, unpaved and winding, but not particularly difficult. Finally, you will arrive at a well

**Babyfoot Lake**     37

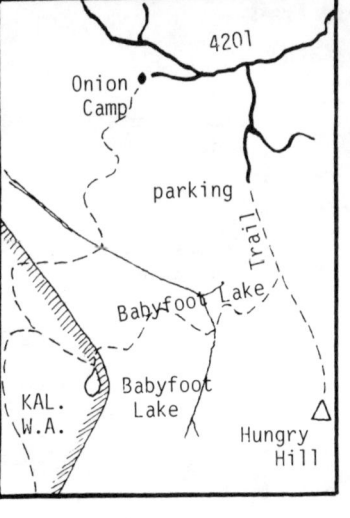

**Length:** 1½ miles
**Water:** A little
**Access:** 2
**Season:** May through Nov.
**Difficulty:** 2
**Elevation:** 4000 ft.
**Scenic Qual.:** 2
**Use:** Non-motorized only.
   X-C ski

marked side road denoting the Babyfoot Lake Trail. If you end up at Onion Camp, you've gone too far.

The trailhead parking area has recently been moved and the trail slightly rerouted. It used to begin right off Eight Dollar Road but is now located a quarter-mile up a logging road.

The trail follows an old logging road along a narrow ridge for a quarter-mile or so, towards Hungry Hill. Then a side trail drops down into the woods and lake. The views from the ridge are impressive but a little disorienting. There used to be a couple steep, slippery spots on the trail but I understand these are gone. All in all, it's pretty easy going.

The lake sits in a little wooded glacial cirque with a headwall on one side. The area below the headwall is flat, with many campsites. Fishing and swimming in the lake are good.

Babyfoot Lake is an officially designated Botanical Area, largely because of its Brewer spruce. I've gone to some lengths in other chapters to extoll the beauty and rarity of this unique tree. But the fact is, the Botanical Area was created before scientists realized how widespread Brewer spruce actually was. It's in no way endangered and reproduces prolifically within its limited range. The exceedingly rare Del Norte daisy supposedly also grows at Babyfoot Lake.

From the lake, there is supposed to be a trail to the top of the cliff which loops back up to the ridge you came in on. Another trail allegedly connects with the Onion Camp and Chetco Rim Trails. I've never found either.

# 20. Umpqua Joe Trail
## (Indian Mary Park)

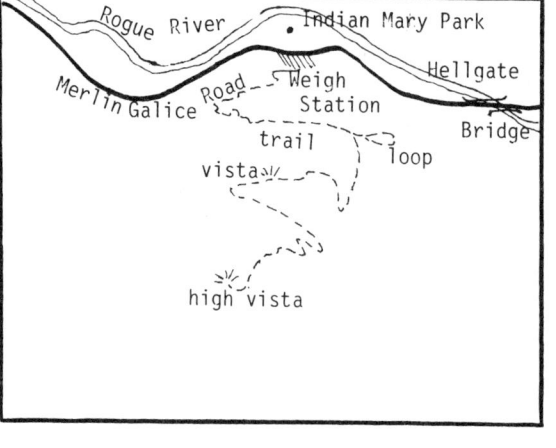

**Length:** 2 miles
**Water:** No
**Access:** 1
**Season:** All
**Difficulty:** 2
**Elevation:** 800 to 2000 ft.
**Scenic Qual.:** 1
**Use:** Non-motorized only

For housebound Grants Pass residents with a couple hours to kill on a winter's afternoon, this little excursion is ideal. It's not fabulous scenery but it's good scenery and a pleasant diversion.

Actually, the scenery is frustrating, with frequent glimpses of things you'd like to see more of, like the rocks on the far side of the Rogue near Hellgate. The trail does offer views of Indian Mary Park and a too-small slice of the Rogue River. It also briefly enters one of those brushy canyons which can be seen careening into Hellgate opposite the auto overlook.

The Umpqua Joe Trail is the only one in this book maintained by a county park department. County parks don't often have two miles of land all in one place and their trails tend to be interpretive nature loops, more intensive than extensive. There is, however, a lovely nature trail at Tom Pearce Park in Grants Pass, which winds along the Rogue through slue, swamp, forest and riffle. There are also excellent trails at Wolf Creek Park, Lake Selmac and Cathedral Hills; all Josephine County parks. Jackson County also boasts some excellent offerings.

Umpqua Joe was the father of Indian Mary and a longtime early resident of the Rogue Valley. He was born, not surprisingly, in the Umpqua Valley. Much literature is available on Umpqua Joe and Indian Mary.

His trail is entirely within Indian Mary Park and it ascends a steep, densely forested, north slope mountainside receiving virtually no sun. It's great for cooling off in summer but never warms up in winter.

To reach the trailhead, get off I-5 at Merlin, north of Grants Pass, and take the Merlin-Galice Road past Hellgate to the Indian Mary Park entrance. The trail begins at the weigh station opposite the entrance. The trailhead sign contains the most detailed map I've ever seen carved in wood but gives no indication of scale. I guess with all those scales nearby ...

The route has some fairly steep pitches but is remarkably level considering the steepness of the hill. A short side loop, two-thirds of the way up, offers a view of the park's playground, a sight not visible from the overlook at the trail's end. If you enjoy aerial vistas of playgrounds, don't miss it.

The objective is a small rock overlook with a view of the park and river. The trail continues for another ¾'s-mile, although it becomes less well maintained and much steeper. The ultimate terminus is a mossy rock pinnacle on the ridgetop. The site is pretty but the view is blocked by trees and not as good as the view from the lower overlook.

## 21. Shan Creek

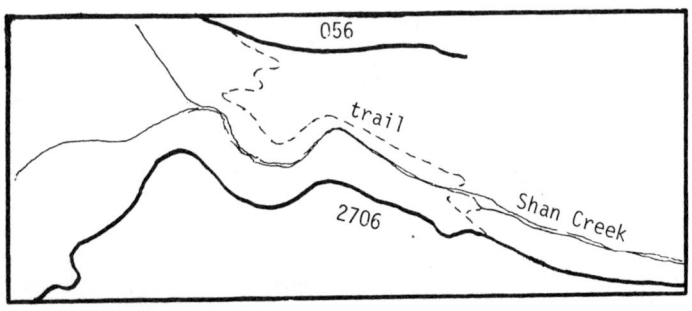

| | |
|---|---|
| **Length:** 2 miles | **Water:** Lots |
| **Access:** 1 | **Season:** All year |
| **Difficulty:** 1 | **Elevation:** 1200 to 2200 ft. |
| **Scenic Qual.:** 1 | **Use:** Any |

Another afternoon quickie to relieve the winter doldrums is the Shan Creek Trail. It's not only easy but fairly close to Grants Pass. Don't be misled by my low Scenic Quality rating. That only means it isn't as spectacular as Mount Shasta or the Illinois canyon.

To reach the trailhead, take Highway 199 to Riverbanks Road. Or take Upper River Road to Robertson Bridge to Riverbanks Road, all out of Grants Pass. Follow Riverbanks to Shan Creek Road. The trailhead is a mile or so past the houses, with a clearly visible sign at a little turnout on the right. The road is paved to the trailhead.

Shan Creek Road also leads to one of the better picnic sites, about eight miles up the hill. There, a lone picnic table overlooks the canyon. The canyon, in turn, perfectly frames Grants Pass and the confluence of the Rogue and Applegate Rivers, with Mt. McLoughlin on the horizon. Past the picnic site is Onion Mountain, whose Forest Service lookout affords excellent vistas.

**40    Mungers Butte**

The Shan Creek Trail begins back near the bottom of the road. From the trailhead, the route descends through the woods and crosses the creek. It's best to take your shoes off crossing the creek because there are usually no dry pathways. Water is likely to be a foot deep in winter and a few inches deep in summer.

A few hundred feet before trail crosses creek, a short side trail shoots down to a huge rock above one of your better swimming holes. It's a favorite picnic spot.

Once across Shan Creek, the trail climbs gradually through Douglas-fir forest, meadows, wooded draws and rock outcroppings. Forested slopes, steep and mysterious, rise all around. Considering the closeness to town and the low elevation, the setting is varied, remote and attractive.

The trail emerges near the end of the dirt road along the top of the ridge north of Shan Creek. There's not much beyond except old logging shows. Before the road was built, the trail climbed all the way to Onion Mountain through some interesting serpentine areas. But the trail above the upper road is now too chopped up to follow. At the top of the trail, there's not much to do except walk back down and admire the flowers.

## 22. Mungers Butte

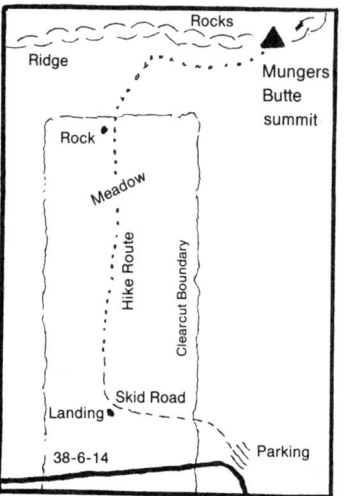

**Length:** 1 mile
**Water:** No
**Access:** 2
**Season:** May thru Nov.
**Difficulty:** 3
**Elevation:** 4300 to 5000 ft.
**Scenic Qual.:** 2
**Use:** Hikers only

The highest point visible from downtown Grants Pass is the 5000 foot summit of Mungers Butte. Conversely, the single best view of the Grants Pass valley may be had from the top of Mungers Butte.

Mungers Butte, south of town, is familiar to Grants Pass residents because of the two narrow, paralleling clearcuts off its summit. Rogue Valleyites know spring has arrived when the snow retreats up the highest clearcut, then disappears.

Our hike also retreats up the highest clearcut. As we shall see, it's a fairly scenic area for a logging unit and in fact is quite interesting. It also offers an opportunity to observe correctly applied forest practices.

To reach the hike's starting point, take Williams Highway south from Grants Pass. At Murphy, turn onto Murphy Creek Road and follow it to the BLM's Spencer Creek Access Road which takes off to the left. A mile or so up Spencer Creek, bear right at the major intersection, following the blacktop up the hill.

Where the blacktop ends and the road cuts sharply left, stay right on road 38-6-14. The sign is down but the sign post isn't. Follow the steep, gravel road around two sharp switchbacks to a gravel pile just beyond the last clearcut. The road swings right at this point and starts downhill. If you proceed straight, past the upper gravel pile, you'll find a pleasant, shady parking spot in the middle of a knobcone pine stand.

This isn't an actual trail but a route. Its main pitch shoots straight up the clearcut and can be grueling. Brush and logging debris abounds so wear your Vibrams. The compensation, aside from a stupendous view, is a profusion of beargrass, fireweed and false-hellebore, three of the Northwest's showiest wildflowers.

Despite the stumps, the clearcut is regenerating beautifully. Planted Douglas-fir and ponderosa pine are thriving alongside natural white fir and western white pine. Growth is slower in the upper reaches where a lovely, if temporary, beargrass meadow had developed amid the rock outcroppings.

On leaving you car, follow the old skid road around to the left to a landing, then make your way up the skid track to the top of the hill. Look for the white flagging I left a few years ago. You should end up at a small landing at the top of the clearcut.

Just below the upper landing, there's a rock outcropping with a lone fir on top. That is the best spot from which to view the valley. Look for Murphy Mountain, Round Top and Manzanita Lookout to the left. Mt. Baldy and Grants Pass Peak lie to the right. Beyond Grants Pass, Walker and Sexton Mountains may be viewed, along with much of the Kalmiopsis area and the Bear Camp ridge. On a clear day, the summit of Mt. Thielsen, north of Crater Lake, adorns the northeast horizon.

To reach the summit, continue uphill above the clearcut a few hundred feet, bearing right towards a rock outcropping in the woods at the ridgetop. Follow the ridgeline to the right, past another cluster of rocks to a third cluster which is obviously the highest point. There are spectacular views to the south of Grayback and Preston Peak, although they're somewhat obscured by woods. Still, it's a lovely spot.

## 23. Rabbit Lake

For years, I stared at Rabbit Lake on the map and at the trail apparently leading to it from the upper Deer Creek area. After several unsuccessful excursions, I concluded that the trail, a principal thoroughfare before the automobile, probably no longer exists. I then attempted, abortively, to find a route up the cliffs on Rabbit Lake Road, above which I suspected the lake was hiding. Meanwhile, I talked to several other people who had tried in vain to find the elusive little pool near Kerby Peak.

## 42    Rabbit Lake

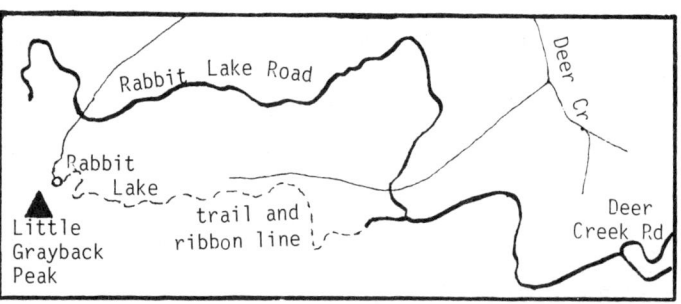

| | |
|---|---|
| **Length:** 2 miles | **Water:** Gobs |
| **Access:** 2 | **Season:** May to Nov. |
| **Difficulty:** 3 | **Elevation:** 4000 to 5100 ft. |
| **Scenic Qual.:** 2 | **Use:** Hikers only (due to terrain) |

Finally, I decided to make my own trail. After studying topographic maps and aerial photos, I set out with machete and survey flagging. Hours later, I arrived at the lake. It is probably still possible to follow my ribbon line but I'm sure the minimal clearing I did is long since overgrown. The route should be evident without a trail, however.

To reach the trailhead, take Highway 199 south from Grants Pass and turn south onto Deer Creek Road at Selma. Follow it to Upper Deer Creek Road and continue to Rabbit Lake Road, which takes off to the right near the summit. Kerby Peak and Little Grayback may be viewed from the road. The trail follows the canyon at the base of the long, gray cliff radiating off Little Grayback.

Be sure to note the Brewer spruce on Rabbit Lake Road. A rare tree confined exclusively to the Siskiyous and Marble Mountains, it can be identified by its long, dangling, branches. This may be the easiest drive from which to view Brewer spruce.

Follow Rabbit Lake Road three or four miles, past the Brewer spruce. It crosses a creek, sweeps right then left around the mountain, then heads into a draw before veering right again. The road crosses two small creeks at the draw. Look for the gray cliff line rising to the left and an obscure side road, also on the left, leading to a clearcut. Park at the end of this road, which is the only turnoff to the left beyond the Brewer spruce.

A trail takes off across a clearcut at the road end. It climbs a hill briefly, enters the woods, hits the creek, then peters out. From there, I attempted to follow the base of the cliff as nearly as possible. The way is steep and brushy, with much climbing. Look for strange, matted clumps of what appear to be dwarf Port Orford cedar. Several rocky, wildflower strewn clearings brighten the path.

Finally, it becomes necessary to ascend a steep slope choked with matted squawcarpet. Follow the ribbon line if possible. If not, head for the low spot just below the peak, taking care not to wander too far right. It helps to head for clusters of trees where possible because they crowd

out the scrub. At times, you may be forced to simply throw yourself over the brush. It's hard work but this portion of the trail isn't as long as it seems.

Before you know it, you'll be looking down on Rabbit Lake, a one-acre pond in a tiny glacial cirque atop a ledge. Upon hiking down to the lake, a short walk reveals Rabbit Lake Road a few hundred feet below. It appears tantalizingly close but trust me that my route is better.

## 24. Kerby Peak

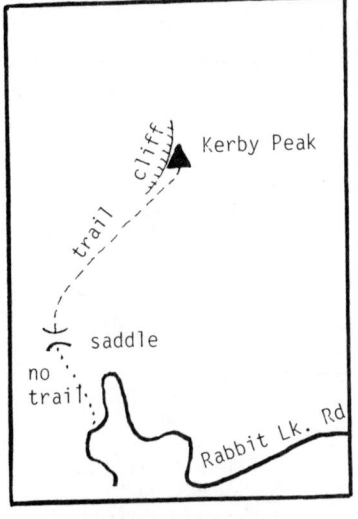

**Length:** 1½ miles
**Water:** No
**Access:** 2
**Season:** May to Nov.
**Difficulty:** 3
**Elevation:** 4860 to 5524 ft.
**Scenic Qual.:** 3
**Use:** Non-motorized only

Kerby Peak is a solitary, 5500 foot outcropping rising from the east side of the Illinois Valley. It is best viewed from Lake Selmac, near Selma, where its often snow-mantled summit gives the lake a postcard quality in winter.

Like Rabbit Lake, I sort of made this trail myself. There is supposed to be a trail to Kerby Peak from White Creek, off Deer Creek Road, but I've never found it. Besides, that route is much longer and steeper. The map also shows a trail off the end of Rabbit Lake Road, which I've likewise been unable to find. No matter, I've devised a simple route requiring no trail.

To climb Kerby Peak, take Highway 199 out of Grants Pass to Selma and turn left on Deer Creek Road. Proceed to Upper Deer Creek Road and up the hill to Rabbit Lake Road. The last few miles of Upper Deer Creek Road afford excellent views of your objective, whose steep, brushy, brown-rock summit looms to the right.

**44**    Big Tree Loop

Take Rabbit Lake Road as far as possible. The last time I drove it, a washout made the road impassable, except to four-wheel drive, about ¾'s of a mile from the end. The road ends at a large clearcut. Begin your hike anywhere between the clearcut and the last road switchback. Best is to hike up one of the skid trails or look for my old ribbon line, if it's still there.

In any event, your objective is a small saddle. It can be reached by gaining 130 feet in elevation from the road while following the hill's contour to the right (facing the hill), for about a half-mile. It's not difficult. Be sure on the return trip not to descend too fast or you might miss Rabbit Lake Road and come out five miles down Deer Creek Road.

From the saddle, life gets much easier, if steeper. Simply follow the ridge uphill to the north (right). It's like climbing stairs. The route is strenuous and exposed but the objective is clear and enticing. Look for Brewer spruce, just below the cliffs to the west.

As always, bring a map and lunch. Thus armed, one can munch on a ham sandwich while picking out such landmarks as Murphy Mountain, Lake Selmac, and Grayback Peak.

## 25. Big Tree Loop
### (Oregon Caves National Monument)

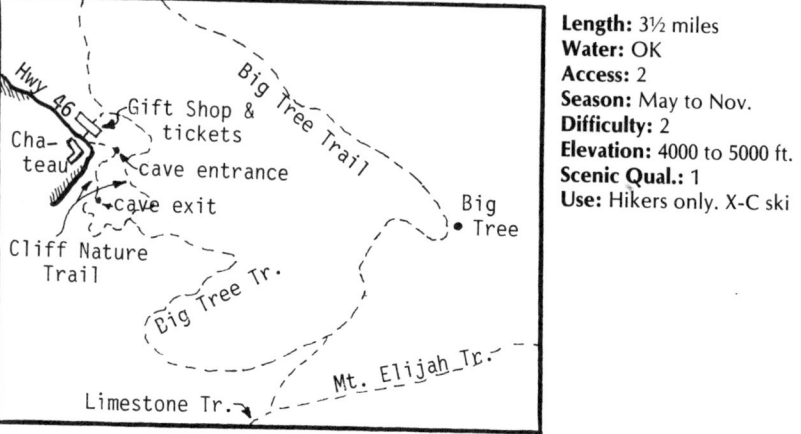

**Length:** 3½ miles
**Water:** OK
**Access:** 2
**Season:** May to Nov.
**Difficulty:** 2
**Elevation:** 4000 to 5000 ft.
**Scenic Qual.:** 1
**Use:** Hikers only. X-C ski

The path around Oregon Caves National Monument may be the most trodden in southern Oregon. Hikers from all over the country return with glowing enthusiasm. The trail is pleasant enough, in my opinion, but manages to miss most of the region's highlights. The experience is greatly enhanced by returning via the Monument's Cliff Nature Trail.

## Big Tree Loop    45

The trailhead is easily reached by taking Highway 199 to Cave Junction and proceeding 19 miles up Caves Highway to Oregon Caves National Monument. At the Monument, park in the lower parking lot and walk up to the gift shop where the book *Trees of Southern Oregon* may be purchased.

The setting around the cave entrance is enchanting. The rustic restaurant, coffee shop and lodge (Chateau), are opened from mid-June to early September. Escorted cave tours leave year round in groups of 16, every few minutes in summer. Tours take about 45 minutes. Although this isn't Carlsbad, it's well worth it. In summer, expect a wait of 30 minutes to an hour for cave tours if you arrive mid-day.

The Big Tree Loop Trail begins under the arch between the cave tour ticket window and the gift shop. The trail may be taken by going either right or left. I recommend left, following the sign which reads, "Big Tree-1.3 Miles."

The trail is moderately steep as it winds through middle elevation woods of Douglas-fir, white fir, grand fir and Port Orford cedar. Don't get lost on the two dead-end trail spurs to the left.

The Big Tree is an immense old Douglas-fir with an oft broken top and an extremely thick trunk. It's what foresters call a "Wolf Tree" — very poor in form and towering above the other trees. Most trees in the vicinity are its offspring.

Beyond the Big Tree, a side trail leads to Mt. Elijah. Although the Mt. Elijah Trail is among the area's most scenic, the route is much shorter from the Bigelow Lake end. The Mt. Elijah Trail offers views of the Siskiyous' high peaks, none of which can be seen from the Monument, the Big Tree Trail or the Caves Highway. It's 1½ miles to the summit of Mt. Elijah from the junction with the Big Tree Trail and another 1½ miles to Bigelow Lakes.

On the two-mile down side of the Big Tree Loop, the trail crosses a meadow of wildflowers, Douglas maple, and the showy but unaesthetically named false hellebore.

A quarter-mile before returning to the trailhead, the trail merges with the Monument's Cliff Nature Trail. The junction is marked by a sign pointing left which says "Chateau." This route adds a half-mile to the journey but is highly recommended. It goes over the top of the marble formation in which the cave is located. There's a terrific vista point halfway along, with a view down Sucker Creek of the Illinois Valley. After that, the trail winds down to the base of the marble, passes the cave exit and returns to the entrance.

Should you take this trail, stop in at the Park Service office and tell them I said, "hello."

## 26. Bigelow Lake/Mt. Elijah

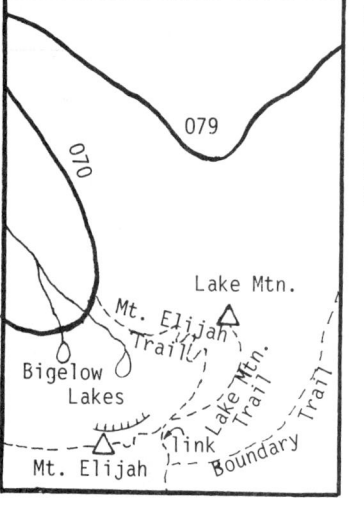

**Length:** 2 miles
**Water:** Lots
**Difficulty:** 2
**Season:** June through Oct.
**Access:** 2
**Elevation:** 5600 to 5978 ft.
**Scenic Qual.:** 3
**Use:** Any

Two of the prettiest high country locations in Josephine County are Bigelow Lake and Mt. Elijah. The Mt. Elijah Trail ends at Oregon Caves National Monument, the only unit of the National Park Service in the Klamath Mountain system. It's 4½ miles from the Oregon Caves Chalet to Mt. Elijah. However, it's less than two miles from the Bigelow Lake trailhead to Mt. Elijah. And that trailhead is only a 15 minute drive from the Monument.

The best route to the trailhead is not from Oregon Caves but from the town of Williams, 20 miles south of Grants Pass on Williams Highway. From Williams, continue south to Caves Camp-Low Divide Road. Low Divide Road winds into the mountains, up steep grades and around the base of Grayback Peak, highest in Josephine County. It is long, slow and unpaved much of the way but not difficult driving. Just remember to bear left whenever the road forks. Eventually, you'll arrive at a cattle grate with the trailhead just before it on the left.

Before starting up the trail, you may wish to visit Lower Bigelow Lake, which occupies a tiny glacial cirque nearby. Walk down the road until you reach the second creek. Make your way up the creek, through the brush, until you find the lake. Along the way, look for Shasta fir, mountain hemlock, Douglas maple and other high elevation species.

The trailhead may also be reached from the Caves Highway out of Cave Junction, off Highway 199 south of Grants Pass. Take Grayback Road from Caves Highway until it merges with Low Divide Road, then bear right. Or, follow the dirt road which begins at the entrance sign marking the Monument boundary. This road is gated but not locked and it's OK to open it as long as you close it again. Bear right at all intersections until you reach the trailhead.

Bigelow Lake/Mt. Elijah    47

**Bigelow Lake (Ch. 26)**                    (Bernstein Photo)

It's a half-mile up the Bigelow Lake Trail to Bigelow Lake; a large, shallow lily pond in a meadow, with white cliffs rising overhead. The lake is off the trail, an eighth-mile to the right. The meadow above is particularly beautiful in spring when water and wildflowers abound. The Forest Service lists 14 sensitive species growing near Bigelow Lake, including practically the only Oregon population of the beautiful Mendocino gentian.

Be prepared to share this beauty with grazing cows. Many high mountain meadows in this area are open to grazing. The drift fence near the road serves to keep them out of the National Monument.

Beyond the lake, the trail winds upward to a small saddle. There, a trail to the left leads to Lake Peak. They tell me that route is poorly marked and difficult to follow. To the right, the trail forks. The downhill fork (left), joins the Siskiyou Boundary Trail after a quarter-mile. The Boundary Trail is a 27 mile walk connecting Tannen Mountain and Grayback Peak. You're standing about halfway between the two.

The uphill fork at the saddle (right) goes to the top of Mt. Elijah. From there, one may look down on Bigelow Lake or across to Whiskey Peak and the Red Buttes. It's a spectacular maze of looming mountaintops, made more impressive by the fact that almost none of the peaks are visible from paved roads. Mt. Elijah itself, despite having Oregon Caves within its bowels, cannot be seen from anywhere in the Monument.

## 27. Tannen Lake
### (Red Buttes Wilderness Area)

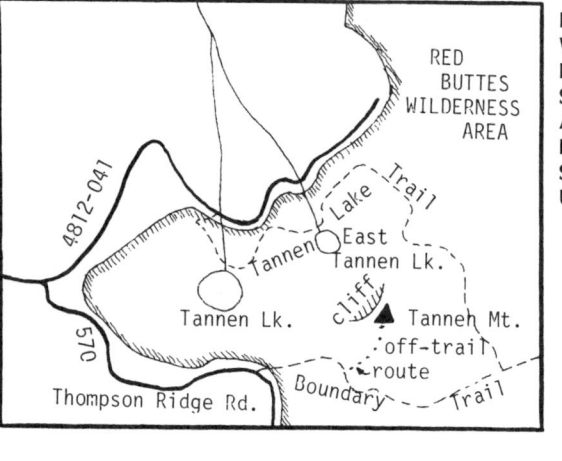

**Length:** 1½ miles
**Water:** Lots
**Difficulty:** 1
**Season:** June through Oct.
**Access:** 2
**Elevation:** 5100 ft.
**Scenic Qual.:** 2
**Use:** Non-motorized only

The best glacial cirque lakes in the Oregon Siskiyous are Tannen and Bolan Lakes. Bolan Lake is seven miles from Tannen Lake and has road access and a developed campground. Tannen is a short, lovely hike. Glacial lakes are infrequent in southern Oregon and generally don't compare to the hundreds which dot the Marble Mountains and Trinity Alps, just to the south. Still, it's worth the drive and hike, especially with an Eastern visitor who's never seen a high mountain lake.

The quickest route to the trailhead is to take Highway 199 south from Grants Pass and turn up the Caves Highway at Cave Junction. Turn right on Holland Loop, right again on Bridgeview-Takilma Road, then left on Happy Camp Road.

The Happy Camp Road is paved but steep and winding, affording good views of the Illinois Valley. The road's summit is in California, as is the Bolan-Tannen turnoff. You may wish to continue towards Happy Camp for a mile or so, to view the Brewer spruce on the downhill side of the road. Also called weeping spruce, the tree is easily recognized by its dark needle-leaves and its dangling, whiplike branchlets. It's one of the country's rarer trees.

Back at the summit, follow the signs to Bolan and Tannen Lakes. Bolan Lake, back in Oregon, is slightly prettier than Tannen but full of people and cars. A short side road leads to Bolan Peak Lookout.

The road from the Bolan Lake turnoff to the Tannen Lake trailhead is one of the region's most scenic. It is usually not passable until mid-June, however. It's unpaved, often bumpy surface snakes around the craggy ridges of Bolan and Althouse Mountain and peers down on Thompson Creek, the Klamath River and the Marble Mountains. The well marked trailhead is a mile past the Thompson Ridge turnoff. Parking is on the shoulder only.

The trail is short, easy, and interesting and it's only a half-mile to the lake. Look for wildflowers, rhododendron and Sadler oak. The latter resembles a rhododendron except its large, evergreen leaves, in a whorled arrangement, have sawtoothed edges. Sadler oak grows only in moist, high elevation areas of the Siskiyou and Marble Mountains. Though considered rare, it is abundant within its range.

Tannen Lake lies in a small, high walled glacial cirque with a creek outlet at one end. It has a steep, willow choked shore with little access other than the campsite near the outlet. Swimming is difficult. The bottom is covered with mushy silt which gives way when stepped on to a 3-D maze of submerged logs. Fishing is supposed to be good.

East Tannen Lake lies a half mile beyond Tannen Lake at the base of Tannen Mountain. It is similar but a little smaller, with an even steeper shore, denser willow brush and a mushier bottom. Fishing is also good there.

# 28. Tannen Mountain
## (Red Buttes Wilderness Area)
### See **Tannen Lake (Ch. 27)** for Map.

| | |
|---|---|
| **Length:** 1 mile plus | **Water:** No |
| **Difficulty:** 2 | **Season:** June through Oct. |
| **Access:** 2 | **Elevation:** 5600 to 6298 ft. |
| **Scenic Qual.:** 3 | **Use:** Non-motorized only |

The summit of Tannen Mountain lies pretty much smack in the middle of the Siskiyou region and affords one of its better overviews. The trail is short but steep and can be undertaken in a couple hours either from Tannen Lake or from the Thompson Ridge trailhead.

The Tannen Lake chapter describes the access road in detail. To summarize, take Highway 199 south from Grants Pass to Cave Junction. From there, follow the Caves Highway and turn onto Holland Loop, Bridgeview-Takilma Road and Happy Camp Road. Proceed up Happy Camp Road past the California state line to the summit and turn left, re-entering Oregon on the Bolan/Tannen Lake Road. Follow the signs to Tannen Lake.

The road between the Bolan Lake turnoff and Tannen Lake is one of the prettiest in the region. It skirts the gray rock faces of Althouse Mountain and looks across the Klamath River canyon to the Marble Mountains.

A mile before the Tannen Lake trailhead, at a small, grassy clearcut, a road takes off uphill to the right. While this road isn't as bad as it looks, be careful. It's narrow and often muddy, with sharp dropoffs. This is Thompson Ridge Road and it ends up in Happy Camp on the Klamath River.

The trailhead, marked by a square post but no sign, is about two miles up, at the edge of the Red Buttes Wilderness Area. From there, the trail ascends through forests of Shasta fir, western white pine, white fir,

**50     Black Butte**

mountain hemlock and incense cedar. If you have a tree book along, look for an occasional noble fir, a rarity in the Siskiyous due to its tendency to interbreed with Shasta fir. A side trail on the left at the trailhead leads down to Tannen Lake.

A mile from the Thompson Ridge trailhead, the trail comes out on a grassy knoll. There it begins a long, steep downhill, rejoining the Tannen Lake Trail a mile later. The Tannen summit may be seen a quarter-mile away on the left, peering above the grass. There is no trail so walk across the grass towards the peak and follow the ridge line up. You should be atop the gray outcropping in about 10 minutes.

The Thompson Ridge trailhead is the beginning of the 27 mile Siskiyou Boundary Trail which snakes along the crest of the range to Grayback Peak and the Red Buttes. Beyond the grassy knoll, the trail drops 1000 feet and it's three or four miles to the next highlight. Unless it were my goal to walk the entire trail, I'd drive around to the Steve Fork access and pick up the trail there to visit such places as Azalea Lake or Swan Mountain.

From the sheltered rock perch atop Tannen, a glacial headwall drops straight down to East Tannen Lake. Tannen Lake cannot be seen but the road to it can, as well as the basin in which the lake is nestled.

Bring a map and look on the eastern horizon for Mt. Shasta and McLoughlin, as well as Pyramid Peak, the Red Buttes, and Whiskey Peak in the Upper Applegate area. Or scan the ridge to the north, past Swan and Lake Mountains to Grayback Peak, highest in Josephine County. To the west, look for Althouse Mountain and the black pyramid of Preston Peak.

I made the climb in Late October when the Illinois and Klamath valleys were filled with fog. It was an hour before I could bring myself to leave.

## 29. Black Butte
### (Siskiyou Wilderness Area)

The most mountainous mountains in the Siskiyous can be explored on this trail. It penetrates the heart of the snow capped crags which pop into view as you enter the Illinois Valley from Grants Pass. The group of summits rise above the head of the South Fork of the Illinois River, just beyond the California state line.

The area has recently been set aside as part of the Siskiyou Wilderness. Young's Peak is the cluster's most interesting because it lies in three National Forests and its slopes drain into the Smith, Klamath and Rogue Rivers. The group's highest is Preston Peak at 7300 feet. The eerie black pyramid, despite being the second loftiest summit in the Siskiyous, is not easily visible from the Oregon side. The view is blocked by the imposing face of El Capitan.

**Black Butte** 51

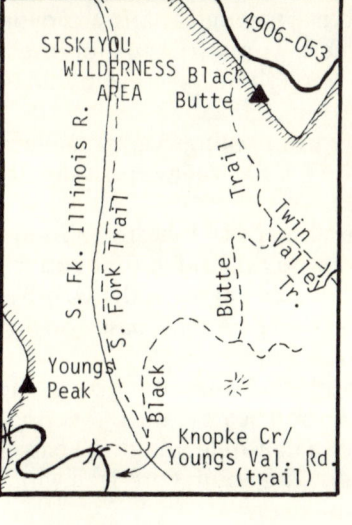

**Length:** 5½ mile loop
**Water:** OK
**Access:** 3 (Youngs Val);
  2 (Bl. Bu.)
**Season:** June through Oct.
**Difficulty:** 2
**Elevation:** 4800 to 5400 ft.
**Scenic Qual.:** 3
**Use:** Non-motorized only.
  X-C ski

The area shows much evidence of glaciation with numerous steep-walled cirques, although only a few lakes. The upper valley of the Illinois River's south fork, however, once contained far more than the usual hanging mountain glaciers which carved the cirques. Rather, there is evidence of a valley glacier. Look for a round bottomed valley with hanging valleys spilling in from the sides. A huge wall several miles long on the north side of the main valley may be viewed from the Young's Valley end of the trail. Its unbroken smoothness could only have been formed by glacial action.

There are trailheads at either end of the Black Butte Trail, with about 30 miles of driving on dirt and gravel between the two. It's probably easier to walk out and back over the same route than to leave cars at both trailheads. Or you could have somebody meet you at the far end, in which case Black Butte is the easier end to find by car.

The Youngs Valley trailhead is reached from the Raspberry Lake road. Take Highway 199 south from Grants Pass into California and turn left up Knopke Creek Road. Follow it to the "T" junction and turn right towards Youngs Valley rather than left towards Sanger Lake. The last couple miles is narrow and rutted. The road is blocked at the pass by a newly constructed gate marking the Wilderness boundary. The actual trailhead is about 1½ miles beyond the gate, at a saddle above Youngs Meadow. The view at the gate of Youngs Valley and Preston Peak is spectacular.

The other trailhead may be reached by taking 199 south from Grants Pass to Cave Junction and going two miles up Caves Highway. Turn right on Holland Loop and right again on Bridgeview-Takilma Road. Follow Takilma Road past the Happy Camp turnoff through the community of Takilma. Turn left at the fork (up 4904), right at the junction with 4906 (which later becomes 053), and proceed to the trailhead. This is a breathtaking drive.

There's no mistaking Black Butte; a narrow, pointed projection towering above the surrounding area. If you have a little time, continue down the road a mile past the trailhead to the first creek, noting the Brewer spruce along the way. The creek flows out of a small, steep walled glacial

## 52    Raspberry Lake

cirque which bears exploring. Follow the creek through a narrow canyon into the cirque. Instead of a lake inside, there's a marsh. Look for insect eating darlingtonia plants in the marsh. If you follow the creek uphill to the left, you'll enter a second cirque with a small lake.

Back at the trailhead, I'd suggest a route from Youngs Valley to Black Butte rather than the other way around. The Youngs Valley end is slightly prettier in case you turn back halfway.

Unfortunately, there are no accurate trail maps of this area. When I walked them, the trails on the ground bore no relation to those on my National Forest map. Furthermore, that map didn't agree with two other National Forest maps and all were wrong. The map herein is based on first hand experience plus examination of aerial photos.

A closed jeep road takes off from a saddle between the gate at the Wilderness boundary and Youngs Valley. It soon bears to the right opposite the glacial wall described earlier. After a half-mile, the route passes the trail down the South Fork of the Illinois. The South Fork Trail winds for nine miles through the woods along the river.

The jeep road crosses the foot wide South Fork, then swings north for about a mile before coming around a rocky point. The Black Butte Trail actually begins a short distance beyond and is clearly marked on the left. The jeep road continues for another mile or two up a beautiful little valley to an abandoned mine. It's horrendously steep beyond the Black Butte intersection.

The next 1¼ miles of the Black Butte Trail is only partially constructed, with areas that have been pioneered only. You'll find flagging and a cleared line but no trail as the route crosses a small valley. Finally, the trail joins the more established Polar Bear Trail to Twin Valley. Twin Valley consists of a pair of meadows a mile to the right, over a ridge. Bear left at Polar Bear junction for the remainder of the Black Butte Trail. The last half-mile traverses a serpentine soil area. Look for an open, park-like forest of Jeffrey and western white pine instead of Douglas-fir and true firs.

The Black Butte Trail has some steep pitches but is surprisingly level considering the terrain. It's one of the most breathtaking 5½ mile walks you're likely to find.

# 30. Raspberry Lake
## (Siskiyou Wilderness Area)

Everything went wrong the day I visited Raspberry Lake but I don't regret any of it. Don't bring a toddler, however. But do bring a camera to this remote pool at the base of Preston Peak, the mysterious black pyramid forming the Siskiyous' second highest peak.

## Raspberry Lake    53

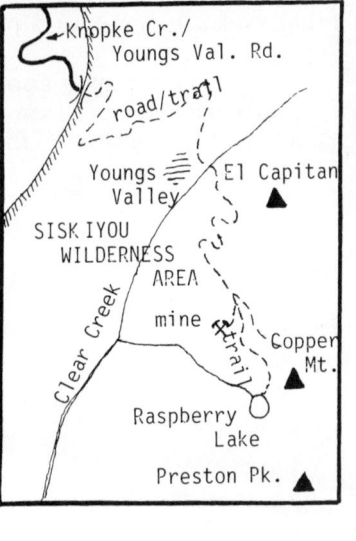

**Length:** 5 miles
**Water:** Lots
**Access:** 3
**Season:** June through Oct.
**Difficulty:** 3
**Elevation:** 4600 to 5400 ft.
**Scenic Qual.:** 3
**Use:** Non-motorized only

Getting to the trailhead isn't easy. Neither is finding the trail. First, locate Sanger Lake, either via Waldo Lookout from Cave Junction or Knopke Creek off Highway 199 in California. Waldo Lookout is more interesting but slower. The road overlooks the tunnel on Highway 199, skirts a beautiful lily pond called Whiskey Lake, ascends a rock face dotted with Brewer spruce, and passes the trailhead to Sanger Peak Lookout. The latter is an easy one-mile side trip.

The Knopke Creek route to Youngs Valley was described in the previous chapter. The two routes meet at the "T" just past Sanger Lake. Turn right if coming from Knopke Creek and left (straight, actually) if coming from Sanger Lake.

Be sure to pause at the overlook where the gated road drops into Youngs Valley, for views of Preston Peak and El Capitan. Clear Creek, running through the middle of Youngs Valley, is a major tributary of the Klamath River. The last time I was there, you could drive past Youngs Valley to at least Clear Creek and probably to the old chrome mine if you had four-wheel drive. The trail from the mine was only 1½ miles. We parked at a beautiful Port Orford cedar grove beyond Youngs Meadow, where the road crossed the creek and started uphill. These days you walk from the gate at the pass.

The actual trail begins at the end of the high road through the mine area. It is poorly maintained, very rocky and badly marked. We put up a few markers and blazes to help out but that was 10 years ago.

The path hits the lake at the top of a tremendous rock fall. I was carrying a pack when I visited so the scramble down was harrowing. Once down, I left the pack at the lake, climbed back up and carried my three year old daughter down. I then made my way up and down yet again, gallantly but

stupidly, to carry my wife's pack for her. I then collapsed in exhaustion until morning.

Covering some 30 acres, the lake is beautiful and deep with good campsites and excellent fishing. Preston Peak disappears as you drop into the basin but a smaller, equally inspiring summit rises sharply out of the lake's eastern shore.

# 31. Devils Punchbowl
## (Siskiyou Wilderness Area)

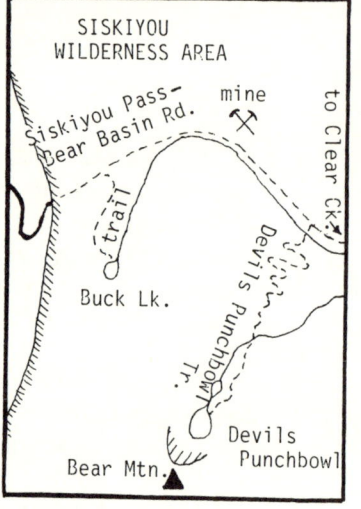

**Length:** 5½ miles
**Water:** Lots
**Difficulty:** 3
**Season:** June through Oct.
**Access:** 3
**Elevation:** 3400 to 4750 ft.
**Scenic Qual.:** 3
**Use:** non-motorized only

I've gone to great lengths to avoid the overuse of superlative adjectives in my descriptions. But Devil's Punchbowl is one of the most awe inspiring glacial cirque lakes I've ever seen, made even more attractive by its isolation and an extremely arduous trail. Situated in the most remote area of the western Siskiyous, no roads and almost no trails cross the ridge for almost 40 miles between the road to Devil's Punchbowl and Bluff Creek Road to the south. The latter is famous for its many bigfoot sightings.

To reach the trailhead, take Highway 199 out of Grants Pass into California, to Little Jones Creek Road. Follow the latter about 15 miles to Bear Basin and Siskiyou Pass. The road is blocked at Siskiyou Pass, which is also the new Wilderness boundary. You used to be able to drive two more miles, to the old mine site. Parking is available at the new trailhead for 10 cars.

There's a primitive camp at the Buck Lake trailhead, on Doe Creek. From there, an easy half-mile trail leads to Buck Lake, a delightful little water body in a small cirque. The lake is worth a visit but doesn't compare with Devil's Punchbowl, 3½ grueling miles away.

The closed Siskiyou Pass road ends at an old mine. From there a trail continues on to the Klamath River. A half-mile down, a side trail crosses a log over the creek and climbs the opposite hillside. There begins a series of endless, steep switchbacks which would challenge even the most experienced hiker.

If you make it to the ridge above the switchbacks, the view is breathtaking with the black pyramid of Preston Peak, second highest in the Siskiyous (7300 feet), rising immediately north. Southward lies the craggy summit of Bear Mountain, the trail's destination. Just below the summit, a tiny "V" notch can be discerned. Devil's Punchbowl is inside the "V".

The trail remains steep even after the switchbacks but the last mile is the most interesting. It crosses creeks and meadows, scrambles over rock surfaces, winds around the edge of a small lake and penetrates the narrow "V" canyon described earlier.

The lake itself consists of 30 acres of crystal water surrounded by perpendicular cliffs up to 1000 feet high. Prettier even than some of the best lakes in the Marble Mountains and Trinity Alps, such beauty is totally unexpected in a range with few other lakes and at an elevation of only 4700 feet.

While I made it in and out in a day, an overnight stay is advised. Ther are few good campsites, however. What the shore lacks in brushiness, it makes up in steepness. Fishing, they say, is excellent and the lake and trail are surprisingly popular. The lake bottom is mostly rock and the water is cold. But a swim in the Punchbowl can be very invigorating.

## 32. Grayback Mountain

Mighty Grayback Mountain, at 7055 feet, is the highest summit in Josephine County. It is one of five Siskiyou peaks over 7000 feet, along with Mount Ashland, Wagner Butte, Preston Peak and Condrey Mountain.

While Grayback is no Shasta or Rainier or even McLoughlin, Grants Pass residents feel a certain fondness for the old gray mound, so aptly named and looking like a beached whale. A trip up Grayback won't guarantee membership in the Explorers Club but it will provide a workout and some pleasant scenery. Bring the kids.

The drive to the trailhead affords no views of the objective. The peak can't be seen from Grants Pass, either, although Sugar Loaf, a subpeak of Grayback, may be glimpsed from town through Luther Divide from the freeway.

To reach the trailhead, first find the town of Applegate, either from Jacksonville or south Grants Pass, via Highway 238. Turn up Thompson Creek Road at Applegate and continue to O'Brien Creek Road. The latter comes in on a hilltop amid a maze of side roads but is clearly marked. Take O'Brien Creek to the end, bearing right at the fork. The last half-mile is steep, rocky and narrow so be careful.

**56**     **Grayback Mountain**

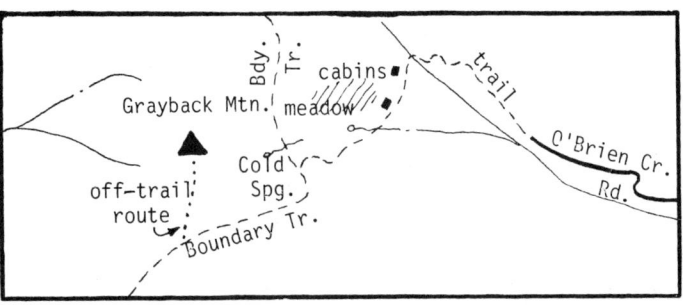

**Length:** 3 miles                      **Water:** A little
**Access:** 2                            **Season:** June through Oct.
**Difficulty:** 2                        **Elevation:** 5000 to 7055 ft.
**Scenic Qual.:** 2                      **Use:** Any. X-C ski

The trail begins at the road end. It winds through the woods for 1½ miles, mostly uphill but not killingly so. After crossing a creek, the path emerges in an enchanting meadow with two rustic cabins. One is a Forest Service structure, the other was built by the people who graze cattle in the area.

The meadow shoots up almost to the summit but is very steep. There used to be a series of markers leading up the meadow to Cold Springs on the boundary Trail. I'm told the trail has been rerouted and is now longer but less steep, following the edge of the trees to the left.

At Cold Springs, take the Boundary Trail left. After a quarter-mile or so, you'll come to a saddle with a sharp ridge rising to the right. To reach the summit, merely walk up the ridge. It's like climbing stairs. Lots of stairs. I left a ribbon line you may wish to follow if it's still there. But it's not necessary.

It's less than a mile from the saddle to the hogback summit. About a third of the way up the ridge, you'll find an overlook of the meadow and cabin below. You can get down quickly by lighting out here and heading towards the cabin. It's fun, if a little mucky certain times of year. Don't try to go up this way.

One of my botanical references indicated Baker cypress on the south face of Grayback, near the trail. In a half-dozen hikes up Grayback, I've never seen them and I couldn't find anyone who has. Many sensitive plant species adorn Grayback, including Lee's lewisia, mendocino gentian and several lilies.

Miller Lake    57

# 33. Miller Lake

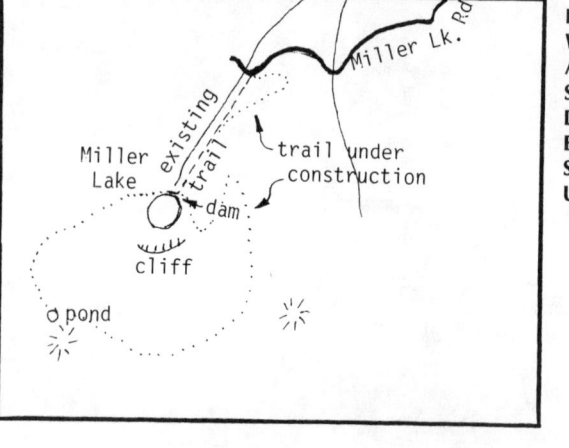

**Length:** 3 miles
**Water:** OK
**Access:** 2
**Season:** June through Oct.
**Difficulty:** 2
**Elevation:** 4900 to 5200 ft.
**Scenic Qual.:** 2
**Use:** Non-motorized only.
  X-C ski

It's difficult to evaluate this little man-made lake in the upper Applegate area because a new trail system is under construction. I'll describe both the old (¾ mile) and new (3 mile) trails. The new is staked and brushed out so it's possible to follow it, although it won't be completed until summer of 1987 or 1988.

Within a mile of Miller Lake, back in the woods away from the trails, is one of the most fascinating botanical oddities in Oregon. But first things first.

To reach the trailhead, take Highway 238, from Jacksonville or south Grants Pass, to the town of Applegate. Turn onto Thompson Creek Road (Road 10) and follow it past the end of the pavement to the next intersection after O'Brien Creek. A sign to the right says "Miller Lake-6 miles." To the left, signs direct motorists to Applegate Lake.

Follow the signs to the trailhead. The present trail is a steep, closed-off logging road. The only trailhead sign is the one prohibiting motorized vehicles. Note the excellent view of Grayback, Josephine County's highest peak, from the trailhead.

The lake, though popular and offering good fishing, is rather foul. Created by a dam, the five acre pool has very steep banks and the water level is subject to much seasonal fluctuation. When the water is down, the bank is muddy and unappealing. So is the water.

The glacial cirque in which the lake sits, on the other hand, is lovely. The main inlet flows down the rocky headwall in a photogenic staircase cascade..

The new trail will commence with a long switchback to the left at the trailhead, then countour around to the lake at a much less steep grade. At the lake, it will ascend uphill to the west fairly steeply, then follow the mountain crest past a little pond and wind back down to the lake on the east side.

58    **Collings Mountain**

**Rare Baker Cypress - Miller Lake (Ch. 33)**    (Bernstein Photo)

Neither the old nor new trails will pass the Baker cypress stand, located a half-mile from Miller lake. This rare tree is limited to four or five small, widely scattered, extremely remote stands in Oregon and a few more in California. The species is centered in the high desert lava country of California's extreme northeast corner. Compared to Baker cypress, Brewer spruce is as common as dandelions.

The Forest service isn't thrilled with the idea of visitors to this fragile site. But if you're truly interested, give them or me a call for details on its location.

## 34. Collings Mountain

Not only is this a good winter hike, it's an easily accessible diversion from the more intensive recreational activity at Applegate Lake. The trail begins at the lake's main picnic, parking and swimming area and offers a good way to burn off a few thousand calories after lunch. After hiking two or three hours, a swim in the lake seems very inviting.

**Collings Mountain** 59

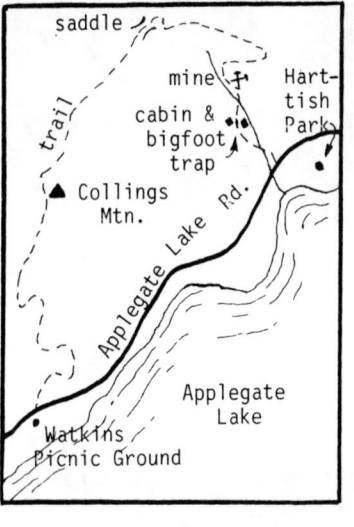

**Length:** 7 mile loop
**Water:** No
**Access:** 1
**Season:** Any
**Difficulty:** 2
**Elevation:** 2000 to 3200 ft.
**Scenic Qual.:** 1
**Use:** Non-motorized only

It should be added that while Collings Mountain may not be the most scenic trail in the upper Applegate area, it boasts some unusual features, one of which is less than a mile from the trailhead.

The trailhead may be reached by taking Highway 238 from south Grants Pass or Jacksonville, to the town of Ruch. From there, take the road up the Applegate Valley, past the dam, to Hart-tish Park on the west shore of Applegate Lake. The trail begins near the parking lot. Bear left so you don't end up on the Grouse Loop Trail.

The Collings Mountain Trail crosses the highway just past the park entrance and is clearly marked. After dropping down to Grouse Creek, it follows the shaded, mossy canyon for a mile before turning uphill. This mile is highly recommended even if you're not seeking a major wilderness experience.

A half-mile along, you'll come to a tiny miner's cabin on a lovely, shaded flat. Built in the 1940's, the cabin remained in use into the 1970's. Near the cabin, a short spur trail to the right leads up the hill to an abandoned bigfoot trap. The trap, a log and plank structure, was constructed in 1974 by a Eugene based group determined to catch the Northwest's most elusive critter. The venture was abandoned in 1976.

The falling iron door is now welded open but one can't help wondering what would have happened if a dog or child had wandered in. The door, triggered by sensing devices, looks like it could crush a child's head. I'm told that before the lake and new road were built, the spot was exceedingly remote.

One also can't help wondering how they expected to entice a bigfoot inside. With soft music, perhaps, or a dummy girl bigfoot in a negligee? Perhaps with a bottle of cognac on the table, along with caviar and a bucket of fried chicken.

Anyhow, it's another half-mile to an old mine opening and a mile beyond that to the ridge. The walk to the ridge is steep, with few level spots. The trail winds through woods of mostly canyon live oak, madrone,

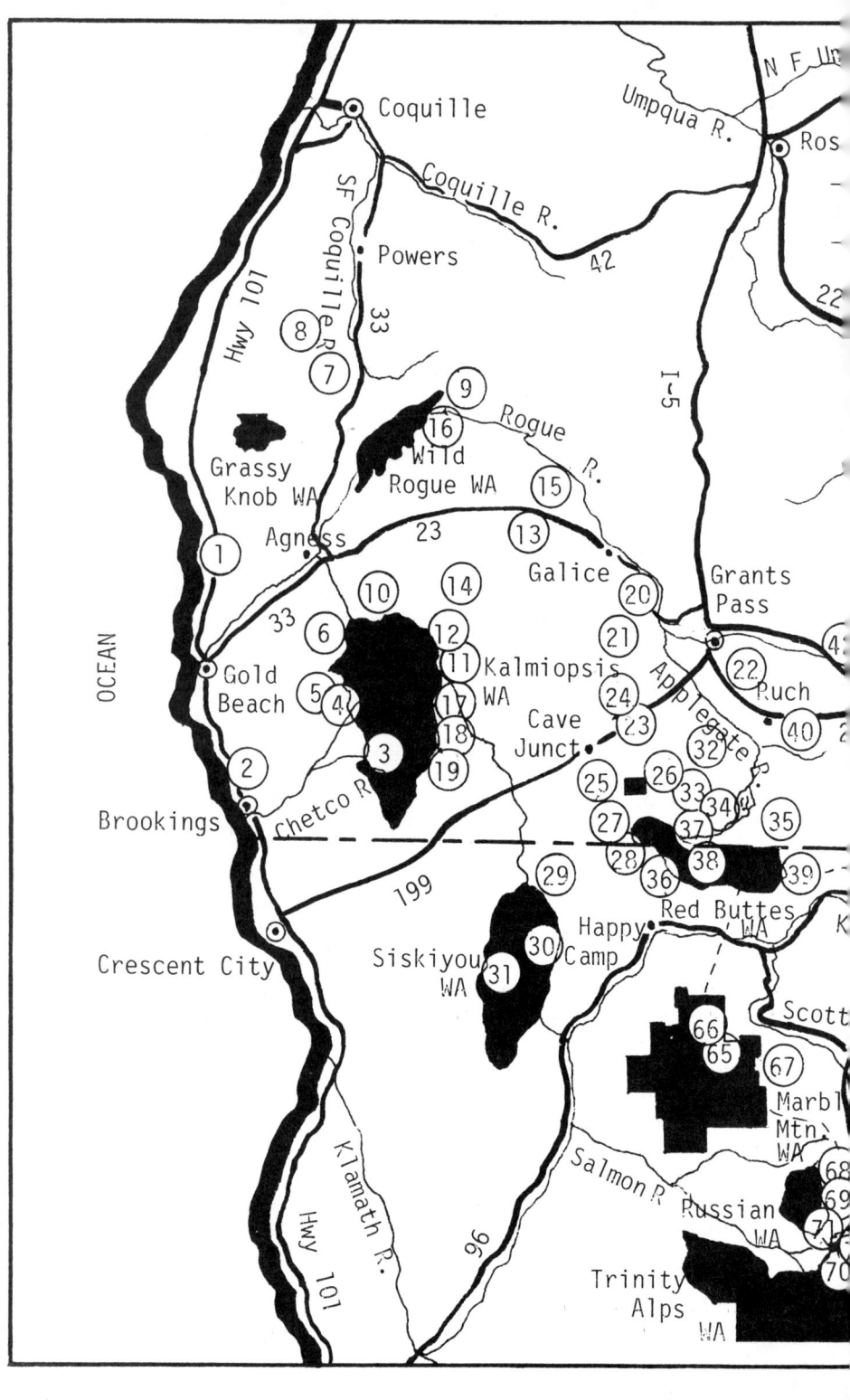

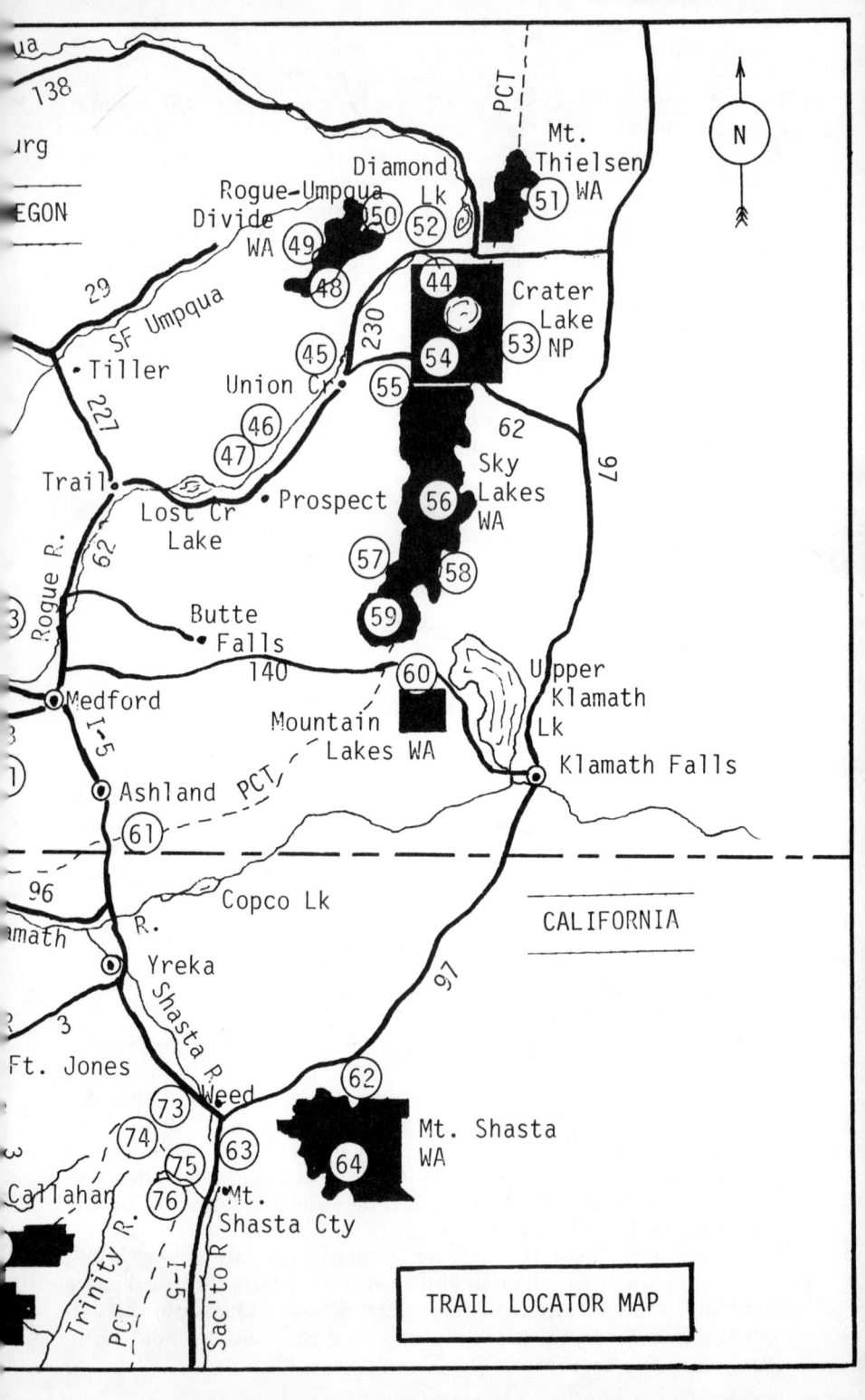

TRAIL LOCATOR MAP

**62    Stein Butte**

and a few pines and Douglas-fir. This is a typical thin soil, south slope, middle-elevation forest. There's a good vista of the lake at one point.

After crossing the ridge, the trail runs just east of the summit for three miles. It's fairly level but mostly in the woods with few overlooks. As impressive as some of the area's peaks are, this is not the best place to view them. There's a great view of the Red Buttes from the highway along the lake and a marvelous panorama from the top of nearby Stein Butte. The Collings Trail does offer at least one excellent look down Carberry Creek.

After a two mile descent, the last part of the trail crosses the site of the major 1981 forest fire. The trail then emerges at the highway, across from the Watkins Picnic Area, 2½ miles down the road from where it started. My advice would be to hike either to the mine (one mile) or the ridge (two miles), then double back and go swimming.

## 35. Stein Butte

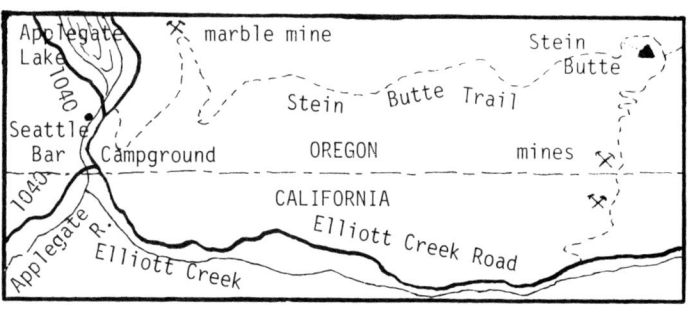

**Length:** 7½ mile loop          **Water:** No
**Access:** 1                            **Season:** All
**Difficulty:** 2                        **Elevation:** 2000 to 4400 ft.
**Scenic Qual.:** 2                    **Use:** Any

For perhaps the best panorama of Applegate Lake and the high peaks of the Red Buttes Wilderness, this easily accessible trail is unmatched. Winter is the ideal viewing time, when the mountains are highlighted by snow. Portions of the upper end of the trail, which crests at 4400 feet, may be under snow as well. Most of the time, this will only enhance the experience, although I'd avoid the Stein Butte Trail if it snowed down to 2000 feet the previous day. If the snow line is 3500 to 4000 feet on the north slope, the trail should be lovely.

To reach the trailhead, take Highway 238 from Jacksonville or south Grants Pass to the town of Ruch and turn onto the road to Applegate Lake. Be sure to stop at the vista point at the dam and check out the sign identifying the surrounding peaks, including Stein Butte. Stein Butte

**Stein Butte** 63

**Bigfoot Trap - Collings Mtn. Trail (Ch. 34)**    (Bernstein Photo)

doesn't seem like much from there, just a small outcropping amid a jumble of higher, forested peaks. The south side is much more impressive.

The difference between north and south slopes are dramatic throughout the Applegate area. The view north reveals peak after peak whose south facing aspect is covered with little besides grass and brush. The view south shows lush north slope forests reaching up to the mountaintops.

The first Stein Butte trailhead is located at the Seattle Bar Picnic Site at the upper end of Applegate Lake. Park, walk across the road and follow the gravel side road 100 feet. The trailhead is on the right.

To reach the far trailhead, proceed past Seattle Bar and the end of the pavement into California. Turn left onto Elliott Creek Road and proceed 2½ miles to the Stein Butte Trail sign. There's ample parking off the road to the right.

For a non-loop route, I'd recommend the Elliott Creek trailhead. It's three miles to the summit and not as steep as one might imagine, considering the trail rises 2200 feet. From the trailhead, one sees only the sheer, tree covered mountainside on the far side of the creek. It's hard to believe you'll soon be peering over the top of that ridge to the high peaks beyond.

**64**    **Azalea Lake**

The trail is fairly easy at first. After a half-mile, it comes around a bend and the rocky, almost perpendicular face of Stein Butte unfurls before you. Don't be discouraged. It's not as far away or as high as it looks and the trail doesn't climb the rock face.

Most of this south slope route winds through forests of Douglas-fir, black oak and madrone. It's rather steep for about a mile as it passes two small mine openings and the unmarked state line.

Eventually, you'll come to a series of switchbacks as the trail painlessly climbs a very steep hill. After that, the path crosses to the north side of the mountain, then hugs a steep, brushy hillside until it reaches the saddle where Applegate Lake comes into view. This segment of the trail needs work. It is badly outsloped, occasionally difficult to follow, and gave me the only blister I've ever had as a result of hiking.

It's a half-mile from the saddle to the top of the trail, through a dense woods and around some snowy (in winter), north slope rock faces. Where the trail starts back down, two ribbons are tied to the trees. To reach the summit, leave the trail here and follow the ridge less than an eight-mile to the old lookout site.

From there, you'll see the lake, Elliott Creek canyon and the Butte Fork canyon. Rising above (counter-clockwise from the northwest) are Grayback, Whiskey Peak, Kangaroo Mountain, the Red Buttes and Condrey Mountain. I'm not sure of the peaks east of Condrey. This is the ony decent view I've ever gotten of Condrey Mountain. At 7200 feet, it's fairly substantial but well hidden.

The trail from Seattle Bar is quite a bit longer and only slightly less steep. It, too, crests after 2½ miles, then levels off for two miles before reaching the summit. The route pases an old marble quarry and maintains excellent views of the lake. Being on a north slope, the woods are denser, with fewer oaks and more conifers.

# 36. Azalea Lake
## (Red Buttes Wilderness Area)

Azalea Lake is the objective of virtually every trail in the Red Butte Wilderness Area. While not as pretty as some of the lakes in the Marble Mountains, it occupies the heart of an outstanding scenic area amid a range fairly devoid of lakes.

Since so many trails converge at Azalea Lake, options on getting there are myriad. The Butte Fork Trail winds eight miles up a wilderness creek before reaching the lake. The Boundary Trail from Tannen Mountain or Cook and Green Pass is rugged, breathtaking and interminably long.

Three trails lead to the lake in five miles or less. We'll concentrate on the Steve Fork and Azalea Lake Trails, which are both fairly easy and about five miles long. The Sweaty Gap Trail is only 3½ miles but much steeper.

Azalea Lake  65

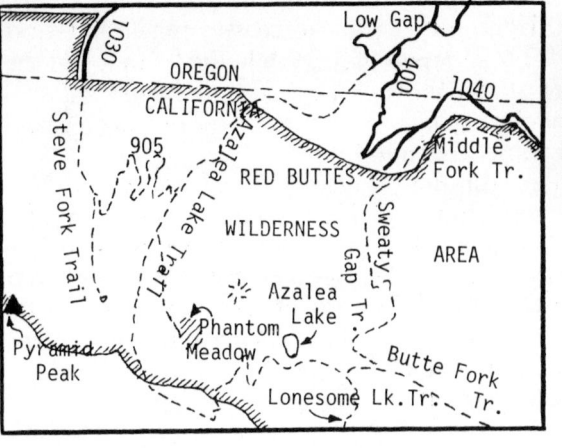

**Length:** 5 miles
**Water:** OK
**Access:** 2
**Season:** June through Oct.
**Difficulty:** 2
**Elevation:** 4500 to 5900 ft.
**Scenic Qual.:** 3
**Use:** Non-motorized only.
  X-C ski

Steve Fork is the easiest trailhead to find at the moment. Take Highway 238 from Jacksonville or south Grants Pass to the town of Applegate. Follow the signs to Applegate Lake on Thompson Creek Road until you reach the Steve Fork turnoff. There, a sign directs drivers over the bridge and to the left for the Steve Fork Trail. Shortly before the road ends, it curves uphill to the right and a poorer road continues along the creek. Follow the creek.

From the well marked, roomy trailhead, the trail follows an old logging road but soon crosses a footbridge and begins a gentle ascent through a forest of Douglas-fir, hemlock, white fir and Shasta fir. Lodgepole pine may also be seen along the trail and in the Azalea Lake basin. I've seen it nowhere else in the Siskiyou Mountains.

It's two miles to a small saddle and 3½ to the main ridge. Just before the saddle, the looming face of Pyramid Peak appears and the route becomes rocky and lined with azalea, rhododendron and Sadler oak. A series of switchbacks leads up to the saddle, then down to the Azalea Lake trail. A side trail peels off shortly after to Phantom Meadows.

From the high ridge above Phantom Meadows and Azalea Lake, look for Pyramid Peak, Buck Peak, the Red Buttes, the Applegate and Klamath River Valleys and a sizeable chunk of northern California and southern Oregon.

Not surprisingly, Azalea Lake may also be reached via the Azalea Lake Trail. Take the road to Applegate Lake from the town of Ruch. Turn right at the fork just past the state line and left just before the Middle Fork trailhead. Follow the road to the Azalea Lake trailhead.

Unfortunately, that road was washed out when I was there last. Before repairs are completed (and after), the trailhead may also be reached from Low Gap Road (400), a major turnoff to the left and over a bridge, five or six miles down Steve Fork Road (1030). Beyond Low Gap, the road passes a rock pit with a sign pointing up a short spur to the trailhead.

The first part of the Azalea Lake trail, to Fir Glade, is a bit steep and scheduled to be rerouted. It's two miles to the intersection with the Steve Fork Trail.

**66    Middle Fork Applegate**

After crossing the high ridge, the trail quickly crosses it again and winds down into Azalea Lake's broad, open basin. While the basin is a glacial cirque, the lake is well away from the rock faces of Figurehead Mountain. Lonesome Lake, two miles away by trail, is a much more typical cirque lake and, I'm told, exceedingly beautiful.

I'll let my friend Joan Peterson-Bratt conclude: "Azalea Lake is large for the Siskiyous, about five acres, but is not deep. It is surrounded by a forest of incense cedar, mountain hemlock, Brewer spruce and lodgepole pine. This is a nice place to have lunch and either hike out as you came in or continue on to Sweaty Gap, a trail best negotiated downhill." At the bottom of Sweaty Gap, you could either have a car waiting or walk two miles back to the Azalea Lake trailhead.

## 37. Middle Fork Applegate

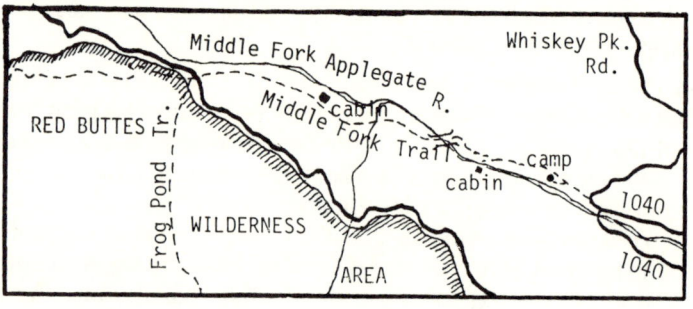

| | |
|---|---|
| **Length:** 2 miles | **Water:** Gallons |
| **Access:** 2 | **Season:** All |
| **Difficulty:** 1 | **Elevation:** 2700 ft. |
| **Scenic Qual.:** 2 | **Use:** Any |

Among devotees of peaceful ambles along gurgling mountain streams, the Middle Fork of the Applegate River is a favorite. This trail must have something going for it because of all the trails on the Applegate Ranger District of Rogue River National Forest, it alone was nominated for inclusion in the National Recreational Trail System. What's more, it was accepted.

To reach the trailhead, take Highway 238 from Jacksonville or south Grants Pass to the town of Ruch. At Ruch, turn up the Applegate River Road towards Applegate Lake. The drive along the lake makes a rewarding Sunday excursion. Look for occassional glimpses of the orange, double-humped Red Buttes, after which the Red Buttes Wilderness Area, which encompasses most of the upper Applegate country, is named.

The pavement ends at the state line and the road forks immediately after. Take the right fork, Road 1040, over the bridge and past the river's many swimming holes. Rock outcroppings and deep pools line this popular section of the river.

Five miles beyond the state line, the road curves sharply uphill in two directions. To find the trailhead, continue straight, past the fork to the left. It's well marked, with parking for 5 or 6 cars.

The trail ultimately ties in with a half-dozen other trails, including the Frog Pond, Sweaty Gap, Azalea Lake, Butte Fork and Boundary Trails. We'll stick to the first two miles, possibly three if you follow the trail to where it comes back out on Road 1040 and connects with the Frog Pond Trail. Road 1040 parallels the river but follows a route high on the hillside, well away from the enchanted canyon bottom.

Joan Peterson-Bratt describes her favorite trail this way: "A rain forest in Oregon?" she asks. "Well, almost. If you're hiking on a hot day, looking for water and shade, this is ideal. There's even a swimming hole less than a half-mile from the trailhead. Two log cabins are also fun to explore along the way. Both are intact enough for visitors to apprciate the work that went into them.

"The trail begins as a wide gravel road at the river's edge. Just before this segment ends, a small path heads up the bank, following the river into a forest of old growth Douglas-fir, white fir, sugar pine and ponderosa pine. Soon after, you'll be able to look across to one of the cabins and, if you care to, descend a little footpath and take a dip in the swimming hole. After a mile, trail again meets river at a log bridge crossing.

"From there on, amid ferns and mosses, the area begins to feel like a rain forest out of the Olympic Peninsula. The old growth stand is a spotted owl management area. After a mile on the south side of the river, you'll come to a second log cabin, a perfect place for a picnic lunch and a good doubling back point. It's another mile to the road and the Frog Pond Trail."

## 38. Frog Pond Loop
### (Red Buttes Wilderness Area)

For a quick introduction to the upper Applegate area, this loop trail is ideal. Each end takes off from the road up the Middle Fork of the Applegate and it's two road miles between trailheads. Unfortunately, the road is presently washed out halfway between so the total trek will be seven miles. They're supposed to repair Road 1040 by late summer of 1987.

**68    Red Buttes**

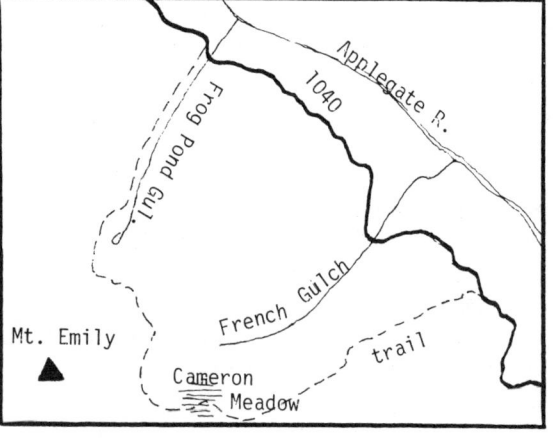

**Length:** 5 mile loop
**Water:** OK
**Access:** 2
**Season:** May through Nov.
**Difficulty:** 2
**Elevation:** 3500 to 5300 ft.
**Scenic Qual.:** 2
**Use:** Non-motorized.
    X-C ski

   To reach the trailheads, take Highway 238 from Jacksonville or south Grants Pass to the town of Ruch. Proceed up the Applegate River past Applegate Lake and Seattle Bar. Turn right at the fork just beyond the state line and left five miles down where the road takes off uphill in two directions. Stay on road 1040 and avoid the Whiskey Peak Road.

   Both Frog Pond trailheads are well marked. The first is about six miles down, the second about eight miles. I suggest beginning at the far trailhead, which requires parking at the washout and walking a mile. From the far trailhead, it's two miles to Frog Pond, up a well maintained trail, at a moderate grade. The trail appears on the map to follow a creek but actually contours along a densely forested hillside amid Douglas-fir, incense cedar and sugar pine.

   Frog Pond itself isn't much but it's set in a lovely meadow below the summit of Mt. Emily. There's an interesting cabin there, built in the 1930's by a gold miner named John Calvin Knox McCoy. McCoy incorporated seven live cedar trees into the structure's frame. It's very photogenic.

   From Frog Pond, it's a mile to Cameron Meadow over a trail with some rather steep pitches. Look for views of the Red Buttes and Whiskey Peak.

   Ben Hamner, of the Applegate Ranger District, describes the loop back down to the near trailhead as "kind of blah." It winds along a forested side ridge for 2½ miles. Ben suggests doubling back at Cameron Meadow and leaving as you came.

## 39.  Red Buttes
### (Red Buttes Wilderness Area)

   The Red Buttes pop up every now and then from many of our area's back roads, although usually just for a second. Their double humped, camelback outline is an instant giveaway. Now that the battle for the Red

# Red Buttes    69

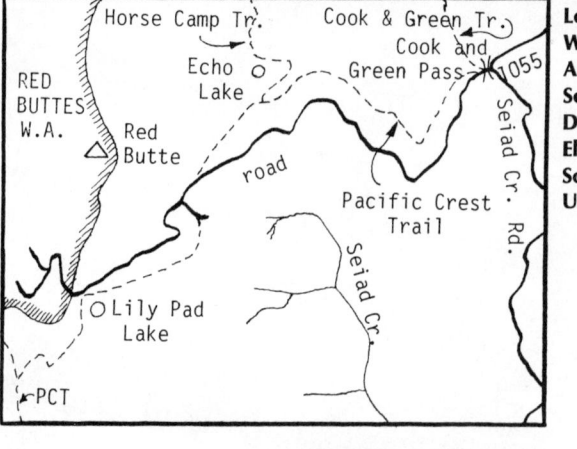

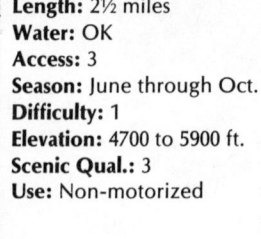

**Length:** 2½ miles
**Water:** OK
**Access:** 3
**Season:** June through Oct.
**Difficulty:** 1
**Elevation:** 4700 to 5900 ft.
**Scenic Qual.:** 3
**Use:** Non-motorized

Buttes Wilderness Area is over and the Pacific Crest Trail is complete, access is fairly easy to this compact little area of great beauty.

The best view from a road of the Red Buttes is from Seiad Creek in California, on the far side of Cook and Green Pass. Motorists should stop and explore the spot where Seiad Creek is crossed. If you have four-wheel drive, take the side road near the bridge to another little bridge. Proceed uphill, bearing right where the road forks. You will end up at an abandoned chrome mine amid a large Baker cypress grove (see the Miller Lake chapter). These trees differ slightly from the Miller Lake specimens. The pearly, ball shaped cones on the Seiad Creek trees are larger and the grove sits entirely on serpentine soil.

To reach the Red Buttes trailhead at Cook and Green Pass, travel to the town of Ruch, out of Jacksonville or south Grants Pass, then take the road up the Applegate River past Applegate Lake where the pavement ends near the California line. Turn left at the fork onto Elliott Creek Road, then right on the Cook and Green Pass Road.

A right turn at the fork near the state line leads to a trailhead on the Applegate which also goes to Cook and Green Pass. It's a fairly popular nine mile trail but violates my rule about hiking to places where one can drive.

The Cook and Green Pass Road is steep, narrow and pretty much second or first gear throughout. Look as you drive for one of the better views of Grayback.

Trails converge everywhere at Cook and Green Pass. It's probably best to take the Pacific Crest Trail to the Red Buttes, although one can also walk up the old road. While the road has remained open, it's among the worst I've ever been on. With four-wheel drive, you might give it a try. The Pacific Crest Trail was rather ruthlessly gouged into the mountain above the road, breaking the hillside's clean, majestic sweep and marring the area's beauty.

70    Tunnel Ridge

**Red Buttes (Ch. 39)**                    (Bernstein Photo)

It's about three miles from Cook and Green Pass to Lily Pad Lake at the Wilderness Boundary. If you've come up the road, look for the Pacific Crest Trail on the right, just before Lily Pad Lake, and follow it uphill to lovely Echo Lake, on the north side of the ridge in a small glacial cirque.

Lily Pad Lake isn't much but the setting is exquisite. From it, you can climb the Red Buttes, follow the road to another old chrome mine, take the Pacific Crest Trail down to Devils Peak and the Klamath, or continue along hte Siskiyou crest to Kangaroo Mountain, Azalea Lake and points north.

## 40. Tunnel Ridge

No other trail I know of is quite like this hike through the brushy foothills of the Little Applegate. It's ideal for a sunny afternoon in summer or winter, with picnic basket and all the kids you can round up.

The main trek follows an old ditch which, from the 1870's to 1930's, channeled water to the gold mines on Sterling Creek. Highlight of the 26 mile engineering feat is the hundred-foot tunnel through Tunnel Ridge.

To reach the trailheads of the four mile loop trail, take Highway 238 from Jacksonville or south Grants Pass to the town of Ruch. Follow the road up the Applegate to Little Applegate Road. Turn left and proceed 10 miles past the Bear Gulch trailhead to the Tunnel Ridge trailhead.

**Tunnel Ridge**    **71**

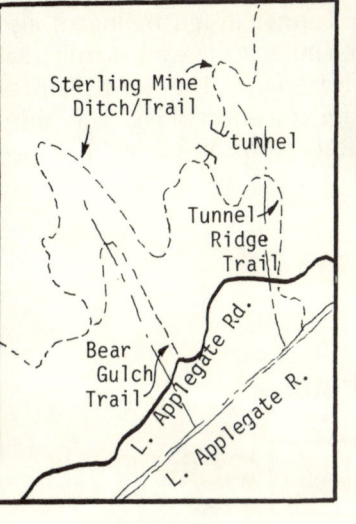

**Length:** 4 mile loop
**Water:** No
**Access:** 1
**Season:** All
**Difficulty:** 2
**Elevation:** 2500 ft.
**Scenic Qual.:** 1
**Use:** Non-motorized only

The drive along the Little Applegate is lovely. At the trailhead, be sure to walk down to the creek before heading up the trail. It's particularly pretty. On the trail, it's an easy mile up a sheltered draw to the ditch and tunnel. Most of the route runs through a forest of young white oak and ponderosa pine; a typical low elevation, south slope forest. The last quarter-mile becomes rather steep as the route loops up an open, grassy area with excellent views of the Little Applegate canyon and 7200 foot Wagner Butte.

The trail passes over the top of the tunnel. The grassy lawn above, surrounded by oaks, makes a fine picnic site. To complete the loop, follow the ditch left for two miles and turn left where the Bear Gulch Trail joins in. It's a mile back down to the road and ¾'s of a mile along the road back to the Tunnel Ridge trailhead.

Actually, it makes most sense to simply explore around the tunnel and return as you came. The Bear Gulch Trail is a little less scenic than the Tunnel Ridge Trail but it is also less steep. The best view of the Little Applegate and Wagner Butte is from where the Bear Gulch Trail meets the ditch.

72    **Wagner Butte**

A third trailhead, 1¾ miles past the Tunnel Ridge trailhead, also connects to the Sterling Mine Ditch after a mile. It's five miles from that trailhead to the tunnel, partly over private land. The BLM plans to relocate this part of the trail away from the inholdings. This third connecting trail, at the Little Applegate Recreation Site, is steeper than the other two.

Watch out for poison oak.

## 41. Wagner Butte

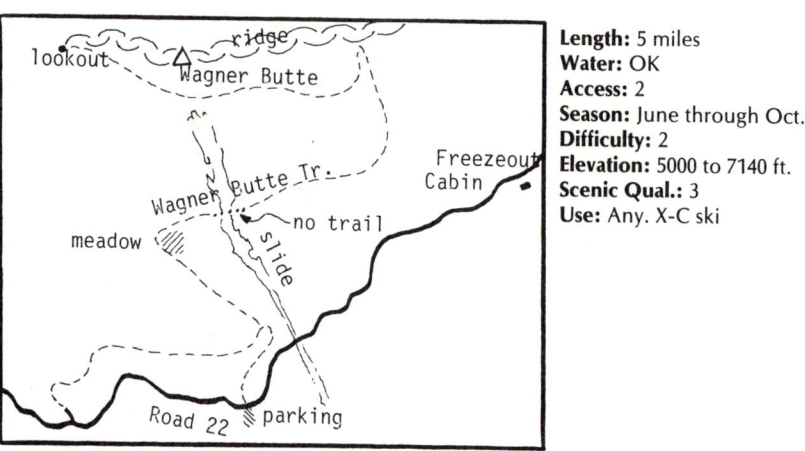

**Length:** 5 miles
**Water:** OK
**Access:** 2
**Season:** June through Oct.
**Difficulty:** 2
**Elevation:** 5000 to 7140 ft.
**Scenic Qual.:** 3
**Use:** Any. X-C ski

One of the most scenic yet ignored trails is southern Oregon is the Wagner Butte Trail. Virtually in Medford's back yard, it should be one of the most popular. Wagner Butte looms immediately west of Medford and Ashland. From Medford, it appears higher than Mt. Ashland, since the latter is father away. At 7200 feet, it's only 200 feet lower than Ashland.

If you've ever wished there was a wilderness trail to the top of Mt. Ashland instead of a network of roads, consider tackling Wagner Butte. The trailhead is only 10½ miles from downtown Talent.

From Highway 99 between Medford and Ashland, follow the signs to the Talent business district, then turn up Main Street. Main Street shortly becomes Wagner Creek Road, one of the area's prettiest drives. Wagner Creek passes through dense woods and alongside moss and fern covered rock slopes. The road is narrow, steep, and winding beyond the end of the pavement and a little slippery in wet weather, so be careful. Also, be extremely alert for oncoming log trucks and stay to the right at all times. Bear left where the dirt road forks and a paved road takes off to the right.

**Lower Table Rock (Ch. 42)**  (BLM Photo)

Beyond Wagner Gap, the road improves. From there to its intersection with the Mt. Ashland road system, the drive is spectacular. It's exactly two miles from the cattle grate at Wagner Gap to the trailhead. Look for a large parking area on the right and a tiny trail sign high up a tree to the left. The parking area is mostly fill and very muddy in wet weather. The Forest Service plans to gravel it over enventually.

The trail snakes through the woods for a quarter-mile, then hits a closed-off logging road. Follow the logging road to the right, up some moderately steep pitches, to a little meadow a mile from the trailhead. The meadow offers good views of the Red Mountain area west of Mt. Ashland. Note the misplaced sagebrush in the meadow and the arrow sign at the end of the meadow.

A quarter-mile beyond the meadow; though some woods, across a grassy gully, and past some more woods; the trail enters a large, grassy area, crosses a small gully and disappears at the edge of a larger gully.

This is the infamous 1984 landslide which wiped out an eighth-mile of the trail. The slide is three miles long and reaches from almost the top of the mountain to well below the road. You're on your own crossing the slide, although Margaret Holman, of the Ashland Ranger Distict, has promised to at least lay a ribbon line across by June or July of 1987.

74    **Lower Table Rock**

The slide area is rapidly turning to grassy meadow cut by a half-dozen gullies. Where the trail first emerges from the woods, sight straight across on as level a line as possible, to the woods on the other side. Pick out a spot there and head for it, negotiating the gullies as best you can. On the far side, look for a small marsh. Follow around the high side of the marsh and pick up the trail immediately beyond.

It's possible to reach the top of the mountain by heading straight up the slide. You'll gain 1200 feet in elevation in a half-mile up a 46% slope. Turn left where the trail skirts the top of the slide and follow it to the lookout. I recommend staying on the trail, not climbing up the slide. It's 2½ miles longer but you're much more likely to make it.

For 1¼ miles beyond the slide, the trail is pleasantly level, with a few steep pitches. It alternates between woods of Douglas-fir, white fir, ponderosa pine and a little Shasta fir; and open, grassy areas.

Some 2½ miles from the trailhead, the route takes off sharply uphill for a half-mile and the Wagner Butte summit appears. Soon after, the trail joins another trail and curves sharply north. There are obviously other routes to the summit, all longer or more difficult.

The last two miles, with the trail running just west of the summit, are stunning. The route is level, with vistas everywhere. The area is mostly brush, broken by picturesque clumps of trees. Look for mountain mahogany and sagebrush. At Cold Springs; a long, wet seep (possibly with grazing cattle); you'll find muddy spots, willow brush and abundant wildflowers.

The trail ends at a lookout. While the elevation of 7140 is slightly below the true summit a mile south, you won't be disappointed. Mt. Ashland can be seen, of course, along with McLoughlin, Crater Lake, Shasta, the Marbles, Grayback, the cities of Ashland and Medford, and so on. Not bad for a 15 mile drive from downtown Medford.


## 42. Lower Table Rock

This "mighty fortress," with the look of a flattop desert mesa, is one of the prominent landmarks along the middle Rogue River. The formation is fascinating in its geology, botany, and history, and the trail is remarkably easy. It's a pleasant afternoon jaunt with the kids in winter or spring. March through June are best for wildflowers.

I only wish they'd think up a more original name. Three-fourths of the flattop rock formations in the world are called "Table Rock." How about something inspiring, like "The Enchanted Mesa," after the one in New Mexico? Or whimsical, like "Ironing Board Butte," or discriptive, like "The Island in the Sky"? Oh well.

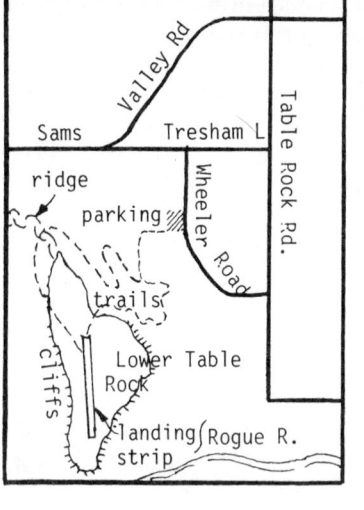

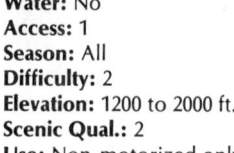

**Length:** 2½ miles
**Water:** No
**Access:** 1
**Season:** All
**Difficulty:** 2
**Elevation:** 1200 to 2000 ft.
**Scenic Qual.:** 2
**Use:** Non-motorized only.

To reach the Lower Table Rock trailhead, take Table Rock Road north from Medford, past Central Point. The route makes a couple right angle turns before reaching the trailhead. From Grants Pass, take I-5 south to Gold Hill and follow the signs to Crater Lake (Sams Valley Road). Turn right either on Table Rock Road or Tresham Lane, which runs into Table Rock Road.

A sign on Table Rock Road directs traffic up the gravel surfaced Wheeler Road to the parking area and trailhead. The trailhead compound was built by The Nature Concervancy, which also maintains the trail and owns a piece of the rock. They've done a commendable job.

There's a wood chip pile with buckets near the trailhead and a sign asking hikers to carry a bucket of chips to be deposited on down. A gravel pile has a similar sign and buckets. It would help if they'd suggest a dumping spot.

The trail parallels a driveway at first, then turns off into a scrubby woods of white oak, madrone and ponderosa pine. Poison oak abounds, along with several species of ceanothus. From the vegetation, it's obvious the place cooks in summer so I'd suggest bringing water in warm weather. The route up the side has some steep spots, a few dusty areas and places which become quite muddy in wet weather. It reaches the top in 1½ miles, ascending a talus slope away from the cliffs.

About halfway up, the trail forks. There's a map posted there which, when I visited, had been severely damaged. To reach the good vista points, bear left at the fork.

Once on top, it's at least another mile before you get anywhere. You'll find a still used landing strip and wind sock and, I should add, a private auto road. The rock surface is amazingly flat and almost featureless. One can walk and walk towards objects appearing a short way off and they never seem to grow closer.

76    **Upper Table Rock**

At the far end of the landing strip, continue straight but bear slightly right, towards the clump of trees. You'll end up on a high point of rock overlooking the Rogue. You may scare off 10 or 20 buzzards from a nearby roost so don't panic if one swoops 10 feet over your head. They don't eat live humans.

There's another vista point due east from the wind sock, which offers a panorama of the valley between Upper and Lower Table Rock. You can see your car from there and most of the trail.

The Table Rock surface is mostly covered with grass. Since I visited in mid-summer wearing sneakers and shorts, I recall it as a mass of cured-out foxtails and star thistles. Walking bare legged through an endless sea of star thistle is one of life's great experiences. It's almost a much fun as picking 50,000 foxtails out of your socks.

Table Rock is the remnant of an ancient, still eroding lava flow which rises 800 feet above the surrounding valley. The former Takelma Indian Reservation (briefly), aside from being home to star thistle and grass, boasts several rare wildflowers. Armed with a good key, look for Brewer's rock cress, scarlet fritilleria and three-bract onion. The entire range on Earth of a plant called dwarf meadow foam is limited to the tops of Upper and Lower Table Rock.

While I've heard countless rumors about rattlesnakes on Table Rock, I didn't see any. But then, in 20 years of hiking, I've only encountered one rattlesnake. He was far more afraid of me than I was of him. Or her.

## 43. Upper Table Rock

A fascinating afternoon diversion for those who have conquered Lower Table Rock yet have not had their fill of flat top rocks, is nearby Upper Table Rock. See the Lower Table Rock chapter for descriptions of these prominent landmarks north of Medford, and their geology and botany.

There are some differences between the two tables. I preferred Upper, ever so slightly. So does Kurt Berger of Medford, who uses it for rock climbing classes. Readers, of course, will form their own opinions.

To reach the Bureau of Land Management's Upper Table Rock trailhead, take Table Rock Road north from Medford and turn right on Modoc Road. From Grants Pass, take I-5 south to the Gold Hill - Crater Lake exit. Proceed towards Crater Lake on Sams Valley Road, turning right onto Table Rock Road then left on Modoc Road. Modoc Road winds briefly through pear orchards and past some old military barracks. Just past the high point, you'll see a Pacific Power transformer on the right. Park in front of it and cross the road to the trailhead.

The day I climbed the 800-foot formation, shortly before Christmas, the entire area was in fog. I missed a lot but gained a lot also. Kurt Berger filled me in on the fair weather details.

# Upper Table Rock                    77

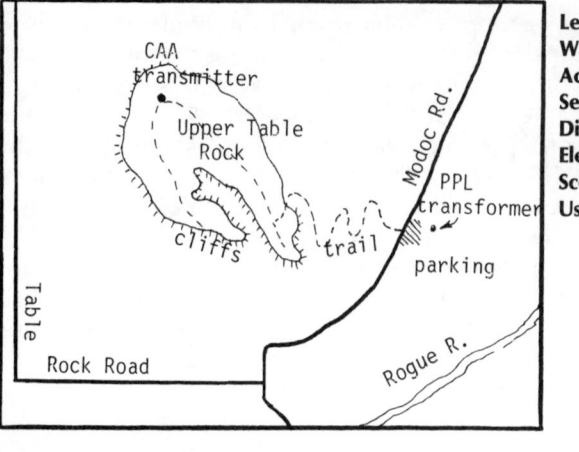

**Length:** 1½ miles
**Water:** No
**Access:** 1
**Season:** All
**Difficulty:** 1
**Elevation:** 1300 to 2050 ft.
**Scenic Qual.:** 2
**Use:** Non-Motorized only

The trail is shorter and less steep than its lower counterpart and a little more open, with better views. The top of Upper Table Rock is 30 feet higher than Lower Table Rock but the Upper trailhead is 150 feet higher. The Upper Table Rock Trail switches back and forth across grass, patches of ceanothus and manzanita and clumps of white oak and madrone. Like its sister (or brother) trail, the rim's bluffs are visible from the trailhead but not from the trail itself until you reach the top.

When I visited, the trail bordered on treacherous, although they tell me it's lovely in dry weather. I found it very muddy. Not a soupy, sticky mud, although there was a little of that, but a very slippery mud. Countless elongated footprints shot off to the side. I walked mostly on the grass alongside the trail, which I'm sure was not the intent of the trail's builders.

About a third of the way up, you'll come to a little wooden bench and a maze of trails. Take the trail the farthest to the right. The bench, intended for sitting, is used extensively in winter as a boot scraper.

The trail comes out only a quarter-mile from the southern tip of the horseshoe shaped mesa. Being in fog, I saw no features whatsoever upon hitting the top so I stayed on the trail until I came to an old jeep road. I turned left on it and followed it to the southern point.

The cliffs aren't quite as high as those on Lower Table Rock because there's more talus (or debris) at the base. But the upper rock has more flat surface and forms a tighter horseshoe. The center of the Upper Table Rock horseshoe is a spectacular rock gorge offering excellent climbing. Look for a huge, detached monolith just around the southern point, towards the center of the horseshoe.

They tell me the view is spectacular. I expect it would be similar to the view from the Lower Table Rock, with a panorama of the Rogue River, Medford, the Siskiyous and Cascades, and so forth.

78    **Boundary Springs**

The seasonal wetlands on Upper Table Rock dry in summer to shallow, flower filled depressions. In winter, collected water is extensive enough to attract hundreds of ducks to use them as a resting site. I scared them off twice and the sky became black with waterfowl.

Away from the seasonal potholes, look for "patterned ground" on the otherwise flat surface. This is typical atop flat lava formations. It consists of bulges of soil one or two feet high and several feet across, sticking up in profusion amid the rocks and cobbles of the general surface.

Spring, of course is the best time to visit as the rock is a haven for many rare, and some not so rare, wildflowers. Still, five days before Christmas, in the fog, I found tiny yellow flowers scattered among the mosses and weeds. I didn't key them out but I did spend considerable time admiring their brave, delicate beauty.

## 44. Boundary Springs
### (Crater Lake National Park)

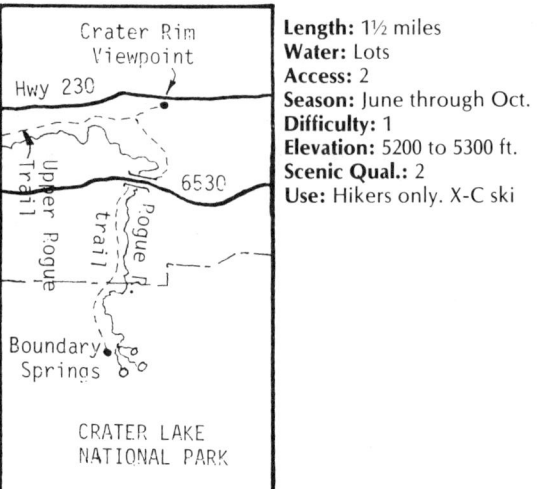

**Length:** 1½ miles
**Water:** Lots
**Access:** 2
**Season:** June through Oct.
**Difficulty:** 1
**Elevation:** 5200 to 5300 ft.
**Scenic Qual.:** 2
**Use:** Hikers only. X-C ski

It's not true that the source of the Rogue River is a hole through the north side of the Crater Lake rim. The water feeding beautiful Boundary Springs, source of the main fork of the Rogue, comes from runoff on Crater Lake's outer slopes, not from the lake.

There are many ways to reach Boundary Springs, located just inside Crater Lake National Park. The longest route is from inside the park. Picking up the Pacific Crest Trail from the North Entrance Road, it's three miles to the Boundary Springs Trail and seven more to the springs.

A better starting place is the Crater Rim Vista Point on Highway 230, the road to Diamond Lake and the Crater Lake North Entrance. Take Crater Lake Highway north from Medford, bear left at Union Creek towards Diamond Lake and park at the Vista Point. It's a half-mile hike through open lodgepole pine forest to the Upper Rogue Trail. Turn left on the Upper Rogue Trail for Boundary Springs and right for Ruth Falls and Hamaker Meadows. The latter is nine miles distant.

The trail towards Boundary Springs follows a bench above the river for a mile, then emerges at a dirt road near a bridge with a developed, if cramped, trailhead area. To reach this spot by car, turn right off of Highway 230 where a green highway sign points to Hamaker Campground. Follow Road 6530 six miles, past lake West, to the trailhead. The gravel road surface becomes dirt after three miles but the road is level and driveable, provided the snow has all melted and things have dried up.

From the bridge on Road 6530 the trail heads south along the river towards the National Park boundary. The crashing stream is bordered by rock and lava formations and the trail remains perched well above the water, although it's possible to climb down if so inclined. The volume of water is surprising, considering the nearness of the river's source.

The Park boundary is a mile from the trailhead and the springs are 1½ miles from the trailhead. Maureen Briggs, of Crater Lake National Park, recommends a fall hike for the color and the profusion of huckleberry bushes at the river's edge.

As you near the springs, the river is bridged by numerous moss covered logs. In mid-summer, look for abundant yellow monkey flowers. At the springs, gushing water bursts from the hillside in several spots. This is an enchanted area of rushing water, flowers, mossy rocks and boulders, willow, and woods.

The magical beauty makes the "hole in Crater Lake" theory seem surprisingly credible. It makes perfect poetic sense that the majestic Rogue should have such a source. Don't be surprised if you find yourself half looking for another opening, possibly quite near, leading to some long forgotten kingdom 2000 feet below the surface of Crater Lake.

Don't walk on the moss.


## 45. Upper Rogue Trail/Winding River

Upon first exploring this quiet section of the Upper Rogue Trail, I decided not to include it since quiet walks in the woods bore me. After thinking about it, however, I decided that the geology is so interesting I couldn't leave it out.

Before taking the trail, some things on the highway should be checked out. "The Highway," is route 230, the road to Diamond Lake. To reach it,

**80**    **Upper Rogue Trail/Winding River**

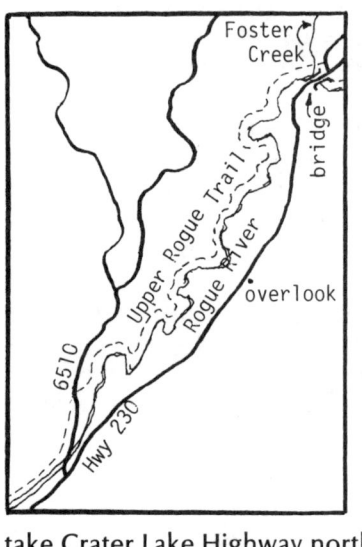

**Length:** 6 mile loop
**Water:** Lots
**Access:** 1
**Season:** All
**Difficulty:** 1
**Elevation:** 3500 ft.
**Scenic Qual.:** 1
**Use:** Hikers only

take Crater Lake Highway north from Medford to Union Creek. Follow the left fork just beyond Union Creek. The trailheads are one and five miles beyond the Diamond Lake/South Crater Lake junction.

Between trailheads, the road passes steep, eroded bluffs of compacted volcanic ash. About halfway along, you'll notice a gap alongside the road where you can pull over and view the river below. It's a wild vista with barren, eroded bluffs shooting down to a placid valley. The bottom is flat and gentle with a forest of old growth lodgepole pine slowly yielding to western white pine and Douglas-fir. Lodgepole is a pioneer species which does well on lava flats. The river is embedded in a much larger river of ash which spewed from Mt. Mazama when its summit collapsed and created the bowl where Crater Lake now resides.

Across the river rises Hershberger Ridge. Two immense volcanic plugs called the Rabbit Ears can be seen sticking out of the ridge.

Whichever trailhead you select, take a look at both before commencing. The south trailhead may be reached by turning left on Hershberger Road, a mile past the intersection of Highways 62 and 230. Cross the bridge and proceed a mile to the clearly marked trailhead. You'll find a little flat there, with a maze of logging roads and plenty of parking. A couple hundred feet away, in the midst of the road maze, hides a second trail sign, about four inches square and covered with moss. Don't worry if you miss it. Just head for the river and the trail will turn up.

The north trailhead is located at Foster Creek, just past the bridge where the Rogue crosses Highway 230 for the last time. To the north, the river disappears into a dark, spooky canyon. You'll find a turnout and parking area on the left.

One must ford Foster Creek after an eighth-mile. In summer, the water is no more than toenail deep. In winter, it may be as high as mid-calf and very cold. Check it out before committing yourself to a six mile walk from the other end.

The trail follows one of the more relaxed river sections. The water has cut broad meanders in the flat ash bed. It's probably great for canoeing. There's not much topography, except for a few undercut bluffs, so the trail is generally level and near the water. The river has changed course frequently so be aware of dry riverbeds called "oxbows," where the water has cut across a meander loop. Some may have water in them.

## 46. Upper Rogue Trail/Natural Bridge

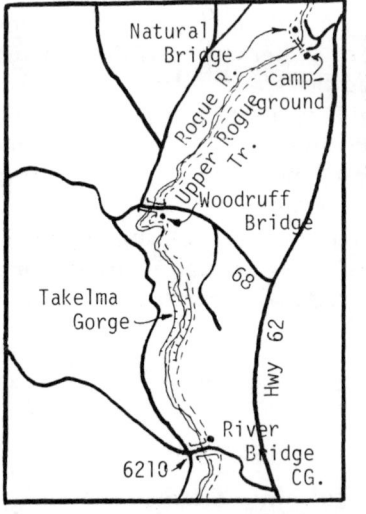

**Length:** 3 mile loop
**Water:** Lots
**Access:** 1
**Season:** All
**Difficulty:** 1
**Elevation:** 2900 to 3200 ft.
**Scenic Qual.:** 2
**Use:** Hikers only

I included this short segment of the Upper Rogue mainly as an excuse to get you to Natural Bridge. Natural Bridge isn't really a bridge but a lava tube. In fact, the entire area is riddled with lava tubes, formed when the outer surface of flowing lava hardened and the inside continued to run. The caves at Lava Beds National Monument are lava tubes and several narrower sections of the Rogue River's channel follow collapsed lava tubes. Lava tubes can be as much as a mile long and big enough to drive a car through.

At Natural Bridge, the Rogue disappears with a roar into a lava tube and re-appears gushing out the side of a cliff, several hundred yards downstream. In between, there's no river, except when water is very high.

One used to be able to walk across the spot where the river disappears. But in summer of 1986, a child fell in and was sucked into the tube. Miraculously, she was spat back out unharmed downstream. The Forest Service has since fenced off the area, paved the trails around it and is building a fancy interpretive display.

82    Upper Rogue Trail/Takelma Gorge

To reach Natural Bridge Campground, take the first left before Union Creek off Highway 62 (Crater Lake Highway), north of Medford. The bridge and interpretive area are impossible to miss. The far trailhead, at Woodruff Bridge, three miles below Natural Bridge, may be found by turning left off Highway 62 where a green sign points to Abbott Camp. Woodruff Bridge is a mile down the side road. It has a small campground and clearly marked trails leading in both directions along the Rogue.

The trail south to Woodruff from Natural Bridge begins on the left just before the footbridge to the Natural Bridge viewpoints. The river walk is quite dramatic for the first mile as the water churns through a formation called Knob Falls, a stretch of whitewater in a collapsed lava tube. The trail is generally level, if a bit rocky here and there, with much opportunity to peer into the chasm. Look for immense, jutting rocks high above the river.

Things quiet down after a mile or so. The river becomes more placid. According to my friend Ernie Thayer, the route below Knob Falls contains "lots of little specatacular things but no big spectacular things." The forest throughout consists of old growth Douglas-fir and western hemlock, with a fair amount of western white pine. The light-starved understory is composed mostly of Oregongrape and princess pine. Princess pine is a tiny herbacious plant, not a tree. Moss sprouts everywhere.

The last two trail miles before Woodruff Bridge cross old logging roads and occassional willow and alder thickets. Finally, the trail emerges near a pretty little waterfall. From there, simply step across the road for the trail to Takelma Gorge and the next chapter.

# 47. Upper Rogue Trail/Takelma Gorge

See **Upper Rogue Trail/Natural Bridge (Ch. 46)** for Map.

| | |
|---|---|
| **Length:** 4 mile loop | **Water:** Gallons |
| **Access:** 1 | **Season:** All |
| **Difficulty:** 1 | **Elevation:** 2900 ft. |
| **Scenic Qual.:** 2 | **Use:** Hikers only |

The Indian tribe after which Takelma Gorge is named seems to spell their name "Takilma" in Josephine County and "Takelma" in Jackson County. And if I had to pick one segment of the Upper Rogue for a day hike, this would be it.

This gorge-ous slit in the earth may be combined with the Natural Bridge section of the upper Rogue, immediately adjacent to the north.

To reach the upper trailhead, take Crater Lake Highway north from Medford to a turnoff on the left marked "Abbott Camp." It's a mile up the Abbot Camp Road to Woodruff Bridge Campground, where the road crosses the Rogue. Trailheads in both directions are clearly marked.

Toad Lake    83

The distances indicated on the signs are a little goofy. The sign at Woodruff Bridge says, "Takelma Gorge 2 Miles - River Bridge 4 Miles." I reached Takelma Gorge in 20 minutes from Woodruff Bridge. After a placid section opposite a road, the river enters a narrow, steep sided chasm. A sign tacked to a tree announces the obvious, that Takelma Gorge has begun.

The trail surface becomes quite rocky here and isn't always easy to follow. But it's difficult to get lost with such clear landmarks. The rocks are full of bubbles and are obviously lava. They're also full of moss.

The far end of Takelma Gorge offers the best views. A little point of land below the trail peers into the dark defile. Inside, water oozes out from between layers of basalt lava into the whitewater below.

Beyond the gorge, the river widens and slows and the trail drops closer to the water. The rest of the walk to River Bridge (a clearly marked turnoff to the left from Highway 62), is pleasant and gentle, with a couple of nice riffles.

I once arrived at River Bridge at daybreak. Light snow highlighted the trail and river bank and steam rose from the water surface. A river otter, the only one I've ever seen in the wild, poked its nose out of the water and smiled at me. They always seem to be smiling and I suspect it's a genuine emotion. The animal performed a few showoff dives and loops and swam off with a grin. I trudged off the same way.

## 48. Toad Lake
### (Rogue-Umpqua Divide Wilderness Area)

If you've never driven to Hershberger Lookout, you've missed one of southern Oregon's great attractions. Straddling the crest of the Rogue-Umpqua Divide, not only is the view great but the juxtapostion of rocky outcroppings, dense forest and gentle meadow is magical. The only place I've ever seen a greater concentration of wildflowers was at Paradise Park on Mt. Rainier.

Before describing the many hiking opportunities from the Rogue side of the Rogue-Umpqua Divide Wilderness, let's first locate the lookout. Drive north on Crater Lake Highway from Medford as though going to Crater Lake. Immediately past Union Creek, take the left fork towards Diamond Lake. A mile beyond the fork, the road to Rabbit Ears and Hershberger Lookout takes off left, dropping downhill and crossing the Rogue River.

Hershberger Road winds through woods and logging shows for several miles, eventually emerging at the base of Rabbit Ears. Stop and explore these two immense volcanic plugs which stick out of a broad ridge. You'll probably notice the view to the southeast but contain your enthusiasm. It gets much better.

**84    Toad Lake**

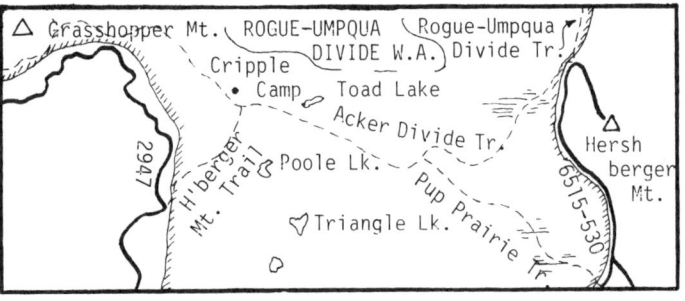

| | |
|---|---|
| **Length:** 2 miles | **Water:** OK |
| **Access:** 2 | **Season:** June through Oct. |
| **Difficulty:** 2 | **Elevation:** 5600 to 5100 ft. |
| **Scenic Qual.:** 3 | **Use:** Non-motorized only. |

Beyond Rabbit Ears, the terrain becomes gentler and more open. You'll soon come around the rocky base of Hershberger Mountain. The last half-mile to the lookout is quite steep but driveable.

From the 6200 foot lookout, Fish Mountain, highest peak in the Wilderness (6800 feet), rises to the northeast. Look also for the ash flow where the erupting Mt. Mazama (Crater Lake) filled up the Rogue River Valley. Other landmarks include Mts. Bailey and Thielsen, the Crater Lake Rim, Devils Peak in the Sky Lakes, Mt. McLoughlin, Mt. Shasta and even Mt. Ashland.

The well marked trailheads are located back at the switchback before the last uphill push to the lookout. The Rogue-Umpqua Divide Trail heads north and connects with Fish Creek Valley after seven or eight miles. The Acker Divide Trail, which is the subject of this chapter, passes Toad Lake after two miles.

The trail to Toad Lake shoots steeply downhill into the woods from the trailhead. It is intimidating at first but soon levels off. After less than a half-mile, beautiful Pup Prairie is crossed, then the junction with the Pup Prairie Trail. Acker Divide weaves in and out between floral meadow and subalpine forest before arriving at Toad Lake. Look for subalpine fir, noble fir and mountain hemlock. Toad Lake sits in another beautiful meadow, although the lake itself is dry or marshy most of the year. Beaver activity is easily oberved.

Cripple Creek Shelter and the Hershberger Mountain Trail lie just past Toad Lake. The Acker Divide Trail continues on to Grasshopper Mountain, Fish Lake and trailheads on the Umpqua side of the Wilderness.

If you feel a need for further exploration before returning home, I suggest returning via the Pup Prairie Trail passed on the way in. The fairly level route winds south for two miles through more forest and meadow along the crest of the divide. The last quarter-mile is rather steep and the trail emerges at the end of a short spur road (525), two miles down the road from the trailhead at Hershberger Lookout.

# 49. Cliff Lake
## (Rogue-Umpqua Divide Wilderness Area)

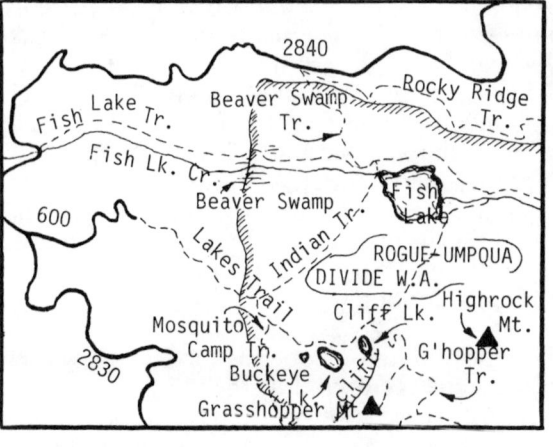

**Length:** 4½ miles
**Water:** Lots
**Access:** 2
**Season:** May through Nov.
**Difficulty:** 2
**Elevation:** 3600 to 4200 ft.
**Scenic Qual.:** 3
**Use:** Non-motorized only.
   X-C ski

To appreciate this short, easy hike from the most popular trailhead in the Rogue-Umpqua Divide Wilderness, one must be aware of an event occurring 6000 years ago. Imagine a 5500 foot mountain, formed by ancient lava flows, suddenly breaking in half and sending millions of tons of rubble into the valley, 2500 feet below.

Such an event created the huge escarpment above Cliff Lake and impounded the waters of Buckeye, Cliff and Fish Lake. Even not knowing the geology, however, this is a beautiful area of lakes, dense forests, steep ridges and jagged summits. Hiking options abound as trails lead in every direction. Hopefully, beginning at the most popular trailhead will make a little sense out of it.

The Skimmerhorn trailhead is the most elaborate I've seen, with parking for at least 50 cars, a picnic ground and pit toilets. To get there, take Crater Lake Highway north from Medford and turn left at Trail. Twenty-six miles later, at Tiller, turn right up the South Umpqua River Road.

The South Umpqua is spectacular and different from the Rogue. Note the abundance of western redcedar, along with the usual middle elevation Douglas-fir and western hemlock. Western redcedar, one of the Pacific Northwest's most common trees, is largely absent in the Siskiyous and southern Cascades. Be sure to stop at South Umpqua Falls.

Umpqua National Forest has attempted to place a trail sign at every road junction. So all you need to do is follow the signs to the Skimmerhorn trailhead, beginning about 25 miles past Tiller. The gravel roads are good and the area is heavily wooded with much logging.

It's two miles to Buckeye Lake from the trailhead, along the Lakes Trail. The path is fairly gentle with slight upgrades in the middle. It's also remarkably wide as summer use is heavy. I visited Buckeye and Cliff

86    Fish Creek Valley

Lakes, believe it or not, in January. Both were frozen over. A dusting of snow adorned the trailhead, with six inches at Cliff Lake. Both lakes sit amid dense forests at the foot of the cliff described earlier. Both also have excellent, level campsites nearby. Buckeye Lake is larger (nine acres), and reveals more of the escarpment than Cliff Lake (four acres).

Just pass Cliff Lake, the Grasshopper Trail takes off uphill to the right while the Lakes Trail continues on to Fish Lake. One and one half miles up the Grasshopper Trail, the Grasshopper Mountain Trail takes off left. It's two miles from Cliff Lake to the lookout site atop Grasshopper Mountain. Since the peak is pretty much a flat mesa, the first part of the climb is steepest. After ascending the cliff, the trail winds through open areas with broad vistas. The extremely jagged peak immediately west is Highrock Mountain. Atop Grasshopper, you can look down 1300 feet on the lakes.

Back at Cliff Lake, there are numerous options in this trail riddled wilderness. Nearby Fish Lake, at 90 acres, is the area's largest. It sits at a lower elevation than Cliff and Buckeye Lakes, in a densely wooded valley. A steep, five mile loop leads to Fish Lake and back. The best route is via the Indian Trail, passed on the left a half-mile before Buckeye Lake. Follow it to the Fish Lake Trail, turn right past Fish Lake, and continue to the junction with the far end of the Lakes Trail from Ciff Lake. It's easier to hike down the Indian Trail than up it.

Two other trails (at least), lead to Fish Lake. The Fish Lake trailhead, passed on the drive to the Skimmerhorn trailhead, follows an easy, 3½ mile route. The Beaver Swamp trailhead is 4½ miles up the road from the Fish Lake trailhead. The trail is shorter, only 1½ miles to Fish Lake, but quite steep on the return trip.

The Beaver Swamp trailhead is worth a visit even if you're not going to Fish Lake since the Rocky Rim Trail also takes off there. It's an almost level mile up the Rocky Rim Trail to probably the best panorama of the Fish Lake area.

## 50. Fish Creek Valley
### (Rogue-Umpqua Divide Wilderness Area)

One of the Cascade Mountains' great "secret places" may be visited immediately north of Crater Lake and west of Diamond Lake. Fish Creek Valley is among the more remote and lovely spots accessible by car while nearby Rattlesnake Mountain, rising to 6600 feet, makes a rewarding day-hike into the Rogue-Umpqua Divide Wilderness.

The region's early explorers obviously were obsessed with fish. Fish Mountain is the Wilderness area's highest, its largest lake is Fish Lake and two of its major streams are Fish Creek and Fish Lake Creek. Something fishy is going on.

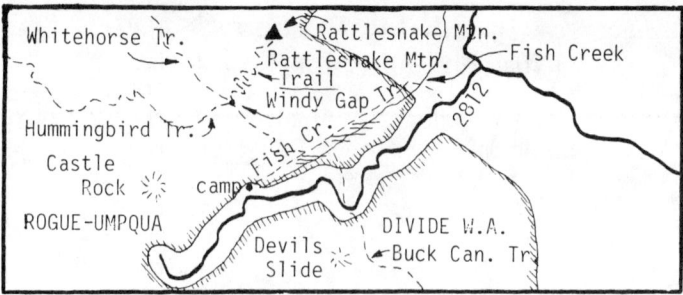

**Length:** 3 miles
**Access:** 3
**Difficulty:** 2
**Scenic Qual.:** 3

**Water:** No
**Season:** June through Oct.
**Elevation:** 5100 to 6600 ft.
**Use:** Non-Motorized only.

To reach Fish Creek Valley, take Crater Lake Highway north from Medford and bear left at Union Creek towards Diamond Lake. Eventually, you'll come to a side road on the right, with a sign pointing to Hamaker Campground. Turn left there, not right, towards Buck Camp. It's complicated and a map helps. Follow this road (6560), over the divide where it becomes Road 37. Turn right on spur 800 past Lonesome Meadow and right again on spur 870, the Fish Creek Valley Road.

Jim Hunt of the Tiller Ranger District describes Fish Creek Valley as a "typical Montana valley-broad and flat with a clear stream meandering through the middle." Mostly meadow and open lodgepole pine forest, rocky crags and forested ridges rise sharply up the valley's sides.

Since the road penetrates the Wilderness Area, they may eventually close it to auto traffic. Meanwhile, it's a rough ride. Begin looking for the trailhead when the aptly named Castle Rock appears. You'll find a nice little campsite, called Happy Camp, and a trailhead sign pointing to the Rogue-Umpqua Divide Trail on the right. This route backtracks down the valley and eventually meets the Whitehorse Meadow Trail on the left.

It's a level mile up the Whitehorse Meadow Trail, another moderately steep mile through woods and meadows to Windy Gap, and a third quite winding but only moderately steep mile to the top of Rattlesnake Mountain. Turn right at Windy Gap onto the Rattlesnake Mountain Trail. The Castle Creek Trail also meets the Whitehorse Meadow Trail at Windy Gap.

The final uphill leg snakes, if you'll pardon the expression, past unusual volcanic rock formation, some of which appear to have been painted yellow. The yellow is lichen.

The summit offers excellent panoramas of the Rogue Umpqua Divide area, Fish Mountain, Mount Bailey and the Crater Lake rim. The route is beautiful but mostly out in the open. Bring water and be prepared to work up an appetite. It's only three miles back down to the car and, hopefully, a waiting picnic lunch.

88    Mt. Thielsen

# 51. Mt. Thielsen
## (Mt. Thielsen Wilderness Area)

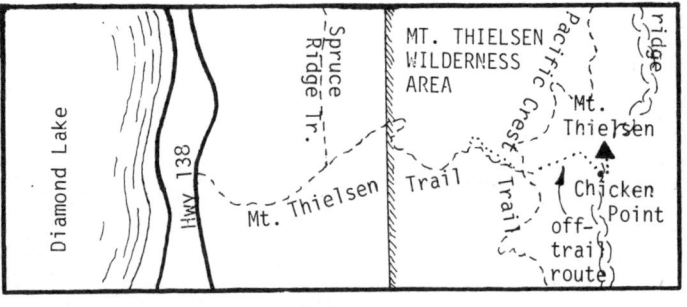

| | |
|---|---|
| **Length:** 4 miles | **Water:** No |
| **Access:** 1 | **Season:** June through Oct. |
| **Difficulty:** 2 | **Elevation:** 5400 to 9182 ft. |
| **Scenic Qual.:** 3 | **Use:** Non-motorized. |
| | X-C ski |

I know what you're going to ask. How can Mt. Thielsen be the most beautiful peak in the southern Cascades when I've bestowed that honor repeatedly on Mt. Shasta? All I can say is when it comes to aesthetics, consistency goes out the window.

Shasta is immense and awe inspiring. Thielsen, no slouch at 9200 feet, is exquisite and unique. Noted for the apparently tilted spire sticking out its top, Thielsen is actually an extinct volcano and the spire is the remnant of the main lava conduit into the peak's molten core. Similar volcanic plugs adorn Mt. McLoughlin. While impressive, those on McLoughlin are off to the side, not at the very top.

The Thielsen Trail has recently been relocated to offer better vista points. To reach it, take Crater Lake Highway north from Medford, bearing left on Highway 230 at Union Creek, towards Diamond Lake. At Diamond Lake, turn left on Highway 138 and proceed 1½ miles to the trailhead. Parking is on the shoulder only. If you have horses and trailers, you may wish to continue north a couple miles to the Thielsen Creek/-Howlock Mountain trailhead.

Back on the Mt. Thielsen Trail, after crossing a stand of lodgepole pine, the path climbs steadily into a forest of Shasta fir and mountain hemlock. After 1½ miles, it passes the Spruce Ridge Trail which connects to the Howlock Mountain Trail. A half-mile beyond this junction, the Thielsen Trail comes around a point and the huge west face of Thielsen emerges for the first time.

The summit remains in view for most of the route beyond this first vista point. Diamond Lake is visible to the Spruce Ridge Trail junction, then disappears for a couple miles. A mile beyond the vista point, the trail curves north through a stand of large timber, then takes a switchback to the southeast, just below a prominent ridge.

**Mt. Thielsen    89**

**Mt. Scott Summit - Crater Lake N.P. (Ch. 53)**          (Bernstein Photo)

Hikers have a choice at this switchback. For the best views of Thielsen and the sweeping basin below, a scramble trail has been marked along the ridge. It's rocky and slow going, however. For the more conservative types (or cross-country skiers), the main, improved trail parallels 50 feet below, down in the trees.

Three miles from the trailhead, the Pacific Crest Trail is joined. This is the end of the Thielsen Trail. The rest of the route to the summit, though fairly obvious, is much more difficult and you may wish to turn around here or content yourself with exploring a couple miles of the Pacific Crest Trail.

A path has been cut above the Pacific Crest Trail at the junction with the Thielsen Trail, through a small brush field. It leads up a prominent east-west ridge radiating from the summit. Follow the extremely steep, rocky ridge a mile to the base of the spire. Then contour around to the right until you come to a boulder field on the main north-south divide between Diamond Lake and the Klamath basin. This is called Chicken Point.

Technical climbing gear isn't necessary to ascend the spire but don't feel bad if Chicken Point lives up to its name for you. Not everyone feels comfortable clinging to narrow ledges above thousand foot dropoffs. If you're in this category, congratulate yourself on making it to Chicken Point and watch the other climbers. Never attempt the spire alone.

**90    Mt. Bailey**

The actual summit is about 10 feet square or less, with a sign-in box. According to Roger Gunderson of the Diamond Lake Ranger District, the views of Crater Lake, Diamond Lake, and the surrounding area are predictably breathtaking. The view straight down is dizzying.

Be sure to stop at the Thielsen View Point on Highway 230 on your way home. You should be able to pick out most of the landmarks passed on the trail. There'll be lots of tourists at the View Point who would love to hear about your ascent of the spire.

## 52. Mt. Bailey

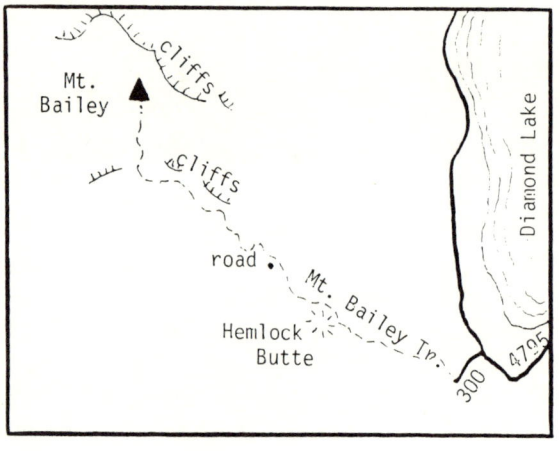

**Length:** 4½ miles
**Water:** None
**Access:** 1
**Season:** June through Oct.
**Difficulty:** 2
**Elevation:** 5300 to 8363 ft.
**Scenic Qual.:** 3
**Use:** Non-motorized only.
   X-C ski

I've sat and stared at Mt. Bailey for hours at a time from across Diamond Lake, either on the beach or in the Lodge. Each evening, the 8400-foot volcanic mass plucks the sun from the sky and gently tucks it away, often with a spectacular display.

Mt. Bailey has always been a favorite of mine. It's not as spectacular looking as neighboring Thielsen but you can't see Thielsen from the Diamond Lake Resort. Bailey is a major, if underrated, Cascade peak with a beautiful and challenging trail to the summit. In winter, Bailey's steep but uniform cinder slopes offer one of the more unusual ski experiences, with mechanized snow cats instead of lifts ferrying skiers up.

Originally named Mt. Baldy because of its domed profile, the peak became Bailey as a result of a cartographer misreading a surveyor's handwriting.

To reach the trailhead, take Crater Lake Highway north from Medford and bear left at Union Creek towards Diamond Lake. Past the summit but before the stop sign where the road from Medford (230), meets Highway 138, look for a road to the left leading to south Diamond Lake. Turn left, then left again on Road 4795. Follow 4795

Mt. Scott    91

around the south end of the lake, past the campgrounds. Just beyond Silent Creek, turn up spur 300. The trailhead is a half-mile up, at a place called Fox Springs. Parking is ample.

It's possible to climb Bailey by taking road 3703 to the left, off Highway 230, three miles before the junction with 138. Follow this road to the far end of spur 300 and walk up spurs 300 and 380, which are closed to traffic. The latter intersects the trail after two miles. You save a half-mile and a fair amount of climbing this way, but miss a spectacular vista at Hemlock Butte.

The Bailey Trail is about the same length and difficulty as the Thielsen Trail except you're more likey to reach the top of Bailey.

The hike begins in a lodgepole pine stand typical of Cascade volcanic regions and works its way into higher elevation Shasta firs and mountain helmocks. Past the vista point at Hemlock Butte and beyond a little wooded flat and spur 380, the route breaks out into the open as it passes treeline clusters of subalpine fir and whitebark pine. The last 1½ miles are above treeline. Watch for unfolding views of Thielsen, the Crater Lake rim, the Rogue-Umpqua Divide, the Rogue Valley, and Bailey's dizzying avalanche bowl which sweeps down to Diamond Lake.

Things become quite steep the last mile. Be sure to bring water. A thousand feet or so before the summit, look for a small crater about 100 feet across and 50 feet deep. It contains a snowfield which has not melted completely in anyone's memory.

The trail peters out a couple hundred yards from the summit and it's necessary to scramble up a pile of loose rocks to reach the old lookout base capping the tip. It's a marvelous view and one is tempted to wait and see if the next mountains over could possibly put on a sunset as well as Bailey does. Unfortunately, I don't recommend descending in the dark and suggest you resist the urge to linger.

# 53. Mt. Scott
## (Crater Lake National Park)

While not particularly difficult, this little trail offers, in my opinion, the ultimate view of Crater Lake. If Crater Lake is the scenic highlight of southern Oregon, the Mt. Scott Trail is the hiking highlight of Crater Lake.

To reach the trailhead, first get to Crater Lake National Park. Any entrance will do. You should have no problems since half the freeway exits in southern Oregon are marked, "to Crater Lake." From Medford, take Crater Lake Highway north. From Grants Pass, get off I-5 south at the Gold Hill-Crater Lake exit and follow the signs.

At Union Creek, you must decide which entrance you want. The north entrance is closer to the trailhead and the road passes Diamond Lake and Mt. Thielsen. The south entrance takes you to Park Headquarters and Crater Lake Lodge. It then goes ¾'s of the way around the lake (one-way), before arriving at the trailhead.

92    **Mt. Scott**

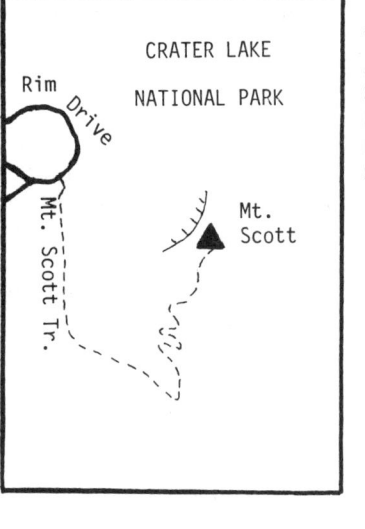

**Length:** 2 miles
**Water:** No
**Access:** 1
**Season:** June through Oct.
**Difficulty:** 2
**Elevation:** 7700 to 8926 ft.
**Scenic Qual.:** 3
**Use:** Hikers only

Crater Lake was one of the original national parks when the National Park Service was created in 1916. Readily available brochures explain how the lake was formed when the summit of an ancient volcano, Mt. Mazama, collapsed on itself, creating a huge, crater-like caldera. Later on, America's deepest lake, at 1900 feet, formed inside it.

I'd guess that 80% of the park's trees are mountain hemlock, with their drooping top leaders. Look also for subalpine fir, Shasta fir and lodgepole pine. The stunted little trees on the high ridges are whitebark pine.

The last time I visited the trailhead, the sign was down and I almost missed it. A second pass would have required driving clear around the lake's one-way road. The Park Service assures me, however, that the trailhead is presently well marked, with lots of parking. To find it, look for the unmistakable rise of Mt. Scott. As you pass the center of its upward sweep, look for the trailhead just beyond the far end of a sharp switchback in the road. If you pass Cloud Cap Road, you've gone too far.

The trail begins to the right of a little hillock between the parking area and the mountain. It stays level for a while, until reaching the backside of the peak. From there, it's a pretty much straight contour up the steep, fairly uniform, sparsely vegetated slope to the lookout on top. There's not much variation until you reach the crest.

At the summit, a long, unbroken sweep of ash and gravel shoots straight down to the parking area. It looks like it could be scrambled down in 10 minutes and presents a tempting return trip alternative. The Park Service would probably advise against this.

Many landmarks may be seen from the Mt. Scott summit but the lake is so overwhelming you'll be hard pressed to notice them. As I said, this is the ultimate view of one of America's ultimate scenic wonders.

Garfield Park    93

# 54. Garfield Park
## (Crater Lake National Park)

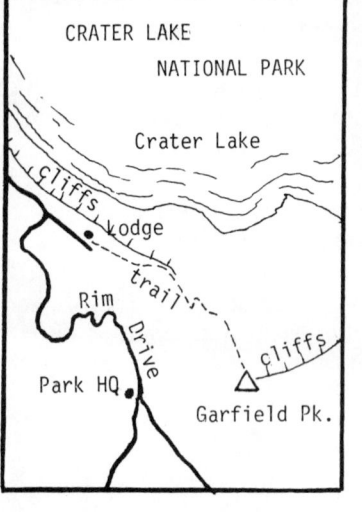

**Length:** 1½ miles
**Water:** No
**Access:** 1
**Season:** June through Oct.
**Difficulty:** 2
**Elevation:** 7076 to 8060 ft.
**Scenic Qual.:** 2
**Use:** Hikers only.

When I mentioned to my four year old daughter that I was writing about Garfield Peak, she got all excited. I never did muster the nerve to tell her the mountain was named for a President, not a cartoon cat.

As you drive up the winding road between Park Headquarters at Crater Lake and the Rim Village, you may catch a glimpse of the Garfield Peak Trail. It can be seen clinging to the side of a mass of tortured, multicolored lava above a spectacular dropoff. My wife usually comments that she's glad she's down here, not up there.

For you "up there" types, the Garfield Peak Trail is one of the most accessible and spectacular within Oregon's only National Park. Shorter and steeper than the Mt. Scott Trail, the Garfield Trail begins, conveniently, behind Crater Lake Lodge in the Rim Village. The summit is part of the actual lake rim. Mt. Scott is 900 feet higher but set back away from the lake.

The National Park service undoubtedly had autos in mind when they designed the park and the best way to view the lake is from the many observation points on the Rim Drive. The Watchman, Cleetwood Cove, and Cloud Cap are of particular interest.

Some outstanding trails adorn the park, however. Most of the longer ones, including the Pacific Crest Trail, follow routes through the sweeping but volcanically pock-marked high country away from the rim. The one-mile Cleetwood Trail is the only route actually leading to the water's edge. The Annie Creek Trail, beginning in the Mazama Campground near the south entrance, is a 1¼ mile loop along a pretty wooded creek. The creek has knifed through a sea of compacted volcanic ash. Sheer ash bluffs tower above both sides of the narrow canyon.

94    Red Blanket Trail

The Garfield Peak Trail is actually part of a longer trail paralleling the road as far as Discovery Point.

To reach the Garfield Peak Trail, take Crater Lake Highway north from Medford until you arrive at Crater Lake. The south entrance is closest to the trail, although the north entrance will suffice. If you haven't been to the park before, do take the Rim Drive.

The steep trail, as noted, is mostly out in the open. After passing high elevation forests of whitebark pine, mountain hemlock and subalpine fir, it soon breaks out onto the crags and bluffs and pretty much stays there. The colorful rock ranges from gray and black to orange, pink and purple. Much of it has that cindery texture typical of extruded lava.

The summit, a huge, flat field with room for 100 people, is 1900 feet above the lake and 1000 feet above the Lodge. All the old favorites can be seen, including Mounts Thielsen, McLoughlin, Shasta and so forth. Look for Devils Peak rising above the Seven Lakes basin immediately south. An observant hiker could probably pick out Mounts Ashland and Grayback in the Siskiyous.

## 55. Red Blanket Trail
### (Sky Lakes Wilderness Area)

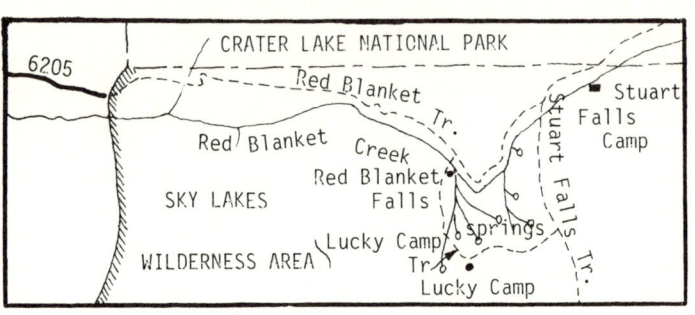

**Length:** 5 miles          **Water:** Fairly gushing
**Access:** 2               **Season:** June throughOct.
**Difficulty:** 2           **Elevation:** 3800 to 5400 ft.
**Scenic Qual.:** 2         **Use:** Non-motorized only.

An alternative entry to the Sky Lakes, away from the crowded Blue Canyon and Seven Lakes areas, may be found via the Red Blanket Trail. The lack of lakes and vistas is compensated by a beautiful creek, green meadows and waterfalls.

Reaching the trailhead is simple. Take Crater Lake Highway north from Medford and follow the signs to the town of Prospect, just off the highway to the right. Take the road out of Prospect towards Butte Falls and turn left a mile later, up Road 6205,

Red Blanket Road. Bear left at the fork 1/3-mile later, where it says "Red Blanket Trail-12 Miles." The road is closed in winter. Follow the rather dusty route to the roomy trailhead area at the end.

The trailhead is located at the Wilderness boundary, very near the southwest corner of Crater Lake National Park. Much of the trail is within a half-mile of the Park boundary.

The trail climbs steadily at first, clinging to the steep, wooded canyon above Red Blanket Creek. The creek rises even more steeply, however, and meets the trail after 1½ miles. After meeting the creek, the trail levels off. The water is peaceful and charming and the walk is very pleasant.

Not quite two miles from the trailhead, the route passes Red Blanket Falls. It's another mile down the Red Blanket Trail to the Stuart Falls Trail and yet another mile to Stuart Falls Camp. Turn left on the Stuart Falls Trail for the falls and camp.

Before the Pacific Crest Trail was built, the main southern Cascades trail was the Oregon Skyline Trail which entered Crater Lake National Park via Stuart Falls. The camp was a popular overnight spot just outside the park boundary.

The area between Stuart and Red Blanket Falls consists of high meadows, abundant wildflowers, many natural springs, much water and much greenery. Trails can be muddy. The lush forest is composed mostly of mountain hemlock, white pine, Shasta fir and Engelmann spruce. It's a good place to observe elk if you're very quiet.

Before returning home, consider taking a short loop trail by continuing south on the Stuart Falls Trail instead of returning to the Red Blanket Trail. It meets the Lucky Camp Trail after a mile. The Lucky Camp Trail runs back into the Red Blanket Trail two miles later. Be sure to turn right past Lucky Camp to return to the Red Blanket Trail. The old Lucky Camp Trail beyond this point has been deactivated.

The entire loop, from the trailhead, around Lucky Camp and back to the trailhead, is nine miles, with an extra two miles to Stuart Falls and back.

# 56. Seven Lakes Basin
## (Sky Lakes Wilderness Area)

Among the many trails penetrating the Sky Lakes Wilderness Area, this is the most popular. People who have hiked it will tell you it contains long, boring stretches, that parts are quite steep, that most of the route is mosquito infested, that the trail is often mobbed and dusty from horses, and that the Seven Lakes area is full of restrictions on where to camp and keep horses.

**96    Seven Lakes Basin**

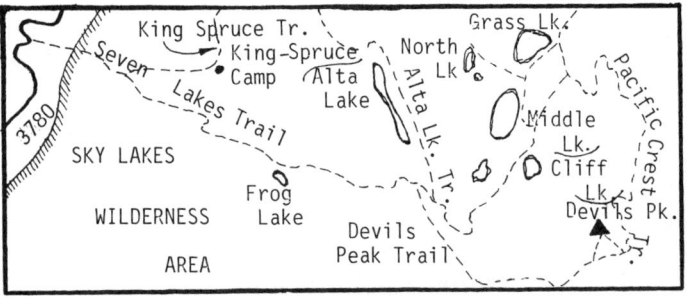

| | |
|---|---|
| **Length:** 6 miles | **Water:** Very little |
| **Access:** 1 | **Season:** June through Oct. |
| **Difficulty:** 2 | **Elevation:** 5300 to 7582 ft. |
| **Scenic Qual.:** 3 | **Use:** Non-motorized only. |
| | X-C ski |

They will also tell you that the Seven Lakes Basin/Devils Peak area is one of the loveliest places in Oregon. Because of the overuse problem, a day-hike is probably the best way to visit, although an early start is recommended as trails are long and there's lots to see. If you do camp, check with the Butte Falls Ranger Station for suggestions as to where. They have certain places set aside for horse pasturing.

Devils Peak is the highest point between Crater Lake and Mt. McLoughlin. At 7600 feet, the steep sided, gray, volcanic outcropping is by far the most prominent peak in the Sky Lakes, although nearby summits are almost as high.

To reach the Seven Lakes trailhead, take Crater Lake Highway north from Medford to the Butte Falls turnoff. Just past Butte Falls, turn left over the bridge towards Prospect. Nine miles down, take a right onto Road 34. Just past the South Fork Campground, the pavement swings left on Road 37 while Road 3780, an all-weather gravel route, proceeds ahead. Follow 3780 through the woods four miles to the roomy, well developed parking area and trailhead.

It's 2½ miles from the trailhead to Frog Lake, the first opening in the dense forest canopy. Camping is prohibited at Frog Lake. A half-mile beyond, the moderately steep, rather dull trail finally emerges at an open saddle above the Seven Lakes Basin. Devils Peak, the Crater Lake rim and several lakes may be viewed from here.

From the saddle, the trail descends sharply, then winds another three miles past at least four lakes before meeting the Pacific Crest Trail. The basin is magnificent, with large meadows, high elevation forests of subalpine fir and mountain hemlock, many bluffs and rocky crags, and a profusion of creeks, marshes and springs. The entire area is a large, north facing glacial cirque between Devils Peak, Jupiter Peak and the saddle.

Cliff Lake is the prettiest body of water, nestled against Devils Peak. The other lakes sit more towards the basin's center, on gentler terrain. Grass Lake is best for camping. Although the lakes are stocked regularly, fishing is only fair.

Blue Canyon Basin    97

The truly energetic might consider climbing Devils Peak. The best route is to follow the Devils Peak Trail which meets the Seven Lakes Trail back up at the saddle. It's a surprisingly level mile from there to the Pacific Crest Trail. Follow the PCT to the left behind Devils Peak. Look for a faint route up the ridge to the left as you approach the pass between Devils Peak and Lee Peak. It's rough going to the summit but not impossible. If you tackle Devils Peak, do it before visiting the basin. You can then continue down the Pacific Crest Trail to the far end of the Seven Lakes Trail and enter the basin from the east.

A side trail to Alta Lake takes off just past the saddle near the beginning of the Devils Peak Trail. It's less than a mile to the long, narrow lake; one of the area's prettiest. A six mile alternate loop returns to the trailhead via Alta Lake. Follow the Alta Lake Trail to the King Spruce Trail and take that back to the Seven Lakes Trail.

However you visit the Sky Lakes, the later the season, the less the crowds and mosquitos. Trails rarely open before mid-June and may not open until July. In fall, the area may become snowed over as early as September or as late as November.

## 57. Blue Canyon Basin
### (Sky Lakes Wilderness Area)

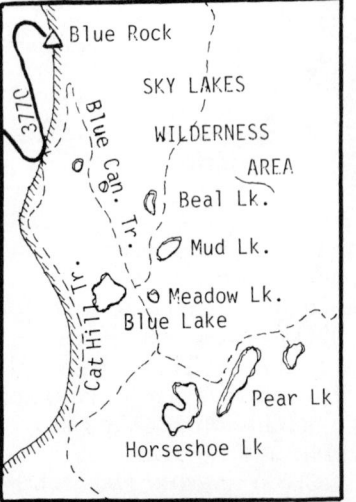

**Length:** 3½ miles
**Water:** Lots
**Access:** 2
**Season:** June through Oct.
**Difficulty:** 2
**Elevation:** 6300 to 5700 ft.
**Scenic Qual.:** 3
**Use:** Non-motorized only

While the Marbles, Siskiyous, and Trinity Alps are a jumble of tortured ridges and canyons, the valleys of the Sky Lakes are broad and gentle. Their volcanic peaks, ranging up to 7400 feet, give an image of elegant

**98    Blue Canyon Basin**

**Seven Lakes Basin - Sky Lakes Wilderness (Ch. 56)**          (USFS Photo)

vastness. The exception, of course, is Mt. McLoughlin, southern anchor of the Sky Lakes Wilderness, a 9500 foot cone dominating the southern third of Oregon.

The Blue Canyon Trail provides the shortest and easiest access to the Sky Lakes. To get there, first find the town of Butte Falls, 15 miles up a clearly marked highway from Crater Lake Highway, north of Medford. A mile or so beyond Butte Falls, another paved road takes off left over a bridge, towards Prospect.

From the Prospect road, take Rancheria Road to the right and stay on it for 15 miles. It becomes Road 32. Road 32 eventually merges with Road 37 and curves sharply to the left. Not long after, a red gravel road, 3770, takes off right. Follow it to the Blue Canyon trailhead. The road system looks very complicated on the map but isn't.

The trailhead is impossible to miss. There are signs everywhere, a fancy parking area and a wooden drift fence. All are courtesy of the Rogue Group Sierra Club.

Before beginning your hike, continue on to the road end at Blue Rock for a panorama of the area and views of Crater Lake, Devils Peak, Smith Rock (not the one near Redmond), and McLoughlin.

Back at the trailhead, signs will try to persuade you to take a loop trail using the Cat Hill Trail one way and the Blue Canyon Trail the other. I concluded that the Cat Hill Trail, which passes no lakes, offers little except extra miles. It affords a great view of the north face of McLoughlin but so does the road. A mile long connecting trail from the Cat Hill Trail meets the Blue Canyon Trail at Meadow Lake.

The Blue Canyon Trail skirts Round Lake after a mile, then two or three smaller lakes. Blue Lake is about two miles down in an impressive, high walled cirque. Meadow Lake is opposite Blue Lake in the middle of a grassy meadow. Between Meadow and Blue Lake, a side trail shoots off northeast, past Mud and Beal Lakes.

Cold Springs Trail    99

A mile or so past Meadow Lake, Horseshoe and Pear Lake are encountered. Both are gentle, shallow giants nestled against headwalls. Island Lake, biggest in the Wilderness, lies 1½ miles beyond Pear Lake. Island Lake is five miles from the Blue Canyon trailhead.

The trail beyond Meadow Lake passes over areas of jumbled rock ripped from the mountainside by glaciers and deposited in mounds called "moraines." Look on the larger boulders for smooth facets and gouges caused by sheets of advancing ice polishing the rock faces. Look also for rocks full of tiny bubbles, as the song goes, formed when gas escaped from the molten lava as it cooled.

Be sure to bring a tree guide. Look for subalpine fir and lodgepole pine at Horseshoe Lake. At Blue Lake, look for western white pine, Shasta fir and mountain hemlock. An alert eye might also spot an occassional Engelmann spruce. All are high elevation species which contrast with the Douglas-fir, ponderosa pine, oak and madrone near Butte Falls.

The Blue Canyon area is exciting and accessible. Unforunately, a lot of people feel this way. In summer, it tends to be mobbed and the endless lines of horses kick up much dust. The road doesn't usually open until mid-June and from then until August, the air is black with mosquitos. September and October, on the other hand are spectacular, highlighted by fall colors around Butte Falls and occassional mountain storms.

## 58. Cold Springs Trail
### (Sky Lakes Wilderness Area)

Okay, so the Cold Springs Trail isn't as scenic as the Seven Lakes or Blue Canyon Trails. And the mosquitos are worse, if possible. But the trail is the most level of all and leads to many large and beautiful lakes. Swimming and picnicing are excellent, although fishing is only fair.

Reaching the trailhead may be a bit difficult as the upper portion of the access road is winding and sometimes muddy early in the year. The last couple miles are rather bumpy. Take Crater Lake Highway north from Medford and turn right on Highway 140 towards Klamath Falls. Forty-one miles later, past Lake of the Woods, a gravel road leading left is called 3651. It's at least 10 miles up 3651 to the small camp and trailhead at Cold Springs.

The trail trails off through woods of mountain hemlock, lodgepole pine and Shasta fir. After almost a mile, at the Wilderness boundary, the South Rock Creek Trail comes in on the right. That's the return route. For now, stay on the Cold Springs Trail.

Its 2½ miles from the trailhead to the Sky Lakes Trail. Follow the latter to the right, then turn left on the Isherwood Loop Trail, returning to the Sky Lakes Trail near Heavenly Lake. Follow the Sky Lakes Trail to the South Rock Creek Trail and return to the trailhead.

**100    Mt. McLoughlin**

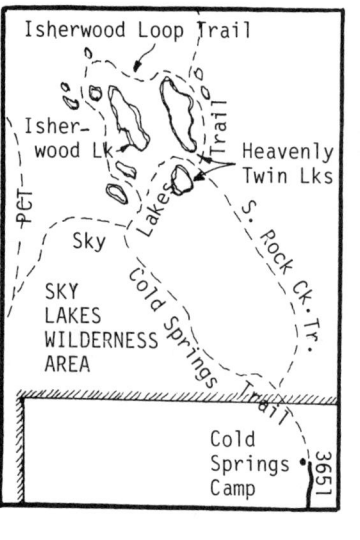

**Length:** 7½ mile loop
**Water:** OK
**Access:** 2
**Season:** June through Oct.
**Difficulty:** 1
**Elevation:** 5800 to 6000 ft.
**Scenic Qual.:** 1
**Use:** Non-motorized only.

This is the Sky Lakes Wilderness Area's largest lake concentration, appropriately called the Sky Lakes Basin. North on the Sky Lakes Trail, it's about three miles to Trapper and Marguerite Lakes, with several smaller lakes in-between. Aside from many lakes and ponds, this part of the Wilderness has little topography, few meadows or vistas and lots of trees. The lakes all occupy the bottoms of a wide basin , lacking the crests and headwalls of the other lake basins. Still, a day in the Sky Lakes is never a waste of time.

## 59. Mt. McLoughlin
### (Sky Lakes Wilderness Area)

The ascent of the southern Oregon's Fujiyama is a major undertaking. Despite the trail's six mile length and steep grades, almost all climbers make it up and down in a day, possibly because the only decent camp sites are at the bottom.

At 9495 feet, McLoughlin is the major summit of the bottom half of Oregon and a landmark second only to Mt. Shasta. It can be seen from as far away as Tannen Mountain, 100 miles distant in southwest Josephine County.

Medford's mountain, while technically a composite volcano composed of ash and lava, is almost entirely one huge cinder cone and is the most perfectly conical of the major Cascades peaks. A huge, colorful basin on the mountain's northwest side has two lava conduits sticking out its middle like giant chimneys. The basin reaches from Fourmile Lake to the summit.

**Mt. McLoughlin** **101**

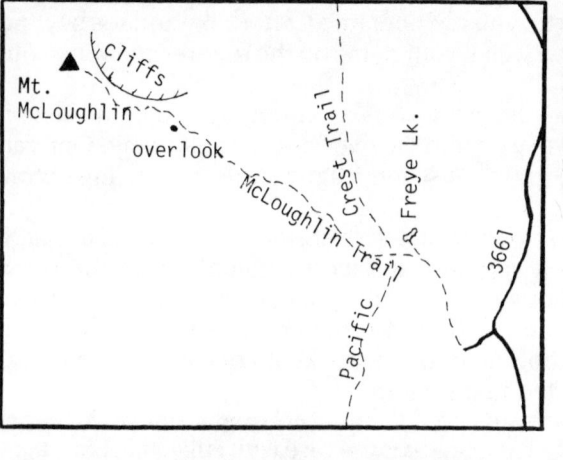

**Length:** 6
**Water:** no
**Access:** 1
**Season:** June through Oct.
**Difficulty:** 3
**Elevation:** 5600 to 9495 ft.
**Scenic Qual.:** 3
**Use:** Non-motorized only.
  X-C ski

To reach the trailhead, take Crater Lake Highway north from Medford. At White City, turn up Highway 140 to Klamath Falls. At mile 37 or so, near Lake of the Woods, Fourmile Lake Road takes off left. The McLoughlin trailhead and parking area are about four miles up and clearly marked.

From the trailhead, the summit appears discouragingly far away. It is. This is no Sunday constitutional so don't worry if you don't make it the first time. Despite the clamoring Boy Scouts who swarm over the rocks on August weekends, many people fail to reach the top. But even if you turn back at the overlook, two miles from the summit, the hike will have been memorable.

As you climb, notice the vegetation changes. The trail begins in Douglas-fir, white fir, sugar pine and western hemlock. It climbs through zones of Shasta fir and lodgepole pine, then subalpine fir and mountain hemlock. The stunted trees on the highest ridges are whitebark pines.

The trail is gentle at first, winding through the woods past a couple side trails including the Pacific Crest Trail. It then begins several miles of steep switchbacks, through less dense woods, with views of Shasta and Lake of the Woods to the south.

Just when you're sure you can go no further, you arrive at the overlook. The overlook is a flat spot on the main ridge at treeline, where you can see north for the first time. Look for the Crater Lake rim, Klamath Lake and Fourmile Lake. The summit still looks far off but this time it isn't.

An enticingly level trail takes off across the loose shale from the overlook. Stay off it. It's a shortcut down and you can't get up it. From the overlook, follow the markers up the rocks. This is where the real work begins. The trail from here scrambles up boulders, skirts narrow ridges and vertical dropoffs, and crosses fields of loose gravel. It may also cross a lingering snow field. The way is steep, often indistinct and entirely over rock with little shade. Altitude may become a factor.

But it's a stunning universe of multihued rock outcroppings, tiny wild-flowers wedged between boulders amid vast desolation; and finally, the summit. The westward panorama doesn't quite extend to the ocean but it

102     Varney Creek Trail

almost does. To the north, you can peer into Crater Lake and see beyond at least to the Three Sisters. Sign your name on the register and watch out for bumblebees.

The hike back down to the overlook takes about 10 minutes, whereas it took well over an hour to get from the overlook to the summit. One can gallop down the loose gravel in seven league strides to the lower trail described earlier.

Be careful on the way down from the overlook as there are a few false trails which can get you very lost. In fact, I wouldn't make the climb without a jacket, matches and a flashlight. Night lows, if you get lost, can be in in the 30's even on the hottest summer days. Also, carry lots of water. A good pair of boots helps on the rocks but one of my ascents was in sneakers and presented no problems.

Every southern Oregonian should climb McLoughlin once. Whether "only a fool would climb it twice," as is the case with Fujiyama, I can't say. I can attest that only a fanatic would climb it three times and I revel in the allegation.

## 60. Varney Creek Trail
### (Mountain Lakes Wilderness Area)

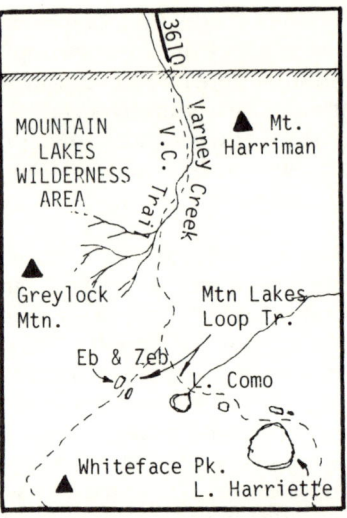

**Length:** 5 miles
**Water:** OK
**Access:** 2
**Season:** June through Oct.
**Difficulty:** 2
**Elevation:** 5520 to 6630 ft.
**Scenic Qual.:** 3
**Use:** Non-morotized only.
   X-C ski

Klamath County's Mountain Lakes Wilderness Area occupies one perfectly square township of six miles by six miles. The square was designated to protect one of the more remarkable formations in the southern Cascades. To get a good look at it before starting up the trail, drive past

## Varney Creek Trail    103

the trailhead into the Klamath basin and watch to the right. You will see a massive wall rising 3000 feet out of a flat, irrigated pasture. The structure is crowned by a ring of jagged, gray peaks surrounding a secluded basin.

The highway view offers an excellent perspective on how the basin came into existence. Like Crater Lake, the area is a volcano whose summit caved in on itself, creating what geologist call a caldera or bowl. There are numerous creek outlets, however. Seven peaks, all between 7700 and 8200 feet, form an obvious ring.

Superimposed on the volcanic history is the area's glacial past. The ice sheets are now gone but most of the lakes rest in glacial cirques and it was glaciers which breached the sides of the caldera, preventing the formation of another Crater Lake. I expect erosion will also breach the wall around Crater Lake within the next half-million years. I only hope it let the water out a little at a time.

The Varney Creek Trail offers the best opportunity to visit the Mountain Lakes basin. To reach the trailhead, take Crater Lake Highway north from Medford and turn right on Highway 140 towards Klamath Falls. A few miles past Lake of the Woods, a green road sign points to the right, up Road 3637, to the Varney Creek Trail. Follow 3637 to 3664. Turn left on 3664 and follow it to the trailhead. This is a new route, not shown on the Rogue River National Forest map. The trailhead is roomy and well developed.

It's 4½ miles of moderate uphill hiking along the creek and through the woods before you get anywhere. After three miles, the trail leaves the creek, passes over a gentle rise, and the basin begins to close around you. Near Eb and Zeb Lakes, life becomes more intersting as you enter a land of lakes, cliffs, lingering snowfields and subalpine forests. Here the Varney Creek Trail ends and the 10½ mile Mountain Lakes Loop begins. Follow it left to Lakes Como and Harriette. Eb and Zeb are less than a half-mile to the right if you wish to check them out also.

Beautiful Lake Como, nestled at the foot of a headwall, is only a half-mile from the junction. Lake Harriette lies 1½ miles beyond Lake Como. Harriette is the area's largest lake, also occupying a glacial cirque surrounded by cliffs and rock falls. The trek into Lake Harriette is short but quite steep. Two miles beyond Lake Harriette, the loop trail takes you to the top of the bluffs above the lake.

The whole experience of lakes, sheer rock faces and wilderness is enhanced by the fact that the cultivated fields of the Klamath basin are never far away and often are visible. It's like a secret childhood hideout wher one can sit in peace and observe the march of civilization without civilization knowing about it.

104    Pilot Rock

# 61. Pilot Rock

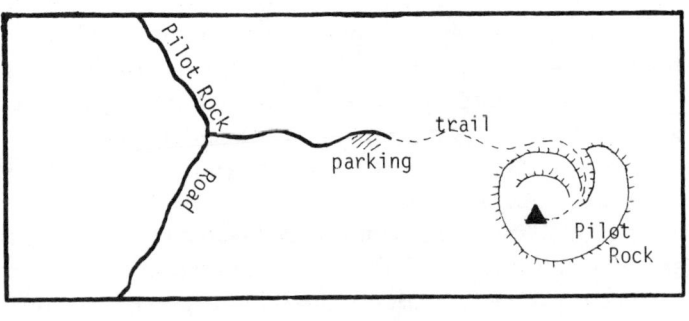

| | |
|---|---|
| **Length:** 1½ miles | **Water:** No |
| **Access:** 2 | **Season:** May thru Nov. |
| **Difficulty:** 3 | **Elevation:** 5500 to 5900 ft. |
| **Scenic Qual.:** 2 | **Use:** Hikers only. |

The sentinel guarding Oregon's border against invaders from the south has long been a landmark to pioneers. Hence its name. Visible for miles from the south and east, it is the first Oregon landmark people notice as they head up I-5.

The rock is an immense volcanic plug, a cylindrical tower of lava remnant of an old volcano. There are other such plugs in southern Oregon. Rabbit Ears in the Rogue-Umpqua Divide comes to mind. Pilot Rock is 500 feet in diameter and 400 feet high. From a distance, its sides appear perfectly perpendicular and the structure seems uniformly round and insurmountable without climbing gear. This is not the case, although the hike up is strenuous.

> The monument stands amid an area of rolling, occassionally brushy hills immediately west of Mt. Ashland and Siskiyou Summit. To get to it, take I-5 south from Ashland and get off at the Mt. Ashland exit. After leaving the freeway, the Mt. Ashland Road takes off to the right after a half-mile. If you go straight instead of turning towards Mt. Ashland, the road crosses the freeway, goes over a pass and returns to the freeway in California.
>
> Just before the pass, a dirt road to the left bears a BLM sign denoting Pilot Rock Road. Follow it towards Pilot Rock. The closeup views are worth the drive. Turn right at the gravel pit and left at the next fork until you find yourself in a wooded area a half-mile from the base. When the road looks too steep and rutted to safely drive, park and walk.

The hike to the base is extremely steep, aggravated by much dirt bike activity. The compacted soil is very slick. As you approach the bottom of the main overhang, the trail, which is very indistinct and braided, trends along the base on the north side.

Shortly, you will discover a huge talus slope emerging from a little canyon, forming a natural entry into the fortress. The talus is made of loose rock at a slope of 70 percent. It's a grueling climb but not very far.

Whitney Falls 105

You will eventually find yourself in a tiny notch, perhaps six feet wide (one foot wide at the bottom), with a rock overhang at about eye level. If you're very agile, this should pose no barrier. If not, climb over it as best you can. A leg up from a friend may help.

Above the overhang, the route emerges into a tiny basin. From there, I'll let you pick your own way to the top. You shouldn't have much difficulty. It's steep in spots and you'll find yourself using both hands and feet to make your way up. But you certainly won't need climbing gear.

The summit is remarkable for its profusion of survey markers, the view of the Shasta Valley and the exhileration of a successful outing.

## 62. Whitney Falls
### (Mt. Shasta Wilderness Area)

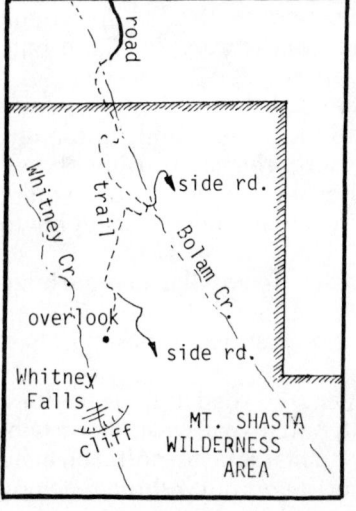

**Length:** 1½ miles
**Water:** No
**Access:** 2
**Season:** June through Oct.
**Difficulty:** 1
**Elevation:** 5600 to 6200 ft.
**Scenic Qual.:** 3
**Use:** Non-motorized only.
  X-C ski

As you head south on I-5 towards Mt. Shasta, you might notice two immense white gashes on the mountain's flank. They're well up the mountain rise—maybe a third of the way—but in the trees just below where the really steep slopes zoom to the summit. The gashes are two mighty river gorges cut through loose ash. The one on the right, class, is the objective of today's hike.

This is the only trail into the new Mount Shasta Wilderness from the north. The trail would appear to have everything: It's dramatic, easy to reach and an easy hike. Shasta-Trinity National Forest plans some development and trail realignment but wishes hikers to be aware that at present, routes are poorly marked and the trails are actually old logging roads which mostly don't go anywhere.

## 106    Whitney Falls

To find the trailhead, take I-5 south to Weed, California, then head out the road to Klamath Falls. After eight or 10 miles, the road passes a formation on the left called Haystack Butte. It looks exactly like a haystack and has a gravel pit at its base. Two or three miles prior, the highway crosses Whitney Creek and an alert driver might catch a brief glimpse of Whitney Falls.

The road to the trailhead is the next right after Haystack Butte. If you arrive at a major intersection with a paved road leading left to Grenada, you've passed the turnoff. A sign at the beginning of the narrow, dirt access road warns that the route isn't maintained or recommended for vehicular traffic. This is nonsense. The road traverses an area underlain by compacted gravel, a perfect road surface. Stay off it during storms, however. It's two miles from the highway to the railroad tracks and three more to the trailhead. The way is well marked.

The trailhead boasts a huge bulletin board, ample parking and signs all over the place pointing to the trail. Despite this, it took me 10 minutes to find the trail. A boulder with the words "Mt. Shasta" spray painted on it and an arrow pointing straight up, should be cleaned off. Since the trail doesn't lead to the summit, one can only conclude that the inscription is for the rare individual unfamiliar with the snow capped, glistening giant towering overhead.

The trail lies to the right, across two creek beds. Both were dry when I visited. The trail is an old logging road most of the way. An eighth-mile up, a sign announces the Wilderness boundary.

The next mile mostly follows Bolam Creek. Where it wanders away from the creek, the terrain is brushy with much manzanita and a few pines and white firs sticking up here and there. The vast brushfield used to be a vast forest. The trees were all hauled away over the road you're walking on. Eventually, the road rejoins the creek then curves uphill to the right.

Bolam Creek is named for the Bolam Glacier. Bolam Glacier is the huge ice fall on the side of the main peak, immediately left of Whitney Glacier. Whitney Glacier occupies the valley between Shasta and Shastina, Shasta's major subpeak.

A quarter-mile after leaving Bolam Creek, the road/trail heads for a small draw but veers left before entering it. A sharp eye will notice a faint trail up the draw. I built a small stone cairn to mark the turnoff. The main road continues for another mile or two, then peters out without reaching any major highlights.

The side trail winds briefly through some woods and across a grassy flat. At the far end of the flat, the world suddenly falls away and you find yourself peering 300 feet down into an awesome canyon with walls of loose, sandy ash. They form an immense "V", sloping down to Whitney Creek at 45-degree angles on both sides. Almost entirely lacking in vegetation, the walls undercut the rim at the top. Several large trees with exposed roots will soon be sucked into the chasm.

Far below, the boulder strewn river bed makes a broad meander, then disappears downhill. The canyon head is blocked by a sheer rock face, 200 feet high, over which the falls tumble.

One slight problem: Both falls and creek are likely to be dry, except in spring. But that in no way diminishes the grandeur of the scene. The trail

skirts the canyon rim towards the falls. According to Gary Oye of the Mount Shasta Ranger Distict, it never gets there and the overlook is considered the end of the trail.

A final word: Shasta not ony can create its own weather, it can do so in a hurry. The October day I visited Whitney Falls was sunny and in the high 60's. On the way back, within minutes, it clouded over around the peak, the temperature dropped 20 degrees and a howling wind came up. I was sweaty, in short sleeves and without a jacket; a perfect formula for hypothermia. It could just as suddenly have snowed.

## 63. Black Butte

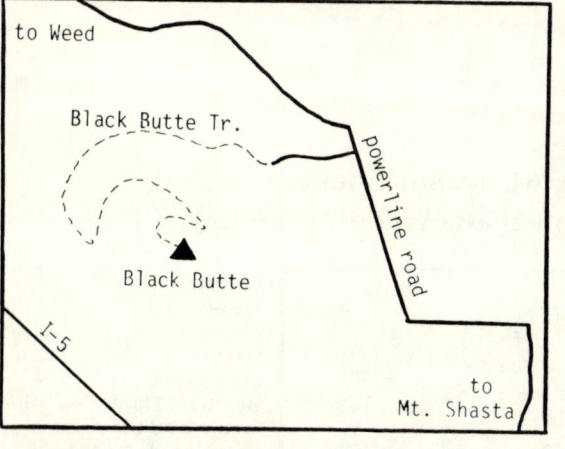

**Length:** 2½ miles
**Water:** No
**Access:** 2
**Season:** May through Nov.
**Difficulty:** 3
**Elevation:** 4400 to 6325 ft.
**Scenic Qual.:** 3
**Use:** Hikers only.

The grim, burnt visage of Black Butte (the one near Mt. Shasta, not the one in the Siskiyou Wilderness), attracts almost as much attention to I-5 travelers in Siskiyou County as does Mt. Shasta itself. In fact, on days when the more famous mountain is fogged in and not visible, tourists can occassionally be seen photographing Black Butte, thinking it to be Shasta.

Black Butte is actually a giant cinder cone on Shasta's west flank, formed when pasty lava and pyroclastic material (pyroclastic means "hot rocks"), shot out of a crack in the unstable volcanic ground. Other smaller cones may be seen along the same fissure radiating from Mt. Shasta. Black Butte's virtually treeless gravel slopes rise 2000 feet, at almost a 45 degree angle, from I-5 at the summit between the towns of Mt. Shasta and Weed.

To reach the trailhead, leave I-5 at Mt. Shasta City and follow the signs to the Everitt Memorial Highway (left off Alma Street). The Everitt Memorial Highway leads to the Bunny Flat trailhead, several campgrounds and the old ski area. About a mile up, a dirt road left (Penney Pines), directs hikers to the trailhead. It's 1½ miles from the Everitt Highway to the intersection with the powerline road. Penney Pines makes a

**108     Mount Shasta**

hard right just off the highway and a 90 degree left a mile later. It's a mile down the powerline road (right), to the half-mile trailhead spur. Parking and turnaround space is limited.

If that's too complicated, you might do as I did the first time. I simply followed roads from the south end of of Weed which seemed to lead to the back of Black Butte. I ended up on the powerline road and located the Black Butte access road immediately after. There were no signs in those days and you could drive almost to the summit if you had the nerve.

The trail offers few surprises as you can see the entire route from the bottom. Very steep and precarious, with loose rock, it reminded me of the evil Mt. Doom in the last chapters of the *Lord of the Rings*. The route is very exposed so carry lots of water if it's hot out.

Along with the base of an old lookout, the summit offers a view that will knock your socks off. Look for Mt. Shasta, obviously, and Mt. Eddy, the Shasta Valley, Weed, Mt. McLoughlin and tourists far below taking your picture.

## 64. Mount Shasta
## (Mount Shasta Wilderness Area)

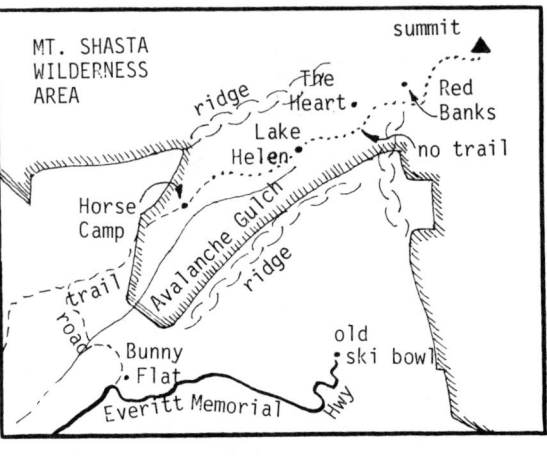

**Length:** 6 miles
**Water:** No
**Access:** 1
**Season:** June through Oct.
**Difficulty:** 4
**Elevation:** 7100 to 14161 ft.
**Scenic Qual.:** 3
**Use:** Non-motorized only. X-C ski

The ascent of Mt. Shasta has been alluded to several times in this book as the "ultimate hike." This is true for two reasons.

First, it is by far the most difficult, although it can be accomplished without technical climbing gear or expertise. It is, however, far more difficult than the climb up Mt. McLoughlin, this book's second hardest climb. But it is far easier than, for example, Mt. Rainier. Climbing Shasta requires "only" stamina, patience, common sense and planning.

## Mount Shasta   109

Second, Shasta is America's most beautiful mountain. Since this is only my opinion, I offer no supporting data. On the other hand, when I once flew from San Francisco to Michigan, Shasta popped into view immediately after takeoff. Located 300 miles north of the airport, the solitary mountain remained visible almost to Utah. That's quite a landmark. Whether the climb qualifies as a day-hike is debatable. The ascent takes about nine hours, the descent three, and you're likely to be utterly exhausted at the end and in no mood for a long drive home. Also, unless you go in October, you'll be hiking in snow a good portion of the route. This is best done in morning when the crust is firm. Most climbers spend the night either at Mt. Shasta City, Horse Camp or Lake Helen. Should you attempt it all in a day from Bunny Flat, plan on hitting the trail by 3:00 A.M. Many hikers carry skis or snow shoes for a fast return trip.

There are dozens of dos and don'ts associated with the Shasta climb, most of which haven't been a factor on other hikes described here: Do climb with someone who's done it before and knows the route. Bring an ice axe and crampons and know how to use them. Know something about snow survival, altitude sickness and hypothermia. Bring at least two quarts of water. Watch for falling rocks, avalanches, and hidden crevaces. Spend a month working out before attempting the climb (jogging and step-ups are good, as are practice climbs up lesser peaks). Bring proper clothing and avoid exposure. Be aware that the mountain creates its own weather and a calm, sunny day can turn into a blizzard within minutes. Bring moleskin, sun glasses, lip balm, lunch, first aid, etc. Do not bring carbonated beverages which may explode in the thin air. Read carefully the Shasta-Trinity National Forest's "Mt. Shasta Climbers Guide." Register at the Mt. Shasta City Police Department before starting out. Don't litter. Etc., etc.

To reach the trailhead, take I-5 south to the cental Mount Shasta City exit. Proceed through town to the Everitt Memorial Highway, which leads to the old ski bowl. The Bunny Flat trailhead is at mile 11.9. Park and hike up the old logging road a mile until you reach a rain guage tower. From there, head north until you reach a trail and follow it to the right 1½ miles through the woods, to the stone shelter at Horse Camp. This is relatively easy going through the heart of Shasta fir country and not a bad trek in its own right. The Sierra Club, which maintains Horse Camp, prefers you spend the night inside only in an emergency. You should find water there.

Alternative to the Bunny Flat route is the steeper but shorter ski bowl route, entirely above tree line. Starting at the ski bowl, it follows the old lift tower line past Green Butte to the ridge, then contours around to Lake Helen where it picks up the route from Horse Camp.

Horse Camp sits at treeline in the bottom of Avalanche Gulch, a long, steep, usually snow filled basin. The trail peters out shortly past Horse Camp. In late summer, when snow is absent, the route is annoying and dusty, over loose scree and rubble. If you're not sure which way to go, follow the dozens of other hikers ahead of you.

110    Marble Valley

At the top of Avalanche Gulch, 3500 feet above Bunny Flat, you'll come to Lake Helen, a large, open depression filled with snow and climbers. There is rarely water in Lake Helen. You're now about 2/3's of the way up, although time-wise, you're only 1/3 of the way up. Elevationally, you're half-way up.

From Lake Helen, head up the steep snowfield towards Thumb rock and the Red Banks, staying to the right of a prominent outcropping in the snow called "The Heart." This is the most arduous pat of the ascent, gaining 2000 feet elevation at a 35% grade.

The Red Banks, a brilliant red escarpment just below the summit, is one of the peak's more interesting formations. In mid-summer or later, they're quite visible from the freeway. Experts recommend ascending to the right and going over the top of the Red Banks. The climb up is difficult, especially at that altitude, but it's safer than the route along the base. Falling rocks are frequent down there. I'd be especially wary of the low route if there's a snow cornice on top of the banks. If there's no snow at all above the banks, the low route may be easier, however.

The top of the Red Banks is slow going but he slope is gentle and you'll soon reach the 14,000-foot summit plateau, a fascinating little flat with sulphur fumeroles. While the fumeroles' warmth once saved John Muir's life during a blizzard, the fumes can irritate your skin and corrode metal. Keep cameras away.

The actual summit is atop a large cinder cone above the summit plateau. It's a quick scramble up loose rock to the top of the world. If the weather is favorable, you're in for the view of your life. You should be able to see not only the Shasta and Klamath basins but the Sacramento Valley and (sometimes, if you have really sharp eyes), the ocean. Look for Lassen, Castle Crags, Mts. Eddy and McLoughlin and so on.

A friend once spent the night on the summit plateau. He reported that the shadow of the mountain moving across the valley as the sun set was one of the great experiences of his life. In the morning, his tent and gear were decorated with horizontal icicles.

# 65.  Marble Valley
## (Marble Mountain Wildeness Area)

Three "ultimate hikes" are described in this book. They are the hike up the Rogue Canyon, the Mt. Shasta climb and the Marble Valley Trail. The latter offers the ultimate journey into the glacial valleys of the Klamath Mountain system. The Marble Valley may be the most beautiful place I've ever been.

A word of caution. The trails I'm about to describe are the most popular in the Mable Mountains. If you visit on a July afternoon, be prepared for

**Marble Valley    111**

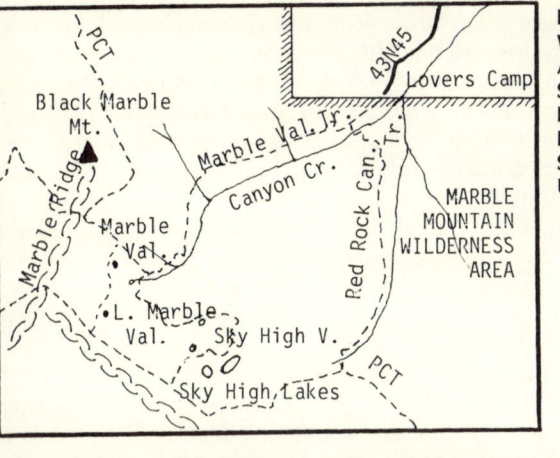

**Length:** 5 miles
**Water:** OK
**Access:** 2
**Season:** June through Oct.
**Difficulty:** 1
**Elevation:** 4300 to 6000 ft.
**Scenic Qual.:** 3
**Use:** Non-motorized only.
  X-C ski

an endless procession of horses, pack animals, Boy Scouts, etc. They can raise much dust. The 15 year old Wilderness Permit system has recently been discontinued.

I've had excellent luck visiting popular places like the Marble Valley in September and October. It's cooler and there are fewer mosquitos or people. But check the weather forecast before leaving and know what time it gets dark.

The Lovers Camp trailhead is easy to find. Take I-5 south to Yreka, get off at the third Yreka exit and proceed to Fort Jones. Turn right on the Scott River Road at Fort Jones by the Sentry Market. Cross the Scott River at Indian Scotty Campground and follow the signs to Lovers Camp. There's a large parking area and horse corral there.

The trail follows a narrow canyon with many side creeks and open meadows. The main stream, appropriately, is called Canyon Creek. The trail's ascent is gradual, with few steep grades and many level stretches.

You'll want to linger in Marble Valley. There are side trails everywhere so bring a map and so some exploring. The valley itself is a little wooded flat but immediately west rises a thousand-foot thick band of white marble called the Marble Rim or simply Marble Mountain. Kings Castle, three miles north, is also sometimes called Marble Mountain. The overlay of black schist capping the north end of the Marble Rim is named Black Marble Mountain.

The Marble Valley side of the rim is a gently sloping expanse. The other side has been deeply cut into a series of steep walled glacial cirques above Elk Creek. Try to get a look at both sides.

Little Marble Valley is even prettier than Marble Valley. Go straight a quarter-mile instead of following the Sky High Lakes Trail. Little Marble Valley has a floor and two sides of white marble. Wildflowers sprout prousely between cracks in the white tile of the valley floor. Geologically, this is a karst area with many sink holes where hollowed out marble has collapsed.

You might wish to continue on to the high trail, which follows the ridge at the south end of Little Marble Valley. From there you should be able to

**112    Paradise Lake**

see not only both sides of the Marble Rim and the major peaks of the Marbles but the Trinity Alps and Mount Shasta.

A final word about the Marble Rim. Marble tends to dissolve into caves and the National Speleological Society's Portland Grotto has mapped over 50 caves within the rim, all containing stalactites and other cave formations. One cave is considerably larger than the one at Oregon Caves National Monument.

Most of the openings are vertical drops and extremely dangerous. Also, the dripstone formations inside are exceedingly fragile and take hundreds of thousands of years to form. The Forest Serice and Speleological Society prefers that only serious cavers visit these sites. For more information, contact the Portland Grotto.

After all that, the Sky High Valley may sound anti-climatic but it isn't. Of the hundreds of glacial cirque lakes in the Siskiyous, Marbles, Trinity Alps, and Cascades, these may be the prettiest. Nestled at the foot of a soaring headwall and surrounded by meadow, the phrase "emerald necklace" comes to mind in describing the two main lakes and several ponds. It's 1½ miles to Sky High from Marble Valley. Lots of trout await catching in the six and 12 acre lakes but many fishermen vie for them.

To return to your car, either double back or loop around to Red Rock Valley which also emerges at Lovers Camp. It's five miles back via that route. Take the Sky High Lakes Trail up to the ridgetop, hang a left on the trail there and follow the signs. Red Rock Valley is a serpentine-type formation with orange cliffs rising above a meadow lined creek.

## 66. Paradise Lake
### (Marble Mountain Wilderness Area)

At 7400 feet, Kings Castle mountain is not the highest peak in the Mountain Wilderness Area. But it is one of the most significant. In fact, it used to be called Marble Mountain and the wilderness was named for it. I guess somebody decided that the "Marble" designation was overused. Kings Castle is a perfectly appropriate name for a magnificent slice of scenery.

Three routes lead to Kings Castle and to Paradise Lake at its eastern base. The Pacific Crest Trail, from the Klamath River or one of the Grider Ridge logging roads, is a major undertaking. You can also come up the old Kelsey Creek Trail from Bridge Flat on the Scott River. The recommended route, however, is up the new two mile trail off Canyon Creek Road.

To reach Canyon Creek Road, take I-5 south to the third Yreka exit and follow Route 3 to Fort Jones. Turn right on the Scott River Road at Fort Jones and follow it to Indian Scotty Campground. Cross the bridge and follow Canyon Creek Road past the Lovers Camp turnoff to the Paradise Lake trailhead. Signs are excellent and the road is beautiful, if steep and winding. Look for good views into the wilderness amid much logging.

Paradise Lake    113

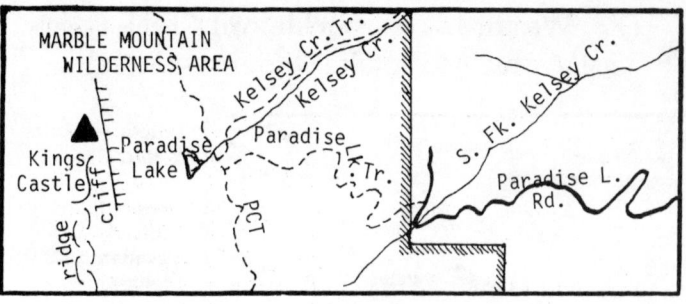

**Length:** 2 miles
**Access:** 2
**Difficulty:** 2
**Scenic Qual.:** 3

**Water:** OK
**Season:** June through Oct.
**Elevation:** 5100 to 6200 ft.
**Use:** Non-motorized only.

A quarter-mile before the trailhead, the road crosses the South Fork of Kelsey Creek where you may wish to park if the water is high. Just before the creek, Kings Castle appears briefly at the head of a canyon. It's easy to understand why this immense, square block of white marble evoked castle images.

The steep trail can be negotiated in an hour or two. It is very popular and not for questers after solitude in mid-summer. But you won't be disappointed. After switching back and forth up a wooded ridge, the route opens into a large, meadowed basin. The shallow, 5 acre Paradise Lake adorns its center.

The lake does have one deep spot, where it nestles against the white face of Kings Castle. Fishing is fair, they tell me, but camping is wonderful. If you enjoy rock climbing, pick your way to the top of Kings Castle for a panorama of the surrounding area including the sheer, glacially cut west face of the Marble Rim.

The Pacific Crest Trail crosses the Paradise Lake Trail just before the lake. The Kelsey Creek Trail peels off the PCT just north of the Paradise Lake Trail. An alternative to doubling back down the Paradise Lake Trail would be to leave a car at the bottom of the Kelsey Creek Trail and return that way. It's seven miles from Paradise Lake to the Kelsey Creek Guard Station, through meadows and rocky ledges, past Maple Falls, then down a beautiful wilderness creek set in a steep sided canyon. The total drop is 3000 feet.

The Kelsey Creek Trail has some historical significance. Built in the 1850's during the gold rush by Chinese labor, it was a military route between Fort Jones and Crescent City. Fort Jones, of course, was then an actual fort. The trail was meticulously constucted and some of the careful stone fill is still in place.

## 67. Wright Lakes/Shackleford Creek Lakes
(Marble Mountain Wilderness Area)

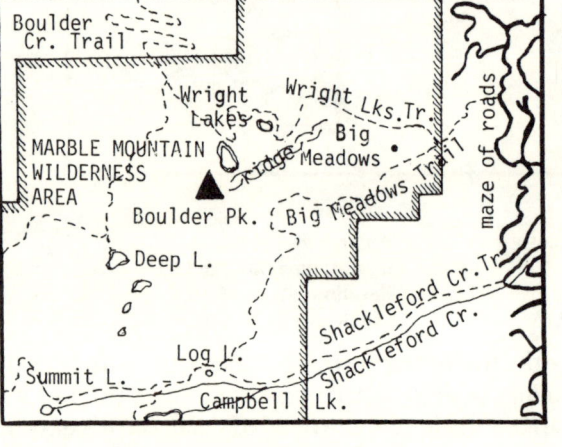

**Length:** 3½ miles
**Water:** OK
**Access:** 3
**Season:** June through Oct.
**Difficulty:** 2
**Elevation:** 5800 to 7400 ft.
**Scenic Qual.:** 3
**Use:** Non-motorized only.

Because of access problems, I shouldn't recommend the Wright Lakes. But I couldn't bring myself to leave them out. Here are the two highest lakes, sitting just below the highest peak, in the entire Marble Mountain Wilderness. The trail is neither too steep nor too long and the lakes are exquisite.

Finding the trailhead, or what's left of it, or its current location, is another matter. Begin by taking I-5 south to Yreka, getting off at the third Yreka exit and proceeding to the Scott Valley town of Greenview, past Fort Jones on Route 3. Turn right, through downtown Greenview, towards Quartz Valley. The orange, boat shaped flank of Boulder Peak, the Marbles' highest at 8300 feet, can be seen overhead with green meadows at its base above the forest.

Eventually, you'll pass a prominent sign directing you to Shackleford Creek Road and the Shackleford Creek Trail. Begin looking a mile or so beyond for Big Meadows Road. There's where we run into trouble. The route to the trailhead runs through an impossible maze of criss-crossing logging roads, some with very bad spots and most on private property. There are no signs and in the past couple years, the trailhead has been obliterated, moved and its access road gated. It's currently ungated, if unmarked, amid much logging activity.

I suggest you inquire at the Scott River Ranger District office in Fort Jones for specific directions. If you still can't find the trailhead, take the Shackleford Creek Trail instead. It's a little longer (5½ miles), and not as breathtaking but definately recommended.

For Shackleford Creek, simply follow the signs to the trailhead. The trail is reasonably level, hugs the creek and stays mostly down in the trees. Just before tiny Log Lake, a side trail takes off left to Wright Lakes. The side trail is faint and the Wright Lakes are eight miles distant.

A mile beyond Log Lake, up Shackleford Creek, 33 acre Campbell Lake occupies a wooded flat. Nearby Cliff Lake, more scenic but a steep climb, is even larger at 52 acres. Summit Lake and the unstocked Jewel Lake are also in the vicinity.

Should you succeed in locating the Big Meadows trailhead, you'll find it ascending fairly gradually up to the ridge, through Big Meadows, then descending steeply into the glacial cirque on the north side of Boulder Peak. Big Meadows is an expanse of creeks, marshy grass, alder and willow thickets, wildflowers and cows. Be sure to turn right on the side trail a mile from the trailhead or you'll end up at Campbell Lake. Several lakes, including Campbell, can be seen from Big Meadows.

It's also possible to reach the Wright Lakes from the road to the Lovers Camp trailhead (see the Mable Valley Chapter). Turn off Canyon Creek Road onto Boulder Creek Road, follow it as far as you can and start walking. The trail is only 4½ miles long but is supposed to be among the steepest and worst in the entire world.

Your day at the 26 acres Lower Wright Lake or the 7 acres Upper Wright Lake may be spent in several ways. You can fish for brook or rainbow trout. You can climb Boulder Peak by hiking back to the ridge. Swimming is possible if you're thick skinned and cold blooded. Or you can simply sit in awe and admiration. Never be afraid to do the latter.

# 68. Paynes Lake
## (Russian Wilderness Area)

If you're unable to locate the nearby Duck Lake trailhead, or even if you are able to, you might try Paynes Lake as an alternative. There's only one lake but it's prettier than any in the Duck Lake area. The trail is a payne, though.

Paynes Lake lies within the new Russian Wilderness Area in an extremely rugged little range separating the Marble Mountains from the Trinity Alps. Before the Wilderness was created, it was known only to local fishermen.

To reach the trailhead, take I-5 south to the third Yreka exit. Proceed past the Scott Valley towns of Fort Jones and Etna to French Creek. Follow French Creek Road to the end where a sign points left to Duck Lake and right to Paynes Lake. Turn right, obviously. It's two miles down the gravel road to the Paynes Lake trailhead, through much timber and across a couple of fast flowing, steep walled creeks. The trailhead is roomy and well marked in the middle of a recent logging partial cut. Skid trails criss-cross the trail's first quarter-mile.

The trail follows a thinly soiled, sparsely wooded granite ridge between two deep valleys. Look for Brewer spruce. Several brush species also adorn the route, including the most northerly evergreen chinkapin I've seen.

**116    Duck/Eaton Lakes**

**Length:** 2 miles
**Water:** No
**Access:** 2
**Season:** June through Oct.
**Difficulty:** 3
**Elevation:** 4400 to 6540 ft.
**Scenic Qual.:** 3
**Use:** Non-motorized only

While the nearly vertical climb to the lake may seem interminable, the trail eventually enters the glacial cirque containing Paynes Lake. As at Duck and Eaton Lake, timber is sparse and the lake occupies a rocky ledge surrounded by cliffs. The 16 acre lake is quite deep and fishing is excellent.

The Pacific Crest Trail crosses the Paynes Lake Trail just below the lake. The seven mile walk along the PCT from Etna Summit to Paynes Lake is fairly level, passes several other lakes and might be considered as an alternate route. Steeper even than the Paynes Lake Trail is the short route to Lower and Upper Albers Lake, a quarter-mile above Paynes Lake. These tiny pools are stocked with trout and are quite beautiful if you have the lung capacity to negotiate the trail. Fishing is better at Paynes Lake.

# 69. Duck/Eaton Lakes
## (Russian Wilderness Area)
### See **Paynes Lake (Ch. 68)** for Map.

**Length:** 3 miles
**Access:** 2
**Difficulty:** 2
**Scenic Qual.:** 3

**Water:** OK
**Season:** June through Oct.
**Elevation:** 4800 to 6700 ft.
**Use:** Non-motorized only.
X-C ski

The mountains containing Duck and Eaton Lakes are a small but formidable cluster between the Marble Mountains and Trinity Alps. The range has a different name on every map. Rising between California's Salmon and Scott Rivers, they were most commonly called the Salmon-

Scott Mountains. The new wilderness area, named for the group's highest summit (8196 feet), suggests as good a name as any. I'm pleased to call them the Russian Mountains.

In 1970, the Russian Mountains were little known and seldom visited except by local fishermen. Back then, there were no trailhead markings at the Duck Lake Trail. I found it by following a maze of logging roads, parking where the highest road was washed out at Duck Lake Creek, and beating the bushes up and down the road.

Today, recent logging and road construction has obliterated much of the lower trail. When I attempted to visit in 1986, the access road was gated three miles from the trailhead. I'm told the gate will be removed soon and that the trailhead is well marked.

To reach the trailhead, take I-5 south to the third Yreka exit and follow the signs to Scott Valley and Etna (Highway 3). A few miles past Etna, turn right on French Creek Road. Follow it until you come to a sign pointing to Paynes Lake (right) and Duck Lake (left). A mile or less left, you'll find an intersection with roads leading in all directions. The hard right up the hill is the now gated road to the Duck Lake trailhead.

The Forest Service plans to extend the trail a mile downhill and locate the trailhead near the "Duck Lake-Paynes Lake" sign. That will make it a four mile trek to Duck Lake. It's presently three and used to be two as some roads were closed off when the Wilderness Area was created. Inquire at the Scott River Ranger District in Fort Jones for the latest information. Or visit Paynes Lake instead.

The trail begins steeply on slopes densely forested with Douglas-fir and sugar pine. The ascent isn't as bad as on the Paynes Lake Trail, however. The lakes occupy a series of granite cirques with towering cliffs. The basins are small and steep and the lakes sit on rock terraces with little meadow and only scattered timber. The main summit, Eaton Peak, can be viewed from French Creek Road as well as from the lakes.

The two Eaton Lakes are up a well marked, ¾-mile side trail, a third of the way to Duck Lake. This side trail is very steep and rocky. Eaton Lake occupies 13 acres, with a much smaller upper lake immediately beyond. Duck Lake, at 26 acres, is one of the area's biggest. Little Duck Lake lies a fairly level ¾-mile beyond Duck Lake. The turnoff is just before Duck Lake. All lakes offer excellent brook trout angling.

Paynes, Duck and Eaton Lakes are included in a proposed Forest Service Botanical Area. It will protect a prime area of what botanists call glacial relics, or remnant populations of plants whose natural ranges became distorted during the last ice age.

You won't see them all from the trail but there are 17 conifer species in the vicinity of Duck Lake, including some of the southernmost Brewer spruce and Pacific silver fir. The latter is generally not found south of Crater Lake. Look also for some of the most northern foxtail pines and for extremely rare California populations of subalpine fir and Engelmann spruce.

# 70. Trail Gulch/Long Gulch Lakes
## (Trinity Alps Wilderness Area)

**Length:** 8 mile loop
**Water:** Lots
**Access:** 1
**Season:** June through Oct.
**Difficulty:** 2
**Elevation:** 5400 to 6400 ft.
**Scenic Qual.:** 3
**Use:** Non-motorized only

I used to wonder how two such lovely lakes ended up with such unaesthetic names. Finally, I concluded that the names were meant to discourage the swarms of hiking humanity who converge on places with more poetic names like Emerald and Sapphire Lake. The secret of Trail and Long Gulch Lakes' beauty is now out as both were recently included in the new Trinity Alps Wilderness Area.

The glacial cirque basin surrounding Trail Gulch is the most noticeable among a cluster of cirques which may be viewed from the road summit between Callahan and Cecilville. Hidden Lake, South Fork Lake and Long Gulch Lake occupy nearby cirques.

To reach Trail and Long Gulch's twin trailheads, take I-5 south to the third Yreka exit and proceed through Scott Valley to Callahan. At Callahan, turn right, up the paved road leading to Cecilville, on the South Fork of the Salmon River.

Beyond the road summit, look for a gravel road to the left which runs along the flat below the main road. It winds past both trailheads, located a mile apart, and passes campsites at Carter Meadow and Trail Creek.

It's 3½ miles up Trail Gulch to the 14 acre lake. The route has some steep spots but isn't too bad as it wanders from woods to meadows along the creek. A side trail left, three miles up, leads to the lake. If you continue straight, it's less than a half-mile to the ridgetop. The ridgetop peers into an area much like the Yosemite high country, with glacially polished granite domes. Look for the 9000 foot summit of Mt. Thompson nearby. It's the one with active glaciers on it.

Trail Gulch Lake rests at the base of a high headwall. The lake is surrounded by woods on the downhill side but boasts a large meadow at the creek inlet. For the best swimming, follow the trail past lingering snowfields to the gap between the headwall and the island.

It's a steep 1½ miles up the rock face to the east, across the ridge and back down to the virtually identical, 10 acre Long Gulch Lake. The trail up from the Long Gulch trailhead is shorter than the one up Trail Gulch but steeper and rockier. That's why it is suggested as the way out, not in. Both lakes are popular these days and offer good brook trout fishing.

## 71. Hidden Lake
### (Trinity Alps Wilderness Area)

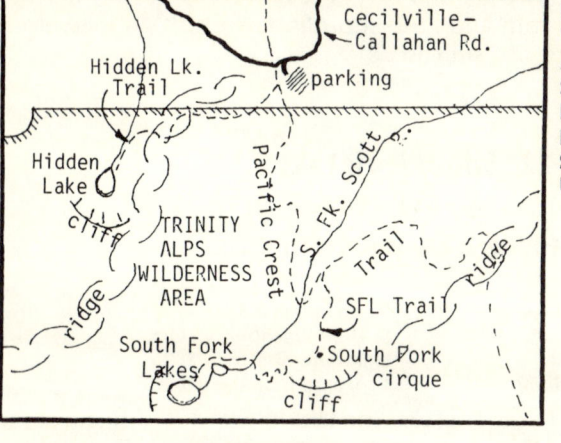

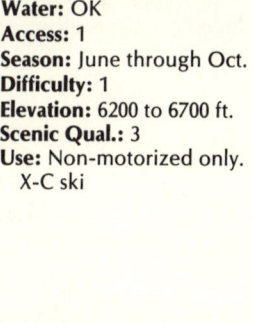

**Length:** 1½ miles
**Water:** OK
**Access:** 1
**Season:** June through Oct.
**Difficulty:** 1
**Elevation:** 6200 to 6700 ft.
**Scenic Qual.:** 3
**Use:** Non-motorized only.
 X-C ski

The objective of my very first hike in southern Oregon or northern California was Hidden Lake. The memorable event occurred in 1970 with my wife, another couple, seven children and a suitcase full of fried chicken.

It was a splendid introduction. The road is paved, the trail is flat and short, the lake is gorgeous and the surrounding scenery is among the most beautiful anywhere. The fishing and swimming are pretty good, also.

To reach this secretive jewel, take I-5 south to the Yreka-Scott Valley exit. Follow Highway 3 through Fort Jones and Etna to the village of Callahan. From there, turn right on the paved Callahan-Cecilville Road.

Approaching the pass between Callahan and Cecilville, a maze of rocky peaks cut by huge glacial cirques appears to the left. This cluster of peaks lies within the Trinity Alps Wilderness Area but belongs to the Scott Mountains. The steep walled cirque basins are far larger than those of the Siskiyous and there are dozens of them. Most obvious are the cirques of the South Fork Lakes and, just beyond the summit, Trail and Long Gulch Lakes. The Hidden Lake cirque is, obviously, less obvious.

There's a little hillock at the pass with a helipad on top and a short dirt road to the left leading to a parking area. Trailheads, sign-in boxes and signs clutter the area. The main trailhead is for the Pacific Crest Trail while only a tiny sign tacked to a tree marks the Hidden Lake Trail.

The route winds through some high elevation woods of Shasta fir and mountain hemlock for a while, then comes out on a brushy ridge. The South Fork of the Scott River lies far below, with the steep granite flanks of the Scott Mountains rising beyond. The maze of cirques described earlier can be seen even more clearly than they could from the road. You'll find yourself taking deep breaths and saying "wow."

120    South Fork Lakes

Finally, the trail reenters the woods and crosses some low, rolling glacial moraines. Then the three acre lake appears gentle and shaded, with the usual cliff rising from the far end. The area near the outlet is relatively flat, with open woods and easy access to the lake. The lake has clear water, a solid bottom and little shoreline brush. It's a marvelous place to eat chicken out of a suitcase.

# 72. South Fork Lakes
## (Trinity Alps Wilderness Area)
### See **Hidden Lake (Ch. 71)** for Map.

| | |
|---|---|
| **Length:** 3 miles | **Water:** Lots |
| **Access:** 1 | **Season:** June through Oct. |
| **Difficulty:** 3 | **Elevation:** 6200 to 6700 ft. |
| **Scenic Qual.:** 3 | **Use:** Non-motorized only |

Both the South Fork Lakes Trail and the Hidden Lake Trail begin at the same point and appear the same length on the map. Since the Hidden Lake Trail is fairly easy and the South Fork Lake Trail follows the Pacific Crest Trail, which avoids steep grades, it is surprising to find that the South Fork Lakes Trail is actually twice as long and far more difficult.

Part of the problem is the Klamath National Forest map. It's been recently down-scaled so some trail configurations may be difficult to interpret. They've also omitted many road numbers. A magnifying glass helps.

To find the two exquisite South Fork (of the Scott River) Lakes, follow the directions in the Hidden Lake chapter. Briefly, take I-5 to Yreka and proceed to the Scott Valley town of Callahan. Take the paved Cecilville-Callahan Road to the summit and park at the trailhead parking area on the left. As you drive, note the towering ridges and glacial cirques.

From the trailhead, follow the Pacific Crest Trail south for 1½ miles. The route affords good views of the surrounding peaks. The trail descends gradually to a creek crossing, amid Shasta fir and western white pine. The creek is actually the South Fork of the Scott. It's a bit muddy and mosquitoey at the crossing. The turnoff to the lakes is just beyond, uphill to the right.

As you approach the trailhead from the highway, an immense glacial cirque looms to the left. This, logically, should contain the lakes. After leaving the PCT, the trail soon enters this cirque and it is found to contain only a meadow surrounded by thousand-foot cliffs. It's quite lovely until it occurs to you that your objective lies in a smaller cirque at the top of the headwall.

Now the fun begins. The really steep push, up rockfalls and cliffs, only lasts a mile but it can be a challenge. I talked to a man with his eight year old daughter before starting up. He warned that the trail was so steep, he was forced to let the daughter rest once.

Caldwell Lakes    121

Amid vertical rock faces on all sides, the trail suddenly disappears over the top into a piney woods on a gentle plateau. The shallow, 3½ acre lower lake soon appears in the middle of a meadow.

It's about five minutes through the woods to the 4½ acre upper lake. You can't miss it, although one could miss the trail to it. The upper lake is nestled at the base of a small cliff in a tiny cirque even more hidden than the one containing Hidden Lake.

It's a long drive from the Rogue Valley and after the tiring hike, you might consider spending the night. Fishing is outstanding, I'm told, and the entire experience is worth the effort. Even if you are forced to rest once. Or even twice.

## 73. Caldwell Lakes

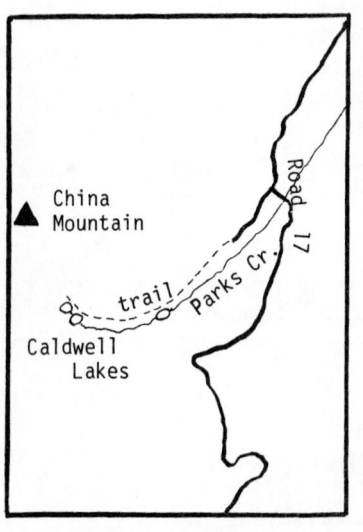

**Length:** 1½ miles
**Water:** Lots
**Access:** 2
**Season:** June through Oct.
**Difficulty:** 2
**Elevation:** 6000 to 7100 ft.
**Scenic Qual.:** 2
**Use:** Any

These three lakes, in the Trinity Divide area between the Trinity and upper Sacramento Rivers, are smaller and shallower than many of the area's other lakes. The two acre pools offer solitude, supurb vistas and fine brook trout fishing.

The trailhead is located 2/3's of the way up the Deadfall Lakes road. Take I-5 south to the Stewart Springs (Edgewood) exit, near the Weed Airport. Make a quick right, then another, then a left up Parks Creek Road towards Stewart Springs. Turn right across the bridge at Stewart Springs. The logging spur leading to the Caldwell Lakes trailhead is clearly marked, five or six miles beyond the bridge. There's ample parking and turnaround space.

The rhododendron and Sadler oak lined trail makes its way up to a little meadow containing the lower lake. Look behind you for an outstanding

**122    Deadfall Lakes/Mt. Eddy**

view of Mt. Shasta framed in a steep walled rock gorge. One of the best photos I ever took of Shasta was from this spot.

The lower lake is shallow and full of logs. The two upper lakes lie a half-mile beyond and are immediately adjacent to one another. In fact, they're more accurately a single hour-glass shaped lake. The charming upper lakes occupy a marshy flat amid an open woods.

I don't believe the setting is a glacial cirque, although a sheer, white rock face rises immediately northwest. The granite monolith looks to me like simply the flank of China Mountain. China Mountain is the second highest peak in the Trinity Divide after Mt. Eddy. Its 8542 foot summit, a mile from the lake, isn't nearly as obvious from a distance as Mt. Eddy. But as you can see, there's more going on at these unassuming little pools than meets the eye.

## 74. Deadfall Lakes/Mt. Eddy

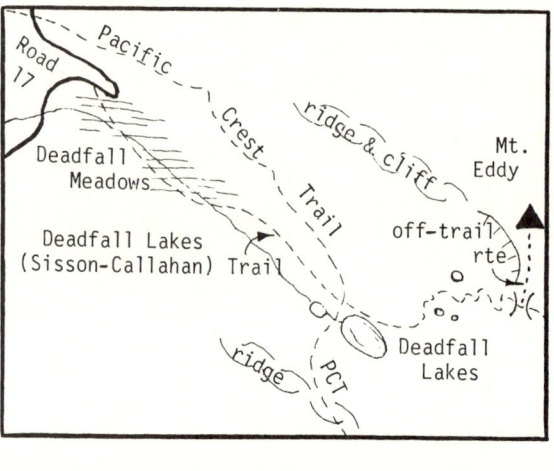

**Length:** 2½ (Lakes),
4 (Eddy)
**Water:** OK
**Access:** 2
**Season:** June through Oct.
**Difficulty:** 1 (Lakes),
3 (Eddy)
**Elevation:** 6400 to 9025 ft.
**Scenic Qual.:** 3
**Use:** Non-motorized only

Motorists heading south past Mt. Shasta may notice a group of snow capped peaks to the right of the freeway. If Shasta weren't to just the left, they would attract much attention. Unfortunately, these other mountains, whose highest point is Mt. Eddy, appear dwarfed beside Shasta's 14,000 foot summit.

At 9025 feet, however, Mt. Eddy is the highest peak in the vast Klamath Mountain system, which includes the Trinity Alps, Marbles and Siskiyous. Eddy is part of a chain called the Trinity Divide, between the Trinity and upper Sacramento Rivers. Its summit is quite accessible, if not a hop and skip through the woods, and its west flank is home to a string of five of the most beautiful lakes anywhere.

**Deadfall Lakes/Mt. Eddy    123**

**Marble Valley - Marble Mtn. Wilderness (Ch. 65)**          (Bernstein Photo)

I've referred to several trails in this book as "among my favorites." This *is* my favorite. It's also my wife's favorite, boasting a challenging climb, lovely lakes, an easy trail and a botanical oddity.

Two trails actually lead to Deadfall Lake. The trailheads are a half-mile apart on Parks Creek Road near Weed, California. To reach them, take I-5 south to the Edgewood-Stewart Springs exit. See the Caldwell Lakes Chapter for details. Continue up Parks Creek Road past the Caldwell Lakes turnoff to the summit. You'll find a spacious parking area at the summit, where the Pacific Crest Trail takes off for Deadfall Lakes.

A half-mile beyond the summit, the road makes a switchback at Deadfall Meadow. There's ample parking on the right and a trailhead sign on the left. The Deadfall Lakes Trail from the meadows is actually the start of the Sisson-Callahan National Recreation Trail.

The Pacific Crest Trail reaches Deadfall Lake in 2½ miles. The route is mostly level, mostly wooded and gouged into a steep mountainside. The lower trail is shorter but moderately steep. The beginning of the lower trail traverses meadow and marsh, with occasional wooded patches. You'll find more wildflowers per square foot along this lower trail than any place I can think of except Hershberger Mountain.

I suggest hiking in on the Pacific Crest Trail and returning via the lower trail. Elect somebody to take the high trail back and drive the car down.

However you go in, you'll eventually reach a crossroads between the PCT and the Sisson-Callahan Trail. To reach the main lake, continue on the PCT, or turn right onto it. For Mt. Eddy and the upper lakes, continue on the Sisson-Callahan Trail or turn left onto it from the PCT. Sisson-

## 124    Deadfall Lakes/Mt. Eddy

Callahan ends after nine miles near Lake Siskiyou. Aside from a brief flirtation with Deadfall Lake and Mt. Eddy, most of its route parallels the North Fork of the Sacramento.

It's a few hundred yards from the trail junction to Lower and Middle Deadfall Lakes. The lower lake is a short scramble right while the middle is a short scramble left. At 25 acres, the middle lake is second in size in the Trinity Divide to Castle Lake. It occupies a large basin with steep grassy slopes and few trees except for some pines and scattered clumps of Shasta fir. Trails lead around the lake to camp sites near both the outlet and inlet. Brook trout fishing is supposed to be pretty good. The lake bottom is solid, if a little rocky, but at 7300 feet elevation, the water tends to be chilly.

If the main lake bores you, which it won't, take Sisson-Callahan to the upper lakes. It's a moderately steep route through open, grassy woods surrounded by orange serpentine rock. Between the middle and upper lakes is a tiny lake with no name. A fifth lake nearby can be seen from Mt. Eddy but not from the trail.

The upper lake is in a small, shallow tarn with clear water and a sandy bottom. Tarns are depressions caused by melting blocks of glacial ice. The shore is level, brush free, and gently shaded by the park-like forest. Of all the natural lakes I've ever visited, this looks the most like a swimming pool.

Above the upper lake, the trail passes a marshy area at the base of a cirque.The headwall rises 1000 feet to the Eddy summit. Beyond this last, colorful meadow, the trail ascends sharply to the ridge.

It's less than a half-mile from the upper lake to the trail crest. In-between, look for stunted little trees with short, stubby needles in closed clusters of five. These are foxtail pines. Foxtail pines are mainly native to high elevation areas of the eastern slope of the southern Sierra, 800 miles away. A few very scattered patches of them have been recorded in the upper reaches of the Trinity Divide and Marbles.

To climb Mt. Eddy, simply follow the ridge left from the trail crest. It's only a half-mile horizontal distance to the summit but much of it crosses loose gravel up an almost 45 degree slope at 9000 feet. Take your time. I rested every few feet the first time while my athletic companion scampered up without missing a step. But he only beat me by 10 minutes.

The summit is wonderful, with an old lookout cabin. Look for the best view of Shasta ever, to the east; the glaciers of Mt. Thompson in the Trinity Alps to the west; the towns of Weed and Mt. Shasta; and the valleys of the Sacramento, Shasta, Scott and Trinity Rivers.

The peak also offers views to the west of the aforementioned 1000-foot headwall and the five Deadfall Lakes. The east face swoops down an avalanche basin. The immense, treeless basin has two glacial cirques cut into its base far below. Dobkins and Durney Lakes may be seen inside the cirques.

## 75. Toad Lake

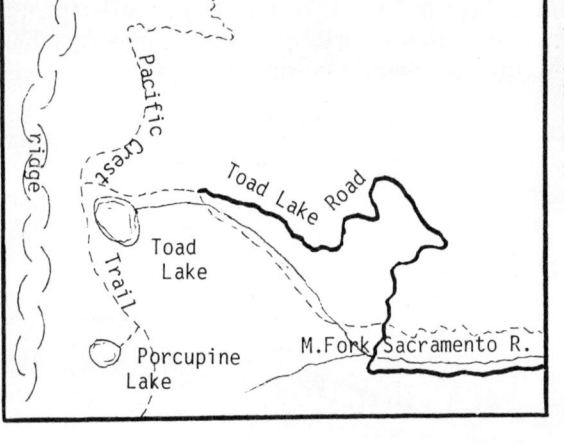

**Length:** 1½ miles
**Water:** Lots
**Access:** 2
**Season:** June through Oct.
**Difficulty:** 1
**Elevation:** 6900 ft.
**Scenic Qual:** 3
**Use:** Any

In the April 16, 1978 edition of *California Living*, I wrote the following: "The chuckhole had been lurking behind a rock, waiting to pounce on the first intruder. Upon spotting my pickup, it leaped out, grabbed a front tire and chucked it in the air, as chuckholes do. Inside, I bumped my head on the ceiling and came down full weight on the accelerator. When I finally regained control, I was inches from a 500 foot dropoff.

"Four creek fordings, six washouts, two patches of axle deep mud, twenty acres of hardpacked snow and fifty rock slides later, I arrived at Toad Lake. It was early May and the 7000 foot high lake was partially frozen over."

I admit to dramatic exaggeration but the quotation does convey an accurate sense of the drive to Toad Lake. The lake itself is a favorite 23 acre fishing spot set high in the crags of the Trinity Divide. The shoreline is level and accessible and the road ends a short half-mile away.

To get there, take I-5 south to Mt. Shasta City. Get off at the central exit but turn right instead of left and follow the signs to Lake Siskiyou, a popular reservoir and resort. Beyond Lake Siskiyou, Road 26 follows the upper Sacramento to its source at Gumboot Lake. The road is mostly paved.

Look for the turnoff to Toad Lake on the right, shortly after Road 26 crosses over to the river's north shore. There should be sign but most of the signs along Road 26 have disappeared. Take a hard left a quarter-mile up the Toad Lake road. After that, simply drive as far as you can, then walk. There's no formal trailhead but you can drive to within a half-mile of the lake.

It's another mile around Toad Lake and up a short but steep and sparsely forested mountainside to Porcupine Lake. This eight acre pool is

**126    Upper Sacramento Lakes**

set in a crater-like depression at the foot of a large rock outcropping. To reach the shore, scramble down the jumble of boulders.

The Pacific Crest Trail crosses the Toad Lake Trail between Toad and Porcupine Lakes. It's about five miles north over the PCT to Deadfall Lake. The route skirts the tops of some fine ridges but Deadfall Lake is another chapter.

## 76. Upper Sacramento Lakes

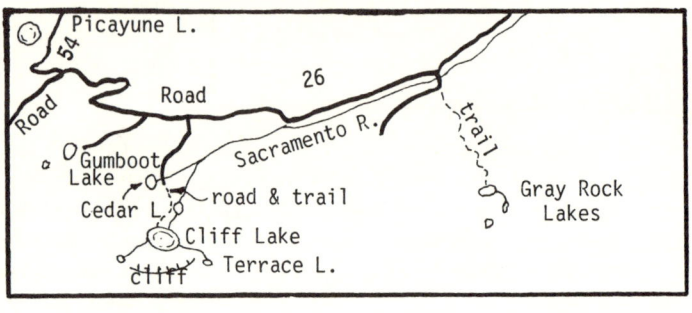

**Length:** 1 mile
**Access:** 1
**Difficulty:** 1
**Scenic Qual.:** 3

**Water:** Lots
**Season:** June through Oct.
**Elevation:** 5600 to 6350 ft.
**Use:** Any. X-C ski

I confess — this whole chapter is a ruse. The Cliff Lake Trail, described in the chapter heading, is actually less than a mile and shouldn't qualify for the book. The Gray Rock Lakes Trails, while more than a mile, would rate a three for difficulty. And you can drive to Castle, Gumboot, and Picayune Lakes.

Let me explain why the area is worth visiting. In the city park in Mt. Shasta, a little spring bubbles into a stone fountain. This spring is supposed to be the source of the Sacramento River, California's longest. From there, the river flows through Shasta Lake into the Sacramento Valley and finally past San Francisco Bay into the ocean.

It's all very charming, except that the South Fork of the Sacramento, branching just south of Mt. Shasta City, continues another 13 miles into the Trinity Divide region between the Sacramento and Trinity Rivers. The source of the South Fork is Gumboot Lake, an excellent fishing spot at the end of an easy, paved or oil topped, road. Gumboot isn't as pretty as some other lakes. Its shore is brushy and it occupies the middle of a sparsely wooded field below a low ridge. Several trailheads take off from the South Fork Road, however.

## Upper Sacramento Lakes 127

To reach the road, take I-5 south to the central Mt. Shasta City exit. Turn right, away from town, then left towards Lake Siskiyou, a large reservoir with campgrounds and a developed resort.

A side road to Castle Lake begins near Lake Siskiyou. Castle Lake is the area's largest natural lake at 47 acres. It's very pretty, set amid dense woods with a headwall on the far side. From there, an easy 1½ mile hike leads to Little Castle Lake, a large puddle with a good view of Shasta.

Past the Lake Siskiyou area, the road soon picks up the river and follows within a few feet of it for several miles. Signs on this road (Road 26) are unpredictable and many have disappeared. I saw no signs for the Sisson-Callahan Trail, which begins off a spur to the right just beyond Lake Siskiyou (see the Deadfall Lakes chapter), or for Gray Rock Lake or Cliff Lake.

Cliff Lake is probably the prettiest. It's a little difficult to find but worth it. As you drive up Road 26, a mass of gray pinnacles appears on the left. Most of the lakes, including Cliff and Gray Rock (surprise!), lie within this formation.

Notice the lodgepole pine. It's quite rare in the Klamath Mountain system and is usually confined to the Cascades. The lower end of Road 26, on the other hand, is dominated by knobcone pine, which tends to usurp the ecological niche of lodgepole pine in the Klamath Mountains. Both species occupy harsh, poor soil sites or recently burned areas. Lodgepole grows at slightly higher elevations so even here the two aren't found side by side. They come close, however.

To find Cliff Lake, take careful note of the point where the road leaves the river and head uphill. That's also where you'll first see the gray rocks. The Cliff Lake turnoff looks like a logging skid road, one of many in the area. This particular one, on the left, is marked by a small bulletin board with a Smokey Bear poster.

Drive in as far as you can or park at the junction. It's a little over a mile to the lake. The access road is muddy at first, then rutted, then it crosses a couple of creeks, then it gets pretty good. I parked after the mud but before the ruts and walked a half-mile. It's possible to drive all the way.

The 15 acre Cliff Lake has a soaring headwall on the far end and jagged peaks above. The shore is brushy and the water is full of snags. Two small lakes are passed on the way in while two more grace the terraces above. Follow the two creek inlets, one on the right of the cliff and one on the left, to reach Terrace Lake and Upper Cliff Lake. Both are difficult, off-trail scrambles.

The nearby Gray Rock Lakes, though harder to reach than Cliff Lake, are among the area's most appealing. Six or seven miles beyond Lake Siskiyou, you'll find a route across the river to the left. The trailhead is supposed to be less than a mile to the right but the map may be confusing. The 1½ mile trail to the 11 acre Lower Gray Rock Lake is very steep. Tiny Timber Lake sits 20 minutes past Lower Gray Rock Lake to the left and is particularly beautiful. Upper Gray Rock Lake lies immediately above the lower lake. All three lakes offer excellent fly fishing.

128    76 Day-Hikes

**Trail Gulch Lake - Trinity Alps Wilderness (Ch. 70)**          (Bernstein Photo)

. . .

As you see, there's lots of hiking to be done within 100 miles of the Rogue Valley — enough to occupy a busy lifetime. I leave it to you to find and explore the many trails I've omitted. My only request is that you don't ask me what a "gumboot" is.

* * *

Art Bernstein is a naturalist and forester who has been exploring the trails of southern Oregon and northern California since 1970. His articles on our back country attractions have appeared in *Northwest, California Living,* the San Francisco *Sunday Examiner* travel section, and the Grants Pass *Courier.* The former Rogue Community College instructor is the author or *Trees of Southern Oregon* and a member of the Southwest Oregon Trails Committee.